DOXED

DOXED

THE POLITICAL LYNCHING
OF A SOUTHERN COP

JOSHUA DOGGRELL

SHOTWELL
COLUMBIA · So. CAR.
EST. 2015
PUBLISHING

Produced in the Republic of South Carolina by

SHOTWELL PUBLISHING LLC

Post Office Box 2592

Columbia, So. Carolina 29202

www.ShotwellPublishing.com

Cover Design: Boo Jackson

ISBN: 978-1-963506-01-3

First Edition

10 9 8 7 6 5 4 3 2 1

Contents

For we wrestle not against flesh and blood, but against principalities, against powers, against the rulers of the darkness of this world, against spiritual wickedness in high places.

—*Ephesians 6:12*

PROLOGUE

"TAKE UP YOUR PEN..."

"Nobody answers him, and his doctrine will there-fore be taken for confessed. For god's sake, my dear sir, take up your pen, select the most striking here-sies, and cut him to pieces in the face of the public."

THESE WERE THE WORDS WRITTEN by Secretary of State Thomas Jefferson to Congressman James Madison on 7 July 1793. This advice resulted from Jefferson's reaction to public writings by Alexander Hamilton (Jefferson's cabinet colleague in the George Washington presidential administration). Hamilton had (inaccurately) implied that Jefferson had authored an intemperate article in a newspaper a few weeks earlier that was hostile both to President Washington and to the Neutrality Proclamation of that Spring.

On 19 June 2015, I was fired from my position as police lieutenant with my hometown City of Anniston, Alabama. I learned that real police were no match for the Thought Police. Not for the first time, I had been targeted by the far-left Southern Poverty Law Center (SPLC), self-professed arbiters of "hate." City leaders had defended and exonerated me in the past. But, this time, two new figures were at the helm of power.

The city manager in Anniston serves as the chief executive of municipal government. The new person at that position was Brian Johnson, a carpetbagger from Georgia looking to use our town as a stepping stone to greener pastures. He had no ties to the city and would soon leave. In the meantime, however, the SPLC's move against me gave him the opportunity to establish his credentials as a crusading social justice warrior in the opening rounds of what would become known as "Cancel Culture." During his short stint in office to that point he had been doing all he could to concentrate power in his office, diminish and dismantle the civil service system which ostensibly serves as a protection for city employees, and striving through intimidation and threats to silence any criticism of his rule that could be transmitted in any form by anyone.

The new police chief was a timid man named Shane Denham. I had worked with him for years. He was the type who desires and strives for more money and a higher position while lamenting the extra responsibilities and trials that come with that. I watched him as he ascended the chain of command and tried to steer around the inevitable confrontations that come with being the head of a department.

A good leader must be one who does not seek out confrontation yet does not run from it when it comes. Shane Denham did not meet this criterion.

The SPLC contacted Chief Denham and Lt. Nick Bowles of Internal Investigations at the Anniston Police Department on 28 May 2015. Their target was me. The city's strategy was, essentially, that (possibly because we had been down this road before, six years earlier) they would sit on it and do nothing, hoping it would go away on its own. On 17 June, the SPLC published their hit piece on me on their website under their "Hatewatch" blog.

The environment was the immediate aftermath of Darren Wilson shooting Michael Brown in Ferguson, Missouri, as well as the resulting riots in cities like Baltimore and North Charleston across the United States. Being a Christian, white, Southern cop accused of "racism" in the Deep South was automatically a hot story. Johnson, whom I had never even met, folded immediately. Denham followed suit. Silence engulfed all other people of influence who could have helped me and defended me because of what was perceived as the unwinnable position of defending a white cop accused of being a "racist" in the climate of 2015. What was a more vile thing to be? It was a time of increased hostility toward police. It was akin to being labeled a child molester. Truth be damned. An accusation had been made. Dung had been hurled. Appeasement was necessary. A sacrifice was in order.

Within hours of the SPLC article, I was placed on administrative leave. At that time, still unsure how far he would sell out (it would be total), Denham told me to expect to be on this leave for "at least a month" while an investigation commenced and went forward. But that would not be good enough to assuage the hounds of race hustlers and professional protesters encircling the municipal seat of government. The press (local, state, and national) had picked up the salacious story and began beating the drums of vengeance. As with so many evil things that proceed from the work of government, immediate action was deemed necessary because "something had to be done."

Then, that evening, something occurred to throw gasoline on a fire that was already raging. While I was leading a Bible study on 1 Samuel at my church in Anniston, a 21-year-old man named Dylann Roof walked into a black church in Charleston, South Carolina, and opened fire. Eight were killed and others wounded. The next day there were two stories on the news: a racist shooter who murdered eight people in Charleston and a racist white cop who had been "outed" by the SPLC in Anniston.

So, the long and thorough "investigation" that I was told would take "at least a month" lasted less than 48 hours. Two days later, on 19 June, in one of those late-Friday-evening press conferences government officials use to release news and then utilize the weekend as a buffer, Johnson and Denham appeared at city hall alongside the mayor and members of the city council to announce my termination as a police officer. Playing to the camera, the city manager, chief, mayor, and councilmen took turns competing to see who could better prove how non-bigoted they were.

Not a positive word was uttered about me.

In what I later determined was a tremendous mistake, I maintained silence on advice of legal counsel. I began attempts to hire an attorney and look toward the chance to present our side on an appeal before the city's Civil Service Board in August and September of that year. I muzzled myself, and I thought we presented our defense well in the face of a three-member board that I firmly believe had made up its mind to uphold the ruling of the city long before any of us walked into the courtroom and were sworn in. The hearing/trial before the board that took place over three days in the summer of 2015 is a matter of public record. At personal expense I obtained a copy of the 580-page transcription of the entire hearing.

I had little allusions that the board would rubber-stamp the city's decision. I did not anticipate the inept and contemptible manner in which the board would conduct the hearings. Two of the three board members verbally indicated they had made their decision before the first day of trial. One board member was absent half the trial and asleep for the majority of the half he was there.

As a public figure, I felt I owed my fellow citizens an explanation. I learned that my co-workers were expressly forbidden to attend any of the hearing while on-duty, and implicitly threatened for attending at all. Many told me privately that most of the officers were very fearful of speaking out in any form concerning this matter ("Look what they did to *you*," was one response). The city manager preferred to rule through arrogance and intimidation. Woe to any employee who did not toe the line, or who dared question him on matters of importance or truthfulness.

The pain of becoming the first Anniston peace officer fired in almost forty years was extraordinary. I had planned on adding at least another twenty years to a career that had spanned over eighteen years at the time. My wife was devastated. Our three young children were confused. Our financial stability and future were, for the first time, in jeopardy. My parents were distraught (my father is a retired Anniston officer). I spent several months unemployed while I worked on my legal defense and applied vainly for work.

Presented in this account are considerations of government transparency and justice. I have committed several wrongs in my life. I have many regrets. I am a sinner, saved by Christ. *But I maintain that my termination by the City of Anniston was not the result of actual wrong doing and policy violations as they publicly claim, but rather a city manager, city council, and police chief calculating that satisfying the small hounds of the perennial professional protesters and race pimps of Anniston was worth sacrificing justice and the reputation, career, retirement, and livelihood of an eighteen-year-officer with an exemplary record.*

The institution of civil government was ordained by God to be a ministry of justice here on earth. It is my firm conviction that justice was *not* served in this incident, and members of the municipal government of the City of Anniston, Alabama, broke criminal law and their own policies in their handling of this matter. Many of the people who attended the proceedings told me, individually, how shocked they were at things they heard in the courtroom. The positions of city manager, mayor, councilman, and police chief are important to citizens. It is important that public light be shined on their conduct.

This was not a private affair. The handling of (non-criminal) allegations of policy violations at a city or county department of government is usually an in-house, quiet process. My allegations, however, were leveled amid a vituperative, circus atmosphere from the beginning of the administrative "investigation." Guilt-by-association got me fired from my job, blackballed from my vocation, and scandalized in local, state, and national media. My name and photo were splashed across the front pages of multiple copies of our hometown newspaper and media outlets throughout the state. The city attorney said inquiries were made by national news outlets, specifically Anderson Cooper. My reputation was blackguarded. My career was ruined.

Who is in a better position than me to adequately answer the calumnies? Government corruption is something that should be exposed. Wrongs should be challenged. The truth still matters. My inner Jefferson stirred me to action... "For God's sake...Take up your pen..."

1.

Scrubbing Sodomite Chalkings

"This ain't your grandfather's University of Alabama."

10 January 1977—17 June 2015

I WAS FOURTEEN YEARS OLD in 1991 when I told my father I wanted to be a cop.

He had not pushed me toward it, and he did not push me away from it. He had been retired for three years at that time. He worked from New Year's Day 1965 to February 1988 for the police department of our hometown, the City of Anniston, Alabama. He began as a motorcycle cop, was promoted to sergeant and then lieutenant, and was the first commander of what was then known as the Special Duty Unit, the forerunner of what would become the county drug task force. "Working vice" or "undercover" was also how it was referenced.

He was only 47 when he retired, but he had always maintained policing was a young man's profession, and he had no desire for a desk job. So, he went from being a part-time to a full-time auto body man, working from the shop next to our home.

We lived (and still live) in the community of Saks in the city of Anniston, the seat of Calhoun County (named for famed Southerner John C. Calhoun) in the northeast section of the state. The patch on the uniform arms of the deputy sheriffs designates it as "The Foothills of the Appalachians."

My father is the hardest-working man I have ever known. My recollection of the first eleven years of my life was him rising early to work in his body shop. He was assisted by friend Jimmy Ogburn, a county deputy sheriff at that time who would go on to retire as assistant chief for the City of Oxford, just south of us. My dad and Jimmy would work until the early afternoon, then roll down the shop doors. My dad went inside to shower, then he would leave in his unmarked orange Chevrolet Nova to begin his shift with the city.

His regular shift was 3-to-11. When it wasn't a school night, I would wait up for him. I remember the thrill of seeing the headlights shine in the driveway. I would meet him at the door. Before I had to go to bed, we would watch Johnny Carson or a rerun of a Jackie Gleason show.

So, I grew up around lawmen. They and their families were often at the house, and we at theirs. Events and gatherings abounded. My father was an active member of the local Fraternal Order of Police (FOP), and I remember fishing and playing with other cops' kids on the grounds and in the lodge there. When I turned sixteen, my friends and I would sneak onto the property late at night to fish and drink beer on the bank while listening to country music. We often spent whole summer nights camping at the lodge.

Until graduation four years later, I only seriously considered two other lines of vocation. I had a hankering to be a newspaper columnist. I had a passion for reading and fancied I might become an author one day, like the legendary Southerner Lewis Grizzard, whose books I consumed during that time.

I also considered being a football coach. I played and loved the game of football fiercely. The first Friday night of November 1994

I played my last game and on the bus ride back refused to take off my shoulder pads. I simply could not imagine never putting them on again. I could not fathom being away from the game.

Sitting on the bus that night was as close as I ever came to not being a cop.

It didn't last long.

I also became an admirer and student of history, particularly American and Southern. The Confederate battle flag still flew atop the Alabama State Capitol building when I was in middle school and I began immersing myself in the history of my people.

After graduating high school in 1995, I moved to Tuscaloosa and enrolled at the University of Alabama on a scholarship. I declared my major as criminal justice. Since being an officer did not require a degree, some suggested I get something broader in case that line of work didn't pan out or in case my mind changed. I did not feel my mind would change and felt strongly enough about it to move forward with it as my major. I wanted to learn everything about the justice system, criminal law and procedure, and policing that I could.

It did not take long surveying the campus to learn that, as one fellow student told me, "This ain't your grandfather's University of Alabama." It had only been thirty-two years since Wallace stood in the schoolhouse door, but things had changed dramatically.

The Greek fraternity/sorority system might have still been considered conservative, but the rest of the student body, the staff, and the administration were overwhelmingly leftists. One of the first weeks of my freshman year, the university sponsored "Coming Out Week." I had never seen such. In my high school, we had a couple of students we suspected of being homosexual, but it was still a time and place that it would have been scandalous to come forward. They stayed in that closet.

The celebrants paraded through the campus, with each day the university designating some different aspect of their gayness. The participants chalked the sidewalks we used to walk to our classes with slogans supporting the lifestyle they had chosen.

Toward the end of that week, I picked up the most recent edition of *The Crimson White* campus newspaper. What I saw on the front page would change my life.

The picture was of a group of young men wearing t-shirts and blue jeans. They were of marked contrast to the latter-day "dirty hippie" look I had grown accustomed to seeing from those chalking sodomite messages on the sidewalk that week. Aside from appearing to have had an adequate shower in the recent past, these young men were clean-cut and well groomed. Their shirts were tucked in their pants. Some were holding Confederate battle flags. Others were on their knees surrounded by mop buckets as they scrubbed the chalked messages off the sidewalks. One of the students interviewed said that his group considered the messages vulgar and offensive to Christian standards. And if one student group thought they had a right to chalk the messages, then another student group had just as much right to clean it off.

This, I immediately thought to myself, was a group I needed to learn more about. They called themselves The Southern League. Young people often "go off to college" and lose their faith, lose their way, and become culturally and politically liberalized due to the influence of the modern academy. Through my affiliation with the League, the Fellowship of Christian Athletes (FCA), and certain professors and friends, my Christian faith blossomed, my vision for the future was made clearer, and my conservative view of culture and politics moved even further rightward.

I attended a few meetings of the campus chapter of the League and liked what I heard. I met older members, many of whom were pastors and educators. Two history professors at the university, **Dr. Michael Hill** and **Dr. Gary Mills**, became mentors of mine. Both were involved with and provided guidance for the university chapter. Both were among many that were cross-members of the Sons of Confederate Veterans (SCV), which my father and I had joined two years prior.

In contrast with the SCV, the League's focus was more concerned with the future than the past. The United States had become too consolidated, with power concentrated in the District of Columbia. The original constitutional republic bequeathed to us by our forefathers had been subverted, and the godless, tyrannical leviathan that had taken its place was beyond reform. Decentralization was the only route to true freedom and Christian liberty. This was a position with which I came to agree.

Writing 28 years later, I still think it was correct then and the only modification I now have with this position is that society, overall, has devolved to the point where such a difficult task is impractical. Scripture tells us mankind will continue to degenerate until Jesus comes back, but many of us did not expect the rapidity of the decline. We still had hope when the League was formed in 1994. Many of us no longer have that same hope in our fellow Southerner. It came to be that we were trying to save people who did not want to be saved. My only hope left in the 21st Century America dominated by the post-Marxist Left, is the body of Christ and His return. The nobility of Southern culture is gone with the wind.

I figured I would attend UA for four years, get my bachelor's degree, and begin looking for a job back home. For practice, I began taking civil service tests. It turns out I was pretty good at taking tests. I scored high on them.

I came home from classes one day in my sophomore year and received a call from my father. I had recently tested for the position of deputy sheriff at the Calhoun County Sheriff's Office, headquartered in Anniston. The sheriff himself called my dad, asking, "When does that boy want to come to work?"

On 28 March 1997, just over two months following my twentieth birthday, still too young to purchase a pistol permit, I walked into the Calhoun County Jail wearing a brown uniform. I worked part-time on the weekends while attending classes in Tuscaloosa during the week. After completing the school year that May, I left behind a full-paid scholarship at my state university and drove to a trailer I had recently purchased in the town of Alexandria. Three days after my last final I began work full-time as a deputy.

Listed on my application was my membership with the Sons of Confederate Veterans and the Southern League (which would soon be renamed the League of the South as a result of a civil dispute with the minor-league baseball franchise with the same name). It was well known throughout my occupation field that I was passionate about my Southern and Confederate heritage and that I was active in advocating for the Southern people and their future. Anyone who would have taken the time to notice or speak with me would have known I was an open secessionist and Southern nationalist. At no time was I told by any superiors that this posed a problem with me being a local peace officer.

In those early days, I never regretted my career decision. I graduated the police academy in November 1997. I was granted my request to go to second shift, which I considered where to find the most action.

I thrived in my position. I met colleagues who became friends, including Matthew Wade. From 1998-2004 we were close friends and spent a considerable amount of time off work together. Nineteen years after meeting him, Wade would become sheriff of Calhoun County. More on that later...

In 2000, we hired a dispatcher that would become my wife the following year. Overall, I would say we treated each other badly. I wanted to do better. She wanted to have children but was physically unable. My walk with Christ was nowhere near what it needed to be. I wanted to get involved in church, but she refused. We became (or always were) incompatible.

In October 2003, I left on a Friday night to attend the Alabama-Tennessee game in Tuscaloosa. It went into four overtimes. By the time I entered our home in Alexandria in the early hours of Sunday morning, I remember thinking, "Man, she finally cleaned up the place." When I flipped on the light and began looking around, I realized she had moved out. I was sad that I had failed at such a serious thing as marriage, but I also experienced relief because I felt released from my obligation to make it work.

One of the last enjoyable things we did together was attend a League of the South national conference in Abbeville, South Carolina, in the summer of 2003.

Over the years my relationship with the sheriff who hired me soured. Many of us felt he treated his employees badly and suffered from a tremendous ego. I was just enough of an independent, young punk to occasionally let him know how I felt about this. As a result, I found myself passed over for promotion every time I was a candidate, despite usually scoring at the top of the civil service test. And after publicly challenging his attempt to circumvent the civil service system in late 2003 by bringing in a sergeant from outside the agency, I found myself reassigned to court services in January 2004. This was one of those moves by a boss who wants to punish you, but does not have anything you have actually done, such as a policy violation, with which he can take punitive action.

Romans 8:28 tells us, "And we know that for those who love God all things work together for good, for those who are called according to his purpose." The sheriff's move was intended to harm me, but God meant it for good [Genesis 50:20].

While working in the courthouse that spring, I met a young woman working as a receptionist for a local law firm. Her name was April Bonner. She had to make frequent visits to the courthouse to file paperwork. We had our first conversation on 18 June 2004. We were married six months to the day later. Our first son, Tyler Emmett, was born the next year. Another son, Nathanael Jefferson, was born 23 June 2008. And our little princess, Shyloh Elisabeth, was born on 3 February 2011.

After the sheriff determined my time in penance was completed, I was moved back to patrol in January 2005. But I knew I was spinning my wheels. I bided my time, looking for a chance elsewhere. Several of my fellow FOP members were municipal officers with Anniston Police Department and courted me. I took their test and became eligible. I accepted a position as police officer with them and was sworn in by Chief of Police John Dryden (who had worked with my father) on 13 April 2006.

Listed on my application with the city was my membership with the League of the South. It was discussed at my interview and my polygraph examination, as would be revealed in trial and depositions nine and ten years later.

I did well at Anniston. After a year and a half as a patrolman, I was made a field training officer. Shortly afterward, in March 2008, I was made a caseworker in the investigative division. In July 2010, I was promoted to sergeant. A year later I was made the investigative sergeant. In January 2013, I was promoted to lieutenant.

In the midst of this, my activity with the League grew. I attended the national conference annually. In March 2009, I began a local chapter of the League in Anniston. At the inaugural meeting and many meetings in the future, several of my fellow officers attended. That first meeting was covered by the local newspaper, *The Anniston Star*. As a result of that publicity, complaints were made by local activists and race hustlers. An internal investigation was commenced by the city. The results were that I was cleared of any wrongdoing and told I was within my constitutional rights to carry on with the group.

On 21 June 2013, I delivered the opening speech at the League's national conference in Wetumpka, Alabama. The title of my presentation was "Cultivating the Goodwill of Peace Officers." Nowhere in the speech nor the question-and-answer session that followed (both totaling together over one hour) was the issue of race mentioned. During the address, I acknowledged one of my co-workers in the audience, Lt. Wayne Brown. Brown had recently become a League member and would accompany me to League events later that year. This acknowledgement and Brown's membership would bring Brown into the fray two years later.

In the years 2013-2015, some of my friends in the League and I detected some problems areas. There was a new sect of people that had begun attending and participating in League events that portended a possible change of direction. I had several conversations with the League president, **Dr.** Michael Hill (an aforementioned professor of mine at the University of Alabama) about these people. He never failed to reassure me that he was keeping tight reins on the newcomers, and that the core principles of the League would not be corrupted.

On 9 August 2014, Police Officer Darren Wilson shot and killed Michael Brown in Ferguson, Missouri. That same month I participated in my last activity with the League at an anti-immigration event in Gainesville, Georgia. Still unsure if the ship would be righted, I decided to withdraw and monitor events inside the League.

On 28 May 2015, I was at work when then-Police Chief Shane Denham walked into my office and closed the door. He said he had been contacted by people with the Southern Poverty Law Center (SPLC) and they were wanting to make an issue with me being a police officer and a League member. My involvement with the League was well known to Denham. We had discussed it numerous times over the years.

At this meeting in my office, he asked if there was anything new, any "smoking gun" that might cause us any trouble. I asked him what he was particularly worried about. He asked if maybe there had been a "hot mic" moment at any of the events I had attended, or if maybe I had said something embarrassing while being secretly recorded. Absolutely not, I told him. In fact, I had scaled back my participation with the League as of late. He said the SPLC had referenced the speech I had given at the national conference in 2013. As has already been referenced, that speech had nothing at all to do with race. I encouraged him to listen to the speech in its entirety and assured him he had nothing to worry about. He said he would.

Before leaving my office, Denham told me he admired how I stood up for what I believed in and told me he would stand up for me. Knowing what kind of man Denham was, I was not put at ease. That evening, I related the incident to my wife and told her that I did not believe Denham would actively throw me under the bus, but he would sure stand on the sidewalk and watch it run over me if it meant any difficulty for him.

After work that day I was running on the treadmill in the department gym. Nick Bowles, the Internal Affairs lieutenant, walked in and was filling up a water bottle from the water fountain near me when he mentioned that he was "about ten minutes" into watching the video of my speech. I do not recall exactly what I replied to him, but it was something like, good, I hope he watched every second of it because there was nothing to be concerned about.

Bowles motioned for me to follow him into the hallway just outside the gym, presumably because there were several other people present. I paused the treadmill and accompanied him.

In the hallway, he pressed me. Was I sure? Was there anything at all that would get me or the department in trouble? I told him he would have to be more specific, seeing how I dealt in issues deemed "controversial" by the left a lot. Being a far-right, Christian, Southern lawman who espoused values traditional with those demographics had already become something harrowing to those occupying the Blue States and on the far-left side of the political aisle. Of what, exactly, was he afraid?

"Do you say 'nigger,' or anything like that?"

Oh, for heavens sake. No, I assured him. If that is your standard, you have nothing to worry about.

That evening, after I had finished my workout and returned home, Bowles called me. He said he had viewed the video in its entirety and then phoned whoever his contact was with the SPLC and told them that, after review, I had not said anything that violated any laws or policies and that I was within my rights.

As will be recounted later, when Bowles took the stand in my civil trial, he would claim he did not say this exactly. He would recount that he was only looking for something egregious and had not found that. He disagreed that his assessment meant that he did not find *anything* that might qualify as a violation of policy.

If there was ever a phone conversation I wish I had taped, that was it. As God is my witness, Bowles told me what I recounted above.

Three weeks passed without a word. I figured the issue had, once again, passed.

On the morning of Wednesday, 17 June 2015, I woke, shaved, and had no idea I would be putting on my badge and gun for the last time. I drove to the police department oblivious to the storm brewing for that day.

At work, I was looking over a front-page article by *The Anniston Star* about a murder defendant getting acquitted in a trial I had testified in the week before. The reporter had made the unprofessional mistake of writing that the defendant had been found "innocent" rather than the quite different and accurate rendering of "not guilty," and I emailed the reporter to call him on his error.

I was eating dinner around midday with some coworkers when the reporter emailed me back. He no longer wanted to talk about the murder trial but wanted my comments about an article released on the SPLC's "Hatewatch" blog about me.

Things began to move rapidly. Within hours, Lt. Brown and I were placed on administrative leave pending another internal investigation. A few hours later, at my local church, I was wrapping up a study on 1 Samuel and speaking with fellow members in the lobby when a troubled young man named Dylann Roof committed his murders in a South Carolina church.

My life would never be the same.

2.

"...A Post-Trayvon Martin Society"

17 June 2015

THE SOUTHERN POVERTY LAW CENTER (SPLC) has long been a nemesis of Christian, conservative causes, people, and organizations. Many on the right have done commendable jobs of exposing their chicanery. Put succinctly, the SPLC is a far-left, ungodly, Marxist, fund-raising machine that masquerades as a law firm seeking justice for the masses who constantly suffer oppression at the hands of what they present as mean, evil white people. For a long time, this group has made a tremendous amount of money from this practice.

On 17 June 2015, the SPLC, apparently unhappy with the City of Anniston's refusal to take disciplinary action against me in light of what they seemed to consider a major revelation, finally made good on their threat to take action of their own. A hit piece appeared on their website's "Hatewatch" blog. It had been twenty days since their minions contacted Chief of Police, Shane Denham, and Internal Affairs, Lt. Nick Bowles, to "alert" them to something they already knew – they had two lieutenants that were members of the League of the South, which was one of the many organizations the SPLC deemed a "hate group."

As will be recounted in more detail in the chapters dealing with their court testimonies, Bowles, Denham, and my immediate supervisor, Captain Greg Feazell, all read what the SPLC sent

13

them in May and/or watched at least portions of the speech I gave in Wetumpka, Alabama, on 21 June 2013. None of them told me they found anything inappropriate in the speech.

The speech had been posted on YouTube not long after it was given by an unknown person, presumably someone at the conference. The fact that I had given a speech at a League conference was not significant or worrisome. I had given several speeches at League events at various places over the years. The content of the speech was mainly about cultivating the good will of peace officers, addressing various issues of gun rights belonging to citizens, and the prospects of possible gun confiscation by the government. The issue of race was not addressed at all.

Anniston Police Department Has Two Hate Group Members on the Force: Southern Poverty Law Center (splcenter.org)

The SPLC article (authored by Keegan Hankes) pointed out that I had given a speech which "has only recently came to the attention of Hatewatch, which immediately sought to bring Doggrell's associations to the city's attention." It was an exercise in character assassination, intended to inflame racial tensions and cause me to suffer. It worked.

I have often been asked if I thought someone sent the speech to the SPLC with the additional information that I was a police officer. It is possible. However, I reckon it is also quite possible that henchmen of the SPLC, tasked with combing the internet looking for some new fountain of "hate" that could be exploited for their uses (financial gain), simply began doing random Google searches about white cops and stumbled across it. Regardless, the issue of how the SPLC came into possession of this information is irrelevant to me, as my position was and is that I was doing absolutely nothing wrong. I was exercising my religious and constitutional rights (which a law officer does not surrender when he takes the oath) and was not breaking any laws nor any departmental policies.

The article and video were simplistic and sophomoric. The logic flowed thusly: I was a member of "a hate group." I had even taken the ghastly step of giving a speech at one of their conferences. I was not only a police officer, but an officer employed in Anniston, Alabama, a Deep-South city where Freedom Riders had been assaulted 54 years prior (and sixteen years before I was born). Therefore, it was unthinkable that the city would continue to maintain my employment considering these horrible connections. I must be delivered up for public flogging forthwith.

What seemed bizarre to me when reading the article were the quotes from City Manager Brian Johnson. The author noted that after the police chief was "alerted" about my membership (which he had already known about for at least nine years), "all further calls were referred to Brian Johnson, Anniston city manager, who told Hatewatch that even if the city was aware of police officers being members of such a 'civic club,' there was only so much they could do. When posed with the hypothetical of a police officer being a member of the Ku Klux Klan (KKK), Johnson elaborated by stating that, 'We could not terminate an employee solely on his or her membership in a legal, lawfully formed, civic club or organization... I do not believe that someone could be terminated solely based on their private sector membership in a properly formed legal organization – as hateful as the KKK might be.'"

The author went on to express that "other cities have not been so *laissez-faire* about extremists and racists in their ranks" and listed examples from across the country.

What occurred here was that Brian Johnson got manipulated by the SPLC, whose devotees know how to play the game so well. Johnson was not prepared for them, and his uninformed and incorrect answers embarrassed him. This made it all the easier for him to sacrifice me when the time came to recompense his gaffe. The SPLC's strategy in these types of head-hunting situations is to contact bosses with these "alerts" that they have "extremists" and "racists" in their ranks, then browbeat them by demanding "something be done" about it. If the punishment offered is considered inadequate, then threats are made to publish articles and bring wider attention to the matter.

Denham told me on 28 May, that when the SPLC contacted him earlier that day to "alert" him he had an officer who was a member of the League of the South, he told them he already knew that, and they reacted as though they were flabbergasted that he could allow such a thing. He told me he definitely felt like the caller was trying to intimidate him into taking action they preferred.

After learning of the publishing while eating dinner with colleagues that day, I returned to my office to check it out. At that time I was the administrative lieutenant at the police department, whose primary area of responsibility was serving as municipal jail administrator. I read the article and watched the accompanying three-and-a-half-minute video. It was pretty pathetic and classic SPLC smear. I had been down this road before, having been investigated and cleared by the city six years prior. However, we now had a new city manager and a new police chief and neither of them inspired confidence in me. Would they do the right thing?

Within a few hours the chief called me to his office. When I entered he was seated behind his desk. Lt. Bowles was standing to his left. Captain Tim Whatley of the uniform division was seated in front of Denham's desk. I took the seat to Whatley's left.

Denham said the three of them had recently returned from Johnson's office at city hall. He said there were "other people" there, but he would not tell me who. He said these "others" were calling for stiff and swift action. There were calls for my termination. My educated guess is that these "others" consisted at least of members of the council, most notably David Reddick, past president of the local National Association for the Advancement of Colored People (NAACP). Reddick would later admit in his testimony that he was involved in these deliberations, which was a violation of Alabama law. The details of this will be included in a later chapter.

Denham handed me a copy of an administrative order from Johnson. I was informed that I had been placed on administrative leave due to "allegations" from the SPLC. The atmosphere of the room was somber, as if the other three men were visiting me on my death bed and were uncomfortable with the situation, perhaps wishing I would just go ahead and pass on, already. I asked Denham what I could expect. He said that I would probably remain on administrative leave "at least a month" while things played out.

I asked to speak to Johnson. I had never had a conversation with him before. I told the three men that I understood and appreciated the stress this was causing them and the department, but I also told them I believed I had done nothing wrong, improper, illegal, or against policy. None disputed that at this time.

I told Denham that Johnson was undoubtedly thinking of some kind of exit strategy. I told him that if I could speak to Johnson, I may could assist with that. Due to my decreased activity with the League and the troubles that I had been monitoring within it, I was considering some face-saving concessions that could be made that *might* satisfy the hounds at the door.

I also laid out something I would most certainly not do. I said that, regardless of the state of the League at that time and mistakes that had been made, I would not denounce them or go on some sort of apology tour like had been seen by so many other people in my situation. The particular word I used – "denounce" – would be centered upon during the upcoming trial.

I was willing to express regret at some actions of the League and, particularly, certain League members. I had already been considering leaving the organization, and, sitting in front of Denham's desk, I was trying to wrap my mind around how that could be accomplished and not seem like it was being driven by agitation from local activists instead of the honest contemplation I had already been giving the issue for about two years. In no way did I want to appear as an appeaser or a sellout.

Again — what I would absolutely not do was "denounce" the League. I would not apologize for joining, or maintaining, my membership with them for twenty years. Overall, I was proud of my membership. I had learned many valuable things, associated with many fine and God-fearing people, fellowshipped with some I still called my friends, adopted positions that I still held. It would have been untruthful and dishonest of me to act like these things were not so, and I was adamant that I would not do it, even if it meant I lost my job.

It was at this point that Lt. Bowles interjected for what I recall were his only comments during this interaction. "Why not?" he asked. "Why not, if it meant saving your job, would you not just flush the whole thing?" I explained to Bowles and the other two men that that would not be the honest nor honorable thing to do, thinking to myself that having to answer this question may portend this might be a concept beyond their grasp.

I thought if I had the opportunity to sit down and discuss this with Johnson, we could possibly find a way to handle it. Denham told me he was headed to Johnson's office as soon as I left and he would convey to him my request.

The request was denied. Johnson had no intention of speaking to me. He fired me two days later without ever giving me an opportunity to address him about this and without ever looking at me face-to-face. In the trial, Johnson testified that he did this because the damage had been done, and nothing I could have said would have made any difference at that point.

I walked back to my office and began collecting my belongings. By that time, the second-shift sergeant had assumed duty at the jail and came to meet with me concerning shift matters. I let him know that I had been placed on leave, the SPLC was coming after me, and I intended on fighting it. He wished me well. It would be the last time I saw Mike Campbell. He died not long after.

I stopped in at the clerk's office before I left the building to turn in some paperwork. One of the clerks, Debbie Rooks, stood up and walked toward me. In a somewhat hushed tone, she asked, referring to our bosses, "Are they not going to back you on this?"

"I guess we'll see," I said. We spoke briefly and cordially a for few more moments and I left.

I drove home from work, my mind consumed with all the possible ramifications of the day's events. It was a third Wednesday, which meant there was a meeting of our local Fraternal Order of Police (FOP) lodge that evening. I was frequently an attendee and had been for many years, but I had missed recent meetings due to leading a Bible study at my church. I briefly considered going to the FOP meeting instead, seeing as my situation would surely be a topic and I needed to start shoring up support. But I felt my obligation was to the Bible study.

When I got home, my wife and three children were in the back yard. The news had already begun picking up the story and she didn't want to see or hear any more of it. The kids were largely oblivious at this point. My wife had the strained, pained expression on her face I have seen a few times over the years when the gravity of things we went through weighed heavily on her.

Six years prior, when I had started the local League chapter, the local newspaper ran two stories on it in the same week. The online publication of those stories allowed for comments from citizens, and many of them were inflammatory. At the time, I was attending a week-long training school in Nashville and not in the middle of the fray. She called me, relating the news and the ire of many of the comments.

I told her that it would be best to stop reading all that. Nothing good would come of it. It was then she told me something I have never forgotten, and which I recalled standing there by the pool speaking to her six years later. "I know you have thick skin and have been through this sort of thing before and can probably get through this again. But have you ever considered that it's not just you now? That you have a wife and kids? Did you ever consider that maybe we can't?"

In 1 Corinthians 7, the Apostle Paul writes of marriages and remarks of the pros and cons of Christian ministry accompanying it. He mentions the advantages single people like himself have when it comes to spreading the gospel. The repercussions and sufferings that come with the ministry are not visited upon the wife and children, therefore the single man has the freedom to conduct himself according to his convictions and not worry about burdening his family with them.

At the pool, my wife asked me, "What are you going to do?"

"I'm going to church, like I usually do."

At 4:17pm, *The Anniston Star* published an online article about the issue. It began: "Two Anniston police officers were placed on administrative leave Wednesday pending an investigation by the city into their participation in what a Montgomery-based civil rights group describes as a hate group." Johnson's quotes in the Hatewatch article were cited, as well as an SPLC representative's characterization of them as "absurd."

David Reddick was quoted. He wailed that he found it "disappointing... [and] disheartening that we've got officers that are sworn to uphold the law that are involved with that...in a post-Trayvon Martin society..."

The flames of racial agitation were being fanned by the usual suspects.

Obviously monitoring very closely the results of their campaign of intimidation, the SPLC at 4:58pm posted an update to their Hatewatch blog which included the fact that Brown and I had been placed on administrative leave. They were well on their way to mission-accomplished, celebratory status.

When I came home from church that evening, I knew I was going to need help. I pulled the information on my status in the FOP's Legal Defense Plan. I figured there was a good chance I would get at least disciplined, if not fired, and I would need an attorney.

None of my family members had the television on or were monitoring internet news. It was swirling around us. We woke the next morning without knowledge of the story from South Carolina, where a gunman named Dylann Roof had walked into a black church and opened fire. So, we had no idea how the intensity of the situation was growing by the minute.

My wife was being very quiet.

I then decided to reach out to my local FOP. I called Ed Akers, who was the president at that time. I had known Ed for years, worked with him prior to his retirement at APD, and had always been on cordial relations with him.

Ed didn't answer. I left a voicemail. Ed didn't call me back.

Before going to bed that night, I thought about how the accusation of being a "racist" was enough to make so many white men today crumble. Nothing seems so likely to make otherwise grown men melt into a glob of goo. I began to wonder how many would wilt in the face of such opposition.

I felt very alone.

3.

"Everyone Said the Proper Things."

18 June 2015

BASED ON WHAT POLICE CHIEF Shane Denham told me the day before, I woke on Thursday morning to what I considered Day One of an extended leave from the department. I had spent much time the previous night and restless moments of unsuccessful sleep trying to calculate what the city would do.

On the one hand, I knew City Manager Brian Johnson and Denham would be under enormous pressure. While I did not know Johnson well, I knew his type. He had no ties to Anniston. In his two years as city manager, he had already demonstrated his proclivity at ruling through fear and intimidation. He did not know me personally, which would make it easier to dispose of me. And he had to be suffering embarrassment from the comments he had made to the SPLC that were now printed in articles published by them and *The Anniston Star* from the previous day.

Denham knew he was in a tight spot. He had known I had been a League of the South member the entirety of my employment with the city. Far from being told I had to give it up, I had been exonerated in an internal investigation and promoted twice since starting a local chapter. Denham had been a member of the administrative command staff throughout all that.

At the time, I was a lieutenant, therefore a member of his own administrative command staff. He told the SPLC when they contacted him on 28 May that he knew I was a member. Initially, he was only worried about a "smoking gun," some new revelation. He watched the video of the speech they sent him. So did Internal Affairs Lt. Nick Bowles. Bowles told me there was nothing there and that he told the SPLC that.

Six years prior, after beginning a local League chapter in Anniston, a complaint from a local citizen had prompted the first city internal investigation. Abdul Khalil'llah, director of an Anniston-based civil rights group called Operation Human Rights, had made a complaint at a city council meeting on 28 April 2009. He sent a written complaint to then-police Chief John Dryden. He said he contacted the U.S. Attorney General's Office and asked that I be fired. I knew of these details at the time, but they were also recorded in an article released by *The Anniston Star* on 4 July 2015 under the headline, "Activist says he complained about officer 6 years ago."

In that article, Denham acknowledged the complaint and admitted the department conducted an internal investigation of me as a result of it. According to the article, "Denham said he couldn't speak much about the investigation, other than that according to the report, it was an involved process. 'It was a lengthy investigation...I've been involved with them, they're very stressful and time consuming...But I can't tell you what the findings were... all I can say is that afterward [Doggrell] was still employed.'"

This investigation will be detailed later, but for now it should be noted that the result of it was that I was cleared of any wrongdoing, told that I was operating within my constitutional rights, and that I was violating no laws or policies. In 2015, the city steadfastly refused to release the file for this internal investigation, and the only official comment anyone would make was that "no action" against me had been taken upon its conclusion.

So, I knew that this was a positive for me. This was an obstacle to my termination. Several people whom I have spoken with about this over the years have related to me that, although they may not agree with my views, or they may have their doubts about some of my positions, they simply cannot understand the justness of an entity firing someone for something they had previously told him was not something for which he could be fired.

Regardless, I woke and dressed that Thursday morning and commenced doing yard work. While doing that, Wayne Brown, the other fired lieutenant, called me. I learned a year later while preparing for federal depositions that Brown waffled on how he intended to handle potential disciplinary action resulting from this. As I understand it, he initially agreed to retire, then changed his mind and wanted to fight it, then after being interviewed by Bowles the next day again agreed to retire.

In our phone conversation, Brown asked what I was going to do, and I told him I was fighting it because we had done nothing wrong. He said he had come to that conclusion, as well, and was going to challenge any disciplinary matter imposed against him.

While I was trying to ease my mind with yard work, things were happening in the city. I learned later during court testimony from Chief Denham that he had several agitators show up at the police department demanding (their sense of) "justice." He was feeling the heat. It was this pressure as well as my characterization of Denham as one who is very uncomfortable with any form of confrontation that leads me to believe that on that Thursday, he changed course dramatically from the day before. He wanted to avoid any difficulties that would accompany doing the right thing. I have no doubt he had his boss, Brian Johnson, "encouraging" him on this path.

I also learned about the groveling of city officials from news accounts.

At 1:17pm, *The Anniston Star* published on its website that Mayor Vaughn Stewart had taken to his Twitter account to address the situation:

> "Like many of you, I was shocked yesterday by the allegations brought against two Anniston police officers. Rest assured, I am working hard to get to the bottom of it. Anniston has no tolerance for racism and hatred. Anniston has come a long way since bigots attacked a bus of Freedom Riders in 1961. We will continue to move forward, not backward."

Stewart probably never bothered to take the time to watch the video of the speech I gave. But he must have seen the three-and-half-minute inflammatory and misleading video the SPLC posted with its Hatewatch hatchet job. In that video, I am seen speaking, followed by images of the Freedom Riders bus being burned in Anniston 54 years prior, as if there was some connection. In some cities, when they want to participate in social justice virtue signaling, they may "wave a bloody shirt." In Anniston, the go-to is to "roll the burning bus." Relevance is not required.

Stewart later gave a phone interview with the *Star* in which he advised the council that he was "trying to let the investigation run its course… It would be easy for any one of us to go out there and speak, but I think we've got to show some restraint and let things take their course." So, the mayor was cautioning restraint and not speaking…after he broadcast three tweets about how hard he was working to make sure "racism and hatred" were eradicated from the city and "rolling the burning bus" for good measure.

At 4:57pm, the *Star* published another article detailing that "Local NAACP officials met with Anniston's police chief Thursday to ensure two of his officers were fully investigated for their ties to what some civil rights organizations describe as a hate group." The coterie (consisting of a grand total of seven people, evidenced by the accompanying photograph) then relocated to city hall to give a press conference.

The two black city councilmen, David Reddick and Seyram Selase, were among the seven. The main speaker was David Baker, listed as being president of the Calhoun County chapter of the NAACP, although later reports surfaced that that entity was defunct, according to the national organization.

Baker, not worried at all about letting "the investigation run its course," said that both Brown and I should be fired. Particularly me, he said. "He should not have the right to carry a badge. He has the right to feel the way he wants to...but as long as he's a police officer, he must hold all he has inside."

In an account published by local news correspondent Dixon Hayes with WLOX 13 at 4:37pm, that same day, Baker was also quoted as saying about me, "Once he took the oath of being a police officer, that dismissed all his rights until retirement."

Just to be clear: Local race hustler David Baker, who led the contingent of seven people who attended the press conference after presumably the same group browbeat and intimidated the chief of police into taking action, went on record that it was his belief that police officers have "all" their rights "dismissed" once they take the oath office.

And these were the people that shouted their way to victory in this situation. Good grief.

The *Star* also interviewed Mark Pitcavage, "director of investigative research and the center on extremism for the Anti-Defamation League." Pitcavage related that his organization also considered the League to be a "hate group." He said the city had the "legal backing" to fire officers for being members of a "hate group," but his reasoning was not mentioned.

What was mentioned was that the SPLC cited a 1985 case from Jacksonville, Florida, as precedent for firing a law officer based on such ties.

The case was *Robert C. McMullen v. Dale Carson*. McMullen had been fired after it was discovered he was a recruiter for the Ku Klux Klan. He sued. A federal court dismissed his suit, and the 11th Circuit Court of Appeals upheld the decision, ruling that a police agency does not violate the First Amendment by discharging an employee who actively participates "in an organization with a history of violent activity, which is antithetical to enforcement of the laws by state officers."

Richard Cohen, president of the SPLC, said that based on *McMullen*, "I think the city would be on firm legal footing" for firing us.

But let us examine *McMullen* as it relates to my situation. I was exercising my First Amendment rights of freedom of speech and freedom of association by my affiliation with the League of the South. Unlike the Klan, the League was not at all "an organization with a history of violent activity." There was no record of this and it was simply not true.

But to groups like the SPLC, ADL, and *The Anniston Star*, painting anything Christian and conservative with a broad brush is standard procedure. The reason the SPLC reported the growing rise of "hate groups" annually is that it continued to expand their definition of what a "hate group" was. Groups like Focus on the Family and individuals like Ben Carson and Rand Paul made their lists. When you *desire* for there to be more "hate groups," your guidelines allow for *anyone* to be compared with the Klan. There's Klan everywhere! We're here to help! Send us your money!

Councilman and past president of the local NAACP David Reddick also spoke, calling not only for my termination, but opportunistically summoning racial sensitivity training for officers and a more racially diverse police force.

The article concluded with Reddick uttering the five words that should make any lover of liberty cringe when they hear it from a government activist: "Something has to be done."

By 6:15pm, the editorial board of *The Anniston Star* had uploaded their opinion on that matter under the headline, "Anniston's Crisis and its Future." Their characterization of me and the city's situation as a "crisis" included the usual leftist fodder, words and phrases like "racist," "white supremacists," "national reputation," and a past "littered with painful memories."

The editorial board lauded the city for its handling of the investigation thus far. This should have appeared odd, since the "investigation" was only about 24 hours old, and nothing of substance had been established or revealed. The only thing that could be established was that the usual suspects, the professional protestors and the cowardly politicians, had fallen all over themselves to find a camera or media outlet in order to brandish their credentials as being against "racism" and "hate."

The penultimate paragraph of the board's assessment consisted of one sentence: "Everyone said the proper things."

Because, see, in a world viewed through the lens of social-justice utopia, truth doesn't matter. Contrary viewpoints do not matter. A thorough and evenhanded investigation is really not necessary.

What matters is whether or not those who do speak say "the proper things."

The Anniston Star has long had the reputation of being a liberal paper in a conservative town. The moniker *The Red Star* is common parlance among the resident working class who read it only because they are the only show in town when it comes to local news.

Thursday evening, when I took time to monitor the online activity, I observed that the printed reactions from the public were overwhelming positive toward me and Brown.

From the "Our Readers" section, posted at 5:58pm, Billy Price from Asheville wrote that, although he was not a member of the League,

> "It is a pro-South group if it is anything. I would like for the Southern Poverty Law Center to produce some evidence where any member of the League of the South has ever committed a hate crime... The SPLC is looking under every rock and behind every tree trying to remain relevant as a 'watchdog group' to find racists and to keep the money flowing in. The FBI finally realized a few years ago that the SPLC is a bunch of phonies and stopped taking its advice and opinions on what is or is not a racist group or individual. If I were the Anniston mayor or police chief, I would consider the source of this 'information' before these two policemen sue the city for false accusations and defamation of character."

Mr. Price brought up a valid point. The SPLC, perhaps once considered a reasonable authority on "hate" crimes and groups, had been removed from the FBI's website as a resource on such matters. It appeared several federal agencies had recently begun distancing themselves from the SPLC after complaints from Christian and family-based organizations which had been tarred and targeted by the lefties in Montgomery.

Yet, in June of 2015, they still had it in them to send shivers down the spine of the city "leadership" of the City of Anniston, Alabama.

It is a custom of mine, when finishing the day's yard work, to grab a beer from the refrigerator in the shop I share with my father (who lives next door) and retire for a respite in the rocking chair on the front porch of my house.

It was as I was refreshing this practice when my cell phone rang and I looked to see it was from Nick Bowles, the Internal Affairs lieutenant. *Ah, here it is,* I thought to myself. *A little earlier than I expected.*

"Can you come see me tomorrow?" he asked, trying to sound friendly and not betray the adversarial position into which we had entered. I agreed. The interview was scheduled for ten o' clock the next morning.

I hung up. Sat back in my rocking chair and gazed over my front yard. Contemplated. Prayed. Mentally prepared.

I had no way of knowing it for sure at that point, but I would not have been too surprised that the next day would be the worst day of my life.

4.

"THE CITY IS REACTING TO THE PUBLIC REACTION. THAT'S WHY THIS IS HAPPENING."

19 June 2015

I HAD NOT RETAINED AN ATTORNEY as Friday morning, 19 June, dawned. At that time, I was not sure I was going to need one. I had been told by the police chief two days prior that I could expect to be on leave "at least a month" before any determination would be made about disciplinary action. If that came, I knew I could then make a firm decision. I was still hopeful that an attorney would not be necessary.

Also, I had phoned the national Fraternal Order of Police's (FOP) Legal Defense Plan the day before and confirmed that my full-protection plan was paid and effective. Administrative leave is not a negative disciplinary action, so none had yet been taken against me. If it was (or so I thought) my friends at the FOP would be there to help.

On Thursday evening I did contact a local attorney who agreed to speak with me and provide guidance. I met with him at 9:00am Friday morning, one hour before I was scheduled to meet with Lt. Nick Bowles at the police department. The attorney said he did not feel it was necessary that counsel attend the interview with me. We talked about a few particulars before I left and went to the station.

There was an unexpected occurrence when I met Nick in his office. Seated with him was Alison Ference, who worked for a state prison that was considering the application of one of my subordinates, Correctional Officer Josh Parker. She was seeking information on his quality as an employee, and Nick asked if I had time to speak to her. I agreed, and he left us alone in his office.

We spoke for what seemed like fifteen-to-twenty minutes about Parker. I remember being preoccupied with the enormity of what was going to follow this and being frustrated at having to deal with this other matter.

I knew Alison as being the wife of Alex Ference, an investigator with the Calhoun County District Attorney's Office. I had known Alex for many years. He was a deputy with the Calhoun County Sheriff's Office when I was hired at that agency in March 1997. We served on that agency's Emergency Services Team (SWAT) together. We were both FOP members. We had been to each other's homes and got to know each other's families.

About two years later, I saw Alex for the first time since the whole ordeal with Anniston at a recreational baseball field in Alexandria, where he and Alison's son was playing. We struck up a conversation and he told me that in the recent past he had considered reaching out to me to see how I was doing. For whatever reason, he didn't.

I remember thinking about all the "friends" in the police field I thought I had all those years. "Friends" who never publicly spoke up for me when my name and reputation were being drug through the mud in June of 2015. "Friends" who offered no assistance when I could not find a job in the aftermath. "Friends" who act like their "brothers and sisters" in law enforcement are so meaningful to them that they would lay down their lives for them.

Words matter. But words can be empty. When the time comes for action, empty words are not worth a damn, except to bring an intense clarity to the chimera that is "The Thin Blue Line."

Living through a tragedy is a way of God showing who and what truly matters in one's life.

As a footnote, I did not recommend Parker. He was not a good employee. Whether that had anything to do with it or not, the prison did not hire him. He was still working as an Anniston correctional officer seven months later when he was arrested for murder. He and a friend had an altercation with 42-year-old Deatrice Barclay at the Anniston Wal-Mart that carried over to Barclay's residence in the Saks community (where I live) and gunshots were exchanged. Barclay was found dead.

I ran into Alex a few years later at a gas station, and he related to me that Alison had divorced him. She had struck up a relationship with a man she worked with at the prison.

The night of 19 June 2015 was rough for me. When I reflected upon all that had happened to me that day, I remember thinking of Alison Ference and Josh Parker. Here I was on my way down, with my reputation in jeopardy and my financial livelihood at stake. But here was my young subordinate with his job intact and at the least the possibility of upward mobility in his career. And there was Alison, a beautiful woman with a loving husband and what appeared to be a healthy family.

Earthly happiness is not always what it seems. And God has shown me that the trials He puts His children through are meant for our good, no matter how impossible that can seem when one is going through it.

Talking with Alison that Friday morning in June of 2015, I could never have predicted where I would be four years later. Parker would still be on bond for murder. Alison would be divorced. And whatever happiness she was chasing on this earth, she apparently never found it. Almost six years to the day after we were sitting together in that office, on 22 June 2021, Alison Ference took her own life.

After Alison left Nick's office, he motioned me outside and we went down the hall and into a suspect interview room. This was another sign to me of the significance of the adversarial nature of this interaction. I wasn't just being taped and recorded, which I expected, I was being sat in "the suspect chair" in an interview room typically used for criminal investigators to interrogate criminal suspects.

Countless times I had sat across from that chair as a case investigator with APD, trying to obtain a confession from a criminal. So, it was hard to escape the feeling that that was how I was being treated by my employer and fellow officers – like a criminal.

The quotes used in this account come from the official transcript of the interview, entered into evidence at my trial by the City of Anniston.

As we entered the interview room, I asked, "I'm showing my ignorance here. Is this standard procedure?"

Nick went on to explain that he had used the interview room "once before," when investigating a suicide by a jail inmate. In other words, when the situation is deemed major, they use the interview room.

Nick asked, "You have never been a part of...an Internal Affairs investigation?"

"Well," I answered, "when we went through this same issue six years ago..."

I wanted to make sure we got it on record that I was being investigated for the same issue I had been cleared of six years prior.

Nick then went on to explain my rights under *Garrity*, which springs from the Fifth Amendment right against self-incrimination. *Garrity* means a government employer can compel an employee to provide testimony about something in an internal affairs investigation that can be used for civil and departmental charges, but not criminal charges.

So, I could have refused to answer Nick's questions. But I could have incurred discipline through that. I could not have been charged with anything criminal as a result of my testimony (and there was nothing criminal I had done, anyway), but I was opening myself up to my testimony being used against me in a disciplinary or civil hearing.

I knew the city was digging. They were trying to find something they could clutch onto in order to justify what they already intended to do – fire me. So, one school of thought was that I should not say anything and therefore provide them with no further ammunition. But the other school of thought which I adopted, and the one I think turned out to be true and more beneficial to me in the long run, was to go ahead and go on record. They were going to fire me regardless. I had an opportunity here to throw some of this back at Bowles, and by proxy Denham, Johnson, and city attorney Bruce Downey, who I knew was watching the video of this in the Investigations room.

Wayne Brown had already been in the same room earlier that morning. Of course, the details of his testimony were unknown to me at the time.

NB: "Let's talk about the League of the South... when did you join them?"

JD: "In the fall of 1995."

NB: "And why did you join them?"

JD: "They...[were] pro-South. They are for the Southern people. They are for the advancement of the Southern people and wanted to promote the independence and wellbeing of the Southern people by any honorable means, and I thought that the Southern people needed that kind of advocacy and that was the group for it."

Nick verified that the national organization was founded in 1994 and I joined in 1995. He asked how many members there were, and I didn't know. He really pressed me on this. I guess the strategy was to hopefully show how "fringe" the League was by showing how few members there were. But I honestly didn't know, and for the first time used the Fraternal Order of Police (FOP), of which Nick and I were both active members, as an analogy.

JD: "It didn't take me long when I joined the lodge [FOP] to learn that there were thirty people who show up but three hundred members, you know?"

NB: "I have no idea."

Exactly, he had no idea. Just like most of my fellow Southerners who are members of a church have no idea how many actual "members" there are. Many members, or people on a roll, do not attend on a regular basis. And many of those who are in attendance are not members. The average member doesn't know these things, and really shouldn't care, as the number of members has no significance on the value of the worship.

Nick then asked if I was a current member of the League and to describe my involvement.

JD: "I am a dues-paying member. I'm not in a leadership position. I don't have a lot of involvement. I go to meetings, sometimes far off, I go to conferences. And that's about it."

Nick asked if I was requested to speak at the national conference in 2013 and I confirmed I was. Then he asked what my major was in college, and I told him criminal justice. My plan was always to become a peace officer. He asked if any of the League people in college had "any reservations about that?"

"No," I answered.

Bowles asked questions about suspicions League people had about my plans to enter the police field. There were none I observed. We covered me moving from Tuscaloosa to Alexandria and beginning my police career in 1997.

Then he asked me a question I knew he knew the answer to, and I was not going to let the opportunity pass to exploit it.

NB: "What year was the local chapter started?"

JD: "That was March of 2009. You were there."

Nick was visibly shaken by this, and, I must admit, I enjoyed watching his discomfort as his gaze shifted to his notes, which he began thumbing through as he completely ignored my last comment.

Nick had spoken to me extensively about the League when he and I worked together in the APD Investigative division in 2008-09. He encouraged my plans about starting a local chapter in the latter part of 2008. And he and his wife at the time attended our inaugural meeting in March of 2009.

Nick stumbled and dodged. "March '09?"

JD: "Yeah."

NB: "When you – you told me what the goal of the national League of the South is. What is the goal of the local chapter?"

As if the goal of the local chapter would be any different...

JD: "Same thing. It has always been the same. It has been twenty years. Two police agencies have hired me. It has been okay all this time until forty-eight hours ago. Nothing has changed."

The city knew it was in trouble if it could not somehow assert that at least *something* had changed since 2009, when my involvement with the League had been allowed. Nick was in a desperate situation of trying to drag something from me to show how the circumstances had changed.

It was at this point I conceded that there were internal decisions and new members of whom I did not approve. However, I emphasized that the "stated goal of the national organization" had not changed. The "core values" (aka policy) of the League was something with which I was still in agreement. And when an institution you love and believe in, be it a heritage organization, a fraternal organization, a church body of Christ, etc., begins to alter their course, the common and understood action of the member who loves it is not to immediately abandon the ship, but to attempt to right it. And that is how I saw my position in relation to the League in 2013-2015. I would elaborate on this further during my court testimony.

NB: "I'm going to ask some pointed questions. What is the League's stance on African Americans?"

JD: "That is on their website under 'Frequently Asked Questions.' I could only try to paraphrase that... That we should work with blacks in a spirit of Christianity to better both races in an independent South."

NB: "Do you agree with that?"

JD: "I do."

We discussed the influence of Christianity on the League, which was immense.

NB: "What is the League's stance on overthrowing the federal government?"

JD: "They are against overthrowing the federal government, against it."

NB: "Do you agree with that?"

JD: "I do."

I then elaborated on the Southern nationalist view of changing things through legal, peaceful secession and means such as State legislation.

Nick asked where I disagreed with League ideas. I said that any organization is going to have individuals who disagree with each other over various things. This was elementary. But at that time I had no disagreement with what the League had put down in writing that served as the official policy/core values. In my upcoming trial, the city would find all sorts of things that League President **Dr.** Michael Hill had written on social media and articles that were outside the boundaries of League policy, especially recent things. The strategy was to create guilt-by-association. Even though I disagreed individually with what **Dr.** Hill or another member said or wrote, because they wrote or said it, and they were part of and even influential in the same organization I was, then the city was going to forward that I must also believe that way.

I know of no one who could stand the scrutiny of such implementation. Under this type of application, no one could ever prudently join any type of association because at some point, someone in that organization would commit an action for which all other members could be held responsible.

I provided Nick a particular example: In the early 2000s, the idea of reparations for Southerners based on how much the War Between the States cost us in money, property, education, and government influence was introduced by the League. It may have been merely a talking point, but some in the League were probably serious about the idea.

I am against the idea of reparations in any form. So, I was against the League pushing this idea. If anyone would have said that, because I was a League member, and the League as an entity was forwarding this idea as a positive, then I must also be on board with it, they would be uttering a falsehood.

One can be a member of something and not agree with all that something does.

An example my attorney came up with and used during my trial was very insightful. It was during 2015 that Donald Trump announced his candidacy for United States president. He wound up, to the astonishment of many people, capturing the nomination for the Republican party the next year. Trump could be characterized as a very polarizing figure, and he was opposed on many different issues by those within his own party.

If someone had tried to use against these Republicans who opposed Trump the same strategy the city used to prosecute me, there would have been howls of protest. And the city also tried to say that **Dr.** Hill was no mere member, he was the president of the League and was, therefore, authorized to speak for it. However, similarly, Trump was the chosen candidate for the Republican party. Yet, there were many Republicans that were against him, and they would have said on any number of issues that Trump did not speak for them, and they were more committed to the party than the party's current candidate.

To further the point, Trump then shocked many on both sides of the aisle when he won the presidency. For the next four years, Trump was the duly elected chief executive of the country and commander-in-chief of the armed forces. But there were certainly those within the country, and, still, many in his own party, who disagreed with many of his words and actions. They did not think it necessary to leave the country or even leave their party so that they would not be branded with complicity in the words and actions of Trump. They worked from within to change things.

Later in the interview, I made the point that, at the time, Barack Obama was the president of the United States. Did that mean that all citizens were responsible for what he said and what his positions were? Because President Obama said something, did that mean citizen Josh Doggrell must be on board with it because I chose to remain a citizen, living in this country?

So it was for me and the League in 2013-2015. The city's position was that I admitted there were problems in the League, but since I did not leave the organization, I became responsible for what individual members, and particularly **Dr.** Hill, did and spoke. My position was that when you are a part of something, especially something you have invested such a large part of your life in and which you believed in so strongly, you first tried to right the wrongs before simply leaving.

But by that time, the city was in the position of tremendous attempts to justify an action they had already taken. I was fired on 19 June, and, until the trial started on 26 August, they were struggling to explain why.

I told Nick, "So, yeah...there are things that the [FOP] lodge does and hasn't done over the years...steps they have taken and not taken...and it has never caused me to stop being a member of the lodge, but it doesn't mean I go along lockstep with everything that the lodge or my church or the League does."

Nick moved on to a list of questions that I figured came straight from the city attorney.

NB: "Have you ever been approached by a League of the South member who asked you to do something illegal?"

JD: "No."

NB: "Have you ever been approached by a League of the South member and asked to do something immoral?"

JD: "No."

NB: "Have you ever witnessed anything done by a League of the South member that is illegal?"

JD: "Illegal? No."

NB: "How about immoral? And, of course, moral is subjective."

JD: "My definition?"

NB: "Yeah."

JD: "No, I haven't."

NB: "Have you ever used your police power to access records not available to the general public for anybody in the League of the South?"

JD: "No."

This list of questions continued with police decisions, race, religion, and sexual orientation. All answers were "No."

Questions then veered to Lt. Wayne Brown and how he came to be a League member. Not only from the questions here, but the testimony of Brown at federal depositions a year later (Brown was not a witness at the civil trial), I learned that Brown was not wholly truthful. He went into a save-his-ass mode. The truth is that Brown excitedly and willfully joined the League. He went to several events with me in 2013. He never once expressed any regret about anything. As a matter of fact, his exuberance continued to grow in our conversations. He told me shortly before the SPLC article that he was planning on attending the 2015 national conference.

Yet, the picture he painted for the city now that the heat was on him was one in which he very tepidly approached the League, and he was filled with reservations. He told them he only joined because he thought one had to be a member to attend the national conference. This was not true. He told city officials that he witnessed and heard things that disturbed him at League events. If this was true, he never once mentioned it to me.

It is my belief that Brown was trying to escape the ramifications of his own, independent actions. In doing so, he abandoned the truth and showed little regard for how this would affect me. But the city rewarded him for his duplicity. He was allowed to retire. I was fired.

Nick began asking me about **Dr.** Hill and recent quotes and posts from him. He asked questions about whether I had ever been to his house or vacationed with him. I answered the questions (I had not) and then asked about their relevance.

It was then that Nick revealed, probably inadvertently, something huge. This was something we would revisit during the trial and when Nick said he did not remember divulging it, we had to show him this transcript to prove he did, at which time he agreed he did.

Here is the exchange in totality:

NB: "You are a police officer."

JD: "Right."

NB: "And I'm going to shoot straight, man, you have been doing this job longer than me, and you were an investigator for about as long as I was."

JD: "Uh-huh."

NB: "The city is reacting to the public reaction. That's why this is happening."

JD: "Uh-huh."

NB: "Had Facebook, Twitter, the news or whatever happened in 2009, this would have happened in 2009... I mean, it's a completely different ballgame."

JD: "Would you agree that the right and wrong of an issue shouldn't be determined by public outcry?"

NB: "That's not my job to determine."

JD: "All I'm asking is would you agree with that?"

NB: "All I do is ask questions, collect facts, just like any investigation –"

JD: "We are deciding an issue on its merits and talking about laws and policies and constitutional rights. Does it matter if public outcry – is it up to public outcry to determine law, policies, constitutional rights?"

NB: "You tell me."

JD: "No."

Imagine, in the world we live in today, if "public outcry" was the deciding factor in determining the right and wrong of any number of issues.

Officer Darren Wilson was not indicted by a grand jury on any criminal charge for shooting and killing Michael Brown in Ferguson, Missouri, in 2014 because the jury found that he acted justifiably and in self-defense when that criminal attacked him in the immediate aftermath of Brown robbing a convenience store and accosting an employee there. Brown attempted to disarm Wilson. Wilson's actions were not only justifiable, but probably saved his own life and other lives that may have been lost to Brown's actions that day.

But because there existed a criminal element and enablers/condoners in the government and their propaganda arm, the mainstream media, a dangerous and destructive riot ensued. The "public outcry" demanded that the facts were not what they were, that the "innocent" Brown had been gunned down by a racist white cop, and that that cop deserved to be charged and convicted of murder.

Had "public outcry" been the determining factor, Darren Wilson would be in a prison cell today.

I never made it to a prison cell, but, as Nick Bowles clearly laid out in this exchange, the reason I lost my job, my career, my retirement, and my reputation was not because anything I had done was wrong (against law, policy, procedure), but because, as he said, "The city is reacting to the public reaction. That's why this is happening."

Nick shifted to asking about particular people in the League and how well I knew them. He asked about the difference between white nationalism and Southern nationalism.

Nick had made several flattering references to me in the interview, an investigative ploy to attempt to get the interviewee to agree with what follows:

NB: "But you understand – you have to understand, because you are a very smart man."

JD: "Thank you. You are a smart man, too. You look very dapper today."

Translation: I know what you're doing.

NB: "You get it that the majority-minority city that we live in–"

JD: "How is that even a [mathematical] possibility?"

NB: "You understand what I am saying. The majority black city that we live in is up in arms about you being a twenty-year member of this group..."

I do not think the seven people that showed up at the press conference at city hall the previous day (two of whom were white) constitute a "majority black city" being "up in arms," but we would also have to consider, again, if a "public outcry" should determine the right and wrong of a situation.

NB: "...that's where the city has to react to that."

JD: "Oh, react to it, yeah. I mean, somebody makes a complaint, you look into it. It doesn't mean you rush to judgment or make irrational decisions or disregard rights, law, policies, or the ultimate things of, does this affect his performance. You don't base those decisions of right and wrong on 'public outcry.' Because, I mean, we are headed to a period of time in the country, too, where the church is going to keep being attacked, and you can see that with things like same-sex marriage..."

And note: Exactly a week after I uttered those words in the interview with Bowles, the United States Supreme Court issued its *Obergefell* decision, for the first time legalizing homosexual marriage throughout the United States.

"...And we will get to the point where that is going to be driven down the throats of churches... The SPLC has this big, long list of hate groups, which they color and paint with a broad brush... keeps...money coming to their pockets...So, yeah, they are going to call all kinds of people 'hate groups.' And...if you go down that list, a large percentage of those are Christian organizations... I talked to my pastor last night...he said, well, you know, I guess I will be the next target. And I said, don't think you are not, because the same things you preach from the pulpit on Sunday morning are the things they say hateful people say. They are in the business of character assassination and attacking people and ruining their lives and taking away their jobs because a certain [amount of] people don't think like they do..."

In response to this, Nick made some more comments we would revisit when he was on the stand. He was referring to the "Intelligence Report," a publication by the SPLC that they sent to police departments. The SPLC deemed it "the nation's preeminent periodical monitoring the radical right in the U.S."

NB: "Well, like I said, I stopped reading [them]... I get them and throw them in the garbage..."

JD: "Good place for them."

NB: "Because I saw, it was just, it was the same ol', same ol' everything, and just the scare tactics, that's all that I personally saw it as."

JD: "That's what this is, a scare tactic, and it's working."

We spoke further about how far the idea that one man speaking for an entity binds or projects that onto the entity as a whole. Then Nick said this:

NB: "I have never witnessed Josh Doggrell make a decision based on race or –"

JD: "Right. That's where I go back to my main points. I have not violated any rights, not violated any laws, not violated any policy...no kind of views that I hold, faith or politics or economics or anything negatively affects the way I do my job... Let me give you another example if I may. We have homosexuals that work here. I know there is a homosexual that's a subordinate of mine. The only reason I know that is because she interjects it into any and every – each and every conversation she can. That's her business. I disagree with the homosexual lifestyle. I disagree with 'shacking up.' That's my personal view based on being a Christian. I disagree with some of my past conduct and am ashamed of it, but in no way has that ever affected the working relationship she and I have nor the subordinate/superior relationship that [we] have...her sexual preference and her lifestyle has in no way affected the way I have treated her as an employee."

I then referenced an article in the paper that day that used the *McMullen* case as justification for my termination. I explained in detail how that case differed from mine.

JD: "I think there are people in city hall looking for – they are stretching and looking to find something – they have already made the decision to fire me... Now they have to come up with a reason to do it..."

NB: "Do you think that your being a member brings discredit on the police department and the members of the police department?"

JD: "No."

NB: "Even in light of the current press hoorah?"

JD: "I believe that anybody can make an allegation and call a name and hurl insults and even in this case engage in character assassination and try to get people's livelihoods and jobs taken away to where they can't support their family anymore and that doesn't make it right... I don't think some of these people out there that are grandstanding and making political points out of this ever... sit and take into account the damage they do to somebody and their families."

I was asked about the Confederate battle flag:

JD: "I'm proud of that flag. It was a flag that the Confederate soldiers carried with them in battle, fought under, died under. Its main feature is the St. Andrew's Cross that represents the cross that St. Andrew died on, so it's a symbol of faith for me as well. It's the same symbol [cross] that's in our State flag, so it has got a lot of heritage for Alabamians and the South, the fact that it was carried by the soldiers in the war. And I think it has become, over the years, from 1863 to the present day, the most identifiable symbol of the Southern people."

Once again, Nick brought up the public outcry:

NB: "Do you understand the uproar, why that they are in such an uproar?"

JD: "...I understand it. It doesn't make it right, and it doesn't mean that we should dictate what we do based on that, but, yes, I understand it..."

NB: "Has many of the League of the South members reached out to you?"

JD: "A whole lot more than police officers."

NB: "I think a lot of them, they don't know..."

JD: "Plenty here know me and know how hard that this has affected me. And I tell you this, I talked to my dad this morning, and he goes, 'If this had happened when I was working, police officers would be on the front steps of city hall raising hell'... You work with people and you think they know you and know the truth..."

NB: "Why do you think that is?"

JD: "Because they are afraid they are going to be sitting in this chair and have their livelihood ruined or their job taken away... the mass of people are just not willing to stand up for something if it's going to cost them something..."

NB: "...Why would it cost you your job?"

JD: "[Denham] said the other day the city manager wanted to fire me."

NB: "But why?"

JD: "Because it's easier to do that and satisfy the wolves than to do the right thing..."

NB: [Referring to the video of my speech] "...there was nothing on the video that I saw, unless I missed something, I didn't see anything in there inflammatory... But I think when you were identified and identified yourself as a peace officer, that's what draws the eye or that's what draws the spotlight. And just like you said with Ferguson and Baltimore and everything, it's cool to hate cops right now, it just is."

The interview concluded with me expressing appreciation for the fact that city officials had to deal with this and come up with a way to sell whatever decision was made to all the public. Nick asked me for a suggestion. Off the cuff, I came up with this:

JD: "Something along the lines of, we have done this investigation... We looked into this. We have talked with Lt. Doggrell. We have examined his relationship with the League... there are several members of the League that [he] doesn't care for and [he] doesn't hold views that individuals within the League [have] said, there have even been positions that the League leadership has taken that [he] doesn't agree with which would be the same...in any organization that [he] has ever been a part of, including the FOP and [his] church. I would ask that we evaluate him on what he [has] said and his actions and his record as a police officer and his relationship with...his coworkers, peers, subordinates, superiors, and the public, and his record does not support the kind of monster the SPLC is trying to make him out to be. We are sympathetic with the concerns of the community, including the black community, that you wouldn't want someone who was a 'hateful person' to be in public service; we wouldn't want that, either. And our investigation has ruled that that's not the case. And, if anything changes, we will take appropriate action."

All of that would have been honest and could have been successful. It had been six years before. It would be five years later.

But the officials in charge of the City of Anniston in 2015 were not willing to go that route.

Following this, I asked to see Chief Denham. I met him in his office. He and I were the only ones physically present.

"I think he's [Brian Johnson] going to fire you, and I think it's going to be today."

Denham had just returned from the funeral of a retired officer. I do not think he had met with Johnson yet that day and had not been able to view my interview with Bowles due to his attendance at the funeral. Thus, my interview counted for little. The decision to fire me was made by Brian Johnson already, probably as soon as he started receiving heat on Wednesday. It was all a matter of going through the motions now and trying to come up with a justifiable reason.

The real reason: Johnson and Denham had been cowed by, first, the SPLC, and second, by a relatively few (but loud) group of local race agitators, who screamed for blood.

I asked Denham for what policy was I going to be fired and he responded, "I don't know."

"I'm going to fight this," I told him.

"I had no doubt you would."

I returned home to be with my family.

Denham texted me about fifteen minutes before the conference to notify me it was going to take place.

From *The Anniston Star's* coverage, all officials present (viewed in their photo are Johnson, Denham, four of the five councilmen, "city spokeswoman" Aziza Jackson, and another unidentifiable person) who spoke were striving to assure all that this did not serve as an indictment on the whole department. They also wanted to make *completely clear* that they themselves were in *no way* racist. They patted themselves on the back for how well they had handled the situation. And some obligatory comments directed to the race hustlers were included.

Mayor Vaughn Stewart: "This city will not tolerate any kind of connection to racism and bigotry."

Councilman Seyram Selase: "The city has taken these allegations very seriously. The city has an obligation to ensure all citizens feel comfortable and safe with people sworn to protect them."

One might have expected one of the officials to grab a guitar under the table and begin singing "Kumbaya" as another lit a candle and the rest joined hands.

Kumbaya, my Lord, Kumbaya...

Councilman David Reddick used the opportunity to suggest the council and other employees attend racial sensitivity training in the future. "We also need to make changes in ourselves."

Kumbaya, my Lord, Kumbaya...

Councilman Jay Jenkins: "It is unfortunate and disappointing that we have to deal with a situation like this in today's world. But we did handle it well, I am comfortable with that."

Kumbaya, my Lord, Kumbaya...

Reaching out to the SPLC for comment, they began their victory dance, probably pleasantly surprised how fast the city had caved. "Director of the Intelligence Project" for the SPLC, Heidi Beirich, offered, "I'm really glad the city responded. You don't want law enforcement officers involved in hate groups."

Johnson said the "investigation" discovered my "active involvement in the group," which he said led to my firing. Johnson said Brown, who had been allowed to retire, had "cut his involvement with the group in 2013." Again — this was *not* true.

Johnson also said plans were then underway to amend the city's personnel policy to prevent city employees from being involved in hate groups. I wondered why that was necessary, since he had just said I had been fired for "being involved in a hate group." If a policy needed to be made or amended to account for such, what, exactly, was the policy for which I had been fired? At no time at the press conference/peace gathering was that mentioned.

The Anniston Star editorial board posted an endorsement of the city's action a few hours later. The SPLC published their mission-accomplished piece on Hatewatch a short time after that.

There is a whole lot of truth to the old adage, "You can't fight city hall." They have a tremendous amount of resources on their side. You do not. They get paid for the time they spend preparing. You do not. They get to prepare on the job. You do not. They have leverage against all the potential witnesses that are city employees. You do not.

Regardless, I prepared to fight.

And, if the city thought the pandering and nauseating supplication they had performed would help keep the wolves away, they were sadly mistaken.

5.

...With the Church Burnings and the Charleston Shooting...

20 June – 26 August 2015

> My orders are to fight;
>
> Then if I bleed, or fail,
>
> Or strongly win, what matters it?
>
> God only doth prevail.
>
> The servant craveth naught
>
> Except to serve with might.
>
> I was not told to win or lose,–
>
> My orders are to fight.
>
> "My Orders" —Ethelwyn Wetherald

WHEN I WAS YOUNG, I would have nightmares. As I began waking up, still groggy from sleep, it would slowly dawn on me that the dream I had been experiencing was not real, and a wave of relief would wash over me.

After 19 June 2015, the worst day of my life, I had the opposite effect. As I would wake in that same state of grogginess, my mind would begin trying to convince me that I had been living a nightmare in which I had been publicly humiliated and lost my career and livelihood. But as the seconds passed and reality began taking hold, instead of a wave of relief, a weighty and horrendous dread consumed me as its reality firmly gripped my soul.

It wasn't a dream. It really happened – and was still happening. And I had to crawl from bed, face it again, and try to find a path to deal with it.

One of things I have related to people when I speak of this experience is how God used it to bring clarity to my life. There were people I thought were my friends who, it turned out, were definitely not. There was help received from unlikely sources. And there were real friends who showed that they were genuine. This was a time when a cost was attached to knowing me and calling me a friend.

The biggest disappointment was the Fraternal Order of Police, which styles itself "The Voice of Our Nation's Law Enforcement Officers." I had been a member of our local lodge in Anniston since I was old enough to be one, and my father was also and had been for decades. That body turned its back on us. The active members I called did not take my calls nor call me back. Being a paying member of that organization's Legal Defense Plan under "full coverage," I applied for help with cost and counsel when I determined to challenge the city's actions against me. My application was ignored.

Due to my Wednesday night Bible class I was leading that spring, I had not been to an FOP lodge meeting in several weeks. Still being an active member, I decided to attend on the first meeting in July.

I had never felt hostility inside those walls before feeling it that night. The members must have been approached and told they had to make a decision to either side with me or side with the department. They chose the department. Mike Reese, a retired officer who now was one of the three civil-service board members who would decide my fate at the appeal trial, was not a frequent attender of lodge meetings. Yet, on this night, just weeks after my firing, here he was passing out the minutes from the previous meeting and sitting at the front table as an apparent lodge officer.

As they say, the fix was in. That was my last lodge meeting.

I learned what a fallacy "The Thin Blue Line" was. It turns out, cops are largely like everyone else. They might talk a good game and lay the fellowship on thick, but when the times get tough, they look out for number one.

The period of time from 19 June to 26 August 2015 was, overall, a dark and uncertain time for me and my family. My wife was very distraught and mentally affected. She did not want to leave our house, fearful of confrontation, media exposure/pressure, awkward interactions.

19 June was the beginning of Father's Day weekend. The city-government circus took the weekend off, but they were back in full swing on Monday, 22 June. As city officials continued to fall all over themselves to prove how racist they weren't, an article was posted to *The Anniston Star's* website reporting that "[t]he state NAACP on Monday called for a deeper investigation by state and federal officials into the Anniston Police Department and its officers' possible ties to hate groups."

The liberal white appeaser in this country never learns. Attempts to placate a mob *do not work*. It only encourages and emboldens them, like sharks tasting blood.

On the very next workday after the press conference where I was fired, the one where the city officials showed their amazing dexterity of being able to pat themselves all on the back at the very same time, the wolves were mobilizing for more. The president of the Alabama State Conference of the NAACP, Bernard Simelton, did not share the good tidings about how well the city had acted. He told the *Star* his "goal is for the investigation to determine how long the police department knew about the officers' ties to the group and if any other officers have connections with similar groups. 'We want to know why they didn't take action.'"

That same day the author of the article, Patrick McCreless, came to my home. I met him on the front porch. Although I really wanted to comment, I continued to follow counsel's advice and did not "at this time." McCreless reported this in his article while mentioning I had a "Confederate-era flag hung from a pole in the front yard."

(Still do.)

There was something revealing in this article. McCreless wrote about me having the right to appeal to the civil service board to overturn the firing. Then he got this comment from a board member:

> "Board member Randy Third said during a Monday phone interview that he had not heard whether Doggrell had filed an appeal... 'We'll listen to it and if he doesn't like the ruling, then he can go across the street to the courthouse,' Third said, referring to Doggrell filing a lawsuit at the Calhoun County Courthouse."

Well, not exactly. Third was referring to the fact that, under State law, if I lost at the board level, I could appeal that to the Calhoun County Circuit Court. However, what was indicative to me was Third's verbiage.

To me, it read like an assumption that I would not like the ruling. There was nothing mentioned about the city not liking the ruling and having the right to take it across the street. It was comments like these (others will be covered later) that led me to my belief that I never had a chance with this board. Their minds were made up before the hearing, and they never wavered. The case we delivered in the courtroom in August and September was a good one. We were right. The city was wrong. But, when it comes to racial intimidation and cowardly leadership, a white man in this country is doomed.

Still, not all citizens were onboard. From the "Our Readers" section of the *Star* dated 21 June, Canaan Elkins of Anniston wrote,

> "It is a sad day...we are going into a downward spiral of totalitarianism that will obliterate personal freedoms and liberties... The decision by the city manager to fire Lt. Josh Doggrell is completely unconstitutional. The officer did not commit any crime. The officer has the same rights as any other American... the SPLC has caused two men to lose their jobs; that sounds more like hate to me. The SPLC is not a court. The SPLC is not a jury. So why is the City of Anniston submitting to the SPLC? The city has committed a grave injustice to these officers."

From the same section on 23 June, a friend of Wayne Brown's, Don Copeland of Anniston, wrote,

> "A cloud has come over his [Wayne's] life. I am stunned and overcome by my friend's troubles... The Southern Poverty Law Center has alone decided that this group is the equivalent of ISIS, the Ku Klux Klan, Al-Qaida and so on... This is an Anniston shame and loss."

On that Monday morning, I was in a state of flux. After having been fired, I really still did not know why. Johnson had said at the press conference it was because I had been a member of the League. But, I still had to have allegedly *done* something that violated a law or policy. I needed to know not only about payment (I was due a last paycheck), I also needed to know about family insurance, as I was the only breadwinner and all my family members were covered under the city insurance.

Furthermore, I had read the State law concerning appealing the decision and it stated I had ten days to file an appeal with the civil service board, which I intended to do. But I needed to know what, exactly, I was appealing, other than the simple fact I had been terminated.

I phoned my immediate supervisor, Captain Greg Feazell, and asked what policy I had violated to be fired. He said he would have to get with the chief and call me back.

A while later, Feazell called me back. He said the chief also did not know what policy I had violated to be fired. He would have to get with the city manager.

A while later, Feazell called again. He said the city manager and city attorney were working on the reason(s) I was fired and would put them on paper to be delivered to me. As of right then, I was actually *not* fired, and still on administrative leave. "You mean," I replied, "that even though it was announced to the whole world three days ago that I was fired, I'm really not fired?"

"Well, not yet," Feazell chuckled, as if this was all a big joke. He said he had also gotten with human resources and I was still drawing full pay and benefits until it was "official."

For the love, I thought. This whole ridiculous charade would probably be comical if it were not so serious. Feazell said I would have ten days from the time I was actually served with papers, giving the reasons for termination, to file my appeal.

"So, let me get this straight," I said. "Those goons are assembled over at city hall, scratching their heads, trying to come up with reasons after the fact why they fired me?"

Feazell gave me more nervous, goofy laughter and said that the chief's position was that this wasn't coming from the police department, but city hall. Right, I thought. This coming from the same guy that was seated at the press conference Friday nodding in all the right places and collecting his "I'm Not a Racist" participatory placard, suitable for framing.

I set about the business of trying to find an attorney. This proved an incredibly difficult task. I spoke to many people and lawyers. I even contacted the ACLU, thinking that, as repulsive as I found that organization, this might be right up their alley. A representative, to his credit, phoned me back and heard me out before explaining that his group was in the business of working against police, not for them. My plea that I was no longer police, and actually going against them, did not seem to matter to him. Apparently I was tainted with a blue haze that had not evaporated yet.

I called and messaged friends, relatives, lawyers I knew, many I did not know. The week ended without anyone willing to take the case. Many were very up front. It was a good case; I had been wronged. But it was 2015, there was a national atmosphere of hostility and angst toward police, I had been accused of being a racist, and therefore, the facts really did not matter. The reality was my case was unwinnable.

On Thursday, 25 June, Feazell called again. He asked if I was available for him to meet with me at my home. I knew that meant he had been tasked with the unfortunate assignment of serving me with my termination papers. Well, I thought. The jackasses finally figured out why they were firing me. I told Feazell I would meet him in my driveway. I was not about to allow him in my home.

Upon meeting, Feazell once again took the opportunity to tell me that the chief's position was that this was not coming from the police department, but from across the street at city hall. I had no reason to believe him, but if he was telling the truth, as we shall see, Denham was sure converted to The Appeasers' mode of operation by the time he testified at my trial two months later.

Dated 25 June 2015, from "BRIAN JOHNSON, CITY MANAGER" in all caps, as seemed appropriate from someone with such a large view of himself, was my "NOTICE OF DISCIPLINARY ACTION."

It took six days to come up with two, double-spaced pages. I was accused of "Engaging in conduct unbecoming of a sworn officer...," "Associating with persons and organizations of ill repute...," "Violating the City of Anniston's Anti-Harassment Policy, including use of social media in a harassing, divisive, offensive and prejudicial manner," "Participating in or conducting speeches...in your capacity as an officer...without prior approval of the Chief of Police...," and "Engaging in conduct, activities, and speech that has (1) impeded the performance of your duties..., (2) interfered and disrupted the operation and efficiency of the Anniston Police Department..., (3) damaged the public perception, confidence and trust in you, as a sworn peace officer..., (4) implicated and associated the Anniston Police Department...with divisive, offensive and prejudicial beliefs and objectives, and (5) caused and exacerbated racial tensions and distrust in the Anniston Police Department and the City of Anniston."

It was all untrue, and easy to combat. If I could just find a lawyer...

I have a friend who likes to joke about his shyness and difficulties with women prior to meeting the woman who would become his wife. "When people ask how I knew she was 'the one,'" he says, "I tell them because she said 'yes' when I asked her out."

When people ask me why in the world I hired Kenneth Shinbaum to represent me, I tell them the truth. He was the only one who said yes.

I had gotten to the point of sending mass messages to law firms specializing in wrongful termination and labor laws. Finally, toward the end of June, Kenneth Shinbaum of McPhillips -Shinbaum in

Montgomery called me back. His first offer was too expensive for us. He came back with a drastically reduced offer and we accepted on 1 July.

Meanwhile, back at city hall, The Appeasers were still racking their brains on new and improved ways they could show how really, *really* non-racist they were for the month of July. On 26 June, *The Anniston Star* ran a story under the headline, "City of Anniston announces partnership with U.S. Justice Department to resolve racial tension." At the city's service was a federal-government initiative "dedicated to helping state and local governments... prevent and resolve racial and ethnic tensions, civil disorder based on race, color, or national origin, and to address and prevent hate crimes..."

The Appeasers were going all in on liberal, social justice farces and virtue signaling. Johnson said, "the partnership was arranged to address the aftermath of the two police officers' departure" and that the feds "help communities move forward after there is actual *or even perceived discrimination."* [Emphasis added]

Note, here, the federal government is always there to help. Why, they can swoop into a local Southern community and help it "move forward" *even if there was no actual discrimination!* They can help you move forward even if bad stuff is even *perceived!*

On the second day of that month, the *Star* reported, again, that the city was entering into a "partnership" with the federal Department of Justice's Community Relations Service (created by the Civil Rights Act of 1964) due to "recent race-related problems." But the pace had hit a snag.

Brian Johnson lamented that "...they're being stretched kind of thin right now with the church burnings and the Charleston shooting, so they're having to pull off to go to those."

How sad that The Appeasers were delayed in getting the feds to teach them how to be better mega-non-racists, especially when those church burnings were already in the process of being proven to be another round in a long history of hoaxes involving accusations of targeted black church arsons.

Church Burnings:
Falsified History Repeats Itself | National Review

Later that same day, the *Star's* editorial board, the Amen Corner for The Appeasers, released a predictable editorial praising the city for bringing in the feds.

Also on 2 July, I filed my notice of appeal with the civil service board. Board secretary Heather Stephens accepted the notice. In subsequent news accounts by multiple sources, a board "representative" reported that I had filed the notice on 25 June. This untruth was probably concocted because the city did not want it to get out that I had not been officially fired until that date. Johnson probably did not want the press and the city to know that he had announced firing someone when he really hadn't. It took away from the theatrics of the press conference.

My appeal was dated 2 July. Dixon Hayes of the WBRC Fox News affiliate reported on 13 July: "We requested a copy of Doggrell's appeal, but Secretary Heather Stephens declined to provide it 'at this time' and gave no reason. This despite the fact a filed civil service appeal usually becomes public record in other cities."

The appeal notice was not the only thing the city was hiding. I was initially denied my personnel file by the department. When they finally turned it over, all my letters of commendation were absent, as was my application to be hired, which had listed my membership in the League of the South. The application would mysteriously reappear at the time of federal depositions a year later. The city also refused to hand over the file of the 2009 internal investigation, or any of its details or findings.

On 8 July, there was an interesting piece on al.com by Brian Lawson, covering how far the First Amendment goes in protecting government employees' actions. My case was mentioned:

> "Anniston officials said Doggrell's association with the League of the South was investigated in 2009, but they determined his membership had not 'crossed over' into his work as a police officer, Anniston City Manager Brian Johnson told AL.com. Johnson said Doggrell's personnel file had been 'without blemish.'"

The article cited two court cases. One was the 1968 Supreme Court case *Pickering v. Board of Education.* The justices said a public employee's speech on matters of public concern were protected "absent proof of false statements knowingly or recklessly made." In my case, the city did not prove that I did that.

In *Garcetti v. Ceballos,* the court ruled "a government entity has broader discretion to restrict speech when it acts in its role as employer, but the restrictions it imposes must be directed at speech that has some potential to affect the entity's operations."

Now, I'm sure the City of Anniston would claim that my speech had "potential to affect [their] operations." However, my speech had been given two years prior, off duty, in a town eighty miles away. City operations had not been affected for two years. They were only affected when the SPLC produced their hit piece with accompanying inflammatory misinformation. Who was responsible?

My speech was primarily about gun control, certainly a "matter of public concern." The City of Anniston had no policy prohibiting one of its employees exercising his First Amendment rights by speaking in such a manner, as practiced under the guidelines of these two court cases.

The article stated, "The City of Anniston did not return calls regarding the specific basis for the officer's firing." Hmm. Wonder why?

On 13 August, I attended the regular meeting of the civil service board. By State law, they had to set a date for my hearing, and they did so. 14 September was chosen. But the board also set a meeting for 26 August to receive testimony from past police chief Layton McGrady, since he was planning on being out of town at the time of the hearing.

My first of several meetings with Shinbaum in his Montgomery office occurred on 7 July. I had been hard at work writing bios and potential questions for each of our witnesses. I soon learned that Shane Denham would also take the stand on 26 August. Sitting at that August meeting, I calculated we had thirteen days.

Approached by Patrick McCreless of the *Star* following the meeting, I decided to break my silence to the media.

> "I'm looking forward to being able to defend myself and get the truth out."

6.

THE TESTIMONY OF
CHIEF LAYTON MCGRADY

"It didn't affect his job performance..."

26 August 2015

WHEN THE ANNISTON CIVIL SERVICE BOARD held its regular meeting in the summer of 2015, a special date of 26 August was chosen for the testimonies of immediate-past Chief Layton McGrady and current Chief Shane Denham because of scheduling conflicts both had with the selected September trial date.

Chief McGrady had been a special person to me for many years. I met him while he was a uniform lieutenant with the Anniston Police Department, and I was a deputy sheriff in the same county. We worked on some inter-agency assignments together and were members of the Anniston lodge of the Fraternal Order of Police, where we both frequently attended meetings. McGrady was the uniform captain when I was hired at APD in April 2006. He was a part of the hiring interview. He was a tough man, but fair. I had a lot of respect for him.

In the immediate aftermath of my termination, I mentioned to several people that, upon reflection, the only person to whom I felt I owed an apology was Layton McGrady. In the much-referenced League of the South speech I gave in June 2013, in a response during a question-and-answer session with the audience, I relayed a small segment of a private conversation that McGrady and I had the previous year. I did not mention him by name, and I felt like even if I had no one in the room would have been familiar with him anyway. I also was not thinking at the time that this speech (one of scores I gave from 2009-2013) would one day become a chess piece in a court proceeding where my vocation was on the line.

It was an off-the-cuff response to a questioner about the general attitude of police administrators regarding their relationship with the federal government and their concern for the gun rights of citizens. What I relayed was a true comment from that conversation and was relevant to the question. Nonetheless, it was an indiscretion for which I later contacted the chief and apologized. He accepted. I could tell he was clearly frustrated with the situation, miffed that he was being drug into the trial, and angry because he felt the reputation of the department had suffered as a result.

Where I disagree with him is the cause of the turmoil: The main reason things went down as they did in June 2015 was the *response* of the city government to the same kind of agitation that had resulted in the spring of 2009, when I was first investigated. Obviously, with a different city manager and police chief, that unrest was nipped pretty quickly at that time, and we all got along with our lives and doing our jobs.

We were planning on subpoenaing the chief as one of our witnesses, so it was a mild surprise to learn the city had already summoned him on their behalf. I feel I can summarize the city's strategy thusly: The city knew it was going to be difficult getting around the fact that nearly everyone in municipal government, from the city council to the police chief to the rank-and-file employees, knew about my affiliation with the League of the South since *at least* the spring of 2009. So, they seized on a comment I attributed to a former chief in the speech (when he told me "we pretty much think like you do") and used it to try to insinuate that my intention was to say that the chief and the city agreed with the positions and beliefs of the League of the South. Never mind that that was not what he said and not what I said he said. The city had to do something to blunt the impact of the city's prior knowledge.

Chief McGrady admitted in the hearing that he did not view the whole speech I gave (City Manager Brian Johnson would admit the same). It is my educated guess that Chief McGrady was tainted by the "muddying of the waters" technique, whereby someone from the city first contacted him about this issue and fed him their own interpretation of it (the "city line") before he ever had a chance to view the speech independently. I imagine the phone call consisted of something like, "Chief, did you know Doggrell gave a speech at a League of the South conference where he mentioned you and said you pretty much supported them?" I can imagine his outrage. And it would have been justified, had that line been the truth.

To me, the most significant part of Chief McGrady's testimony was when he admitted, under cross examination, that the city's interpretation of my comment may not have been correct. My attorney, Kenneth Shinbaum, asked him about my comment and what I meant when I said the chief and my bosses were "supportive."

Chief McGrady responded, "I assumed it was supportive of the views of the League of the South."

Mr. Shinbaum then asked, "Could it have been supportive of his — allowing him to participate in the organization?"

The Chief answered, "Could have been."

The very last words of McGrady's testimony were regarding his admission that the city may not have had the proper interpretation of this comment regarding being "supportive" when Mr. Shinbaum asked him, "...with respect to his membership in the League of the South, you had no objections?"

"No, sir."

"Okay. And could you understand there why Lt. Doggrell might think that you were supportive of him?"

"Because I didn't have any objections?"

"Right."

"Yes, sir. I can see that."

Mr. Shinbaum earlier asked the chief "did he [Doggrell] ever hide the fact that he belonged to the League of the South?"

The chief answered, "No, sir."

He was also asked, "did you ever ask Mr. Doggrell to resign his membership with the League of the South?"

"No, sir." That question was also asked to Chief Denham and City Manager Johnson, both of whom also testified that at no time was I ever asked to leave the organization.

There was one issue McGrady brought up in his testimony that I have answered numerous times in my life, but that I did not expect to address in this trial. McGrady testified that he never received any complaints from my coworkers about my religious or political beliefs or affiliations other than a few officers and Fraternal Order of Police (FOP) members asking him about me not reciting the Pledge of Allegiance during FOP meetings.

I was surprised by this not only because I thought it irrelevant to the matter at hand, but also because, according to FOP bylaws, what occurs at meetings is not supposed to be discussed in public. I have had a few members ask me about this, and apart from one man (who was an associate member and never has been a police officer), they expressed understanding for my reasons.

I do not recite the Pledge of Allegiance. I did as a child, when we were compelled to in school. But, around the age of nineteen, I began researching the pledge.

My short answer when someone asks me why I do not recite the pledge is, because I am not a socialist. The pledge was written by an avowed socialist in the late 19th century. He was also a Yankee and patterned the pledge after the nefarious "loyalty pledges" used by the United States against my Confederate ancestors. Those pledges were the forerunners of the disenfranchisement of the Southern people. I strongly object to the word "indivisible" used in the pledge, since a republic that is supposed to comprise free and independent States would never be "indivisible." An "indivisible" association is more like a mob than a constitutional republic.

The main objection I have to the pledge is that it makes idols out of a government and a secular flag that supposedly represents it. As a Christian, I feel we should pledge our "allegiance" to nothing but the Lord Jesus Christ, Himself.

There was a significant issue to highlight about this day of testimony from the two police chiefs. One of the three board members missed the entire day, and the reasons were never fully explained to me. We were told later that he had "health issues." While I sympathize with Mr. George Bates's health, I do not think I lack compassion by suggesting that, in a matter of this gravity, the board members who were to be voting on my career and livelihood **should have been present**! If Mr. Bates had any issues that prevented him doing his job, he should have been removed or replaced, and certainly not allowed to vote in the final decision (which he did). As will be detailed later, board member George Bates missed roughly half the entire hearing and was asleep most of the time he was physically present.

Moments before the trial was to commence, I was seated at the defendant's table with my attorney, Kenneth Shinbaum. I mentioned to him the absence of Bates. Shinbaum stood up and walked to the plaintiff's table, where he conferred with city attorney/prosecutor Bruce Downey. Downey stood and addressed the two board members present and inquired about the whereabouts of Mr. Bates. Board member Randy Third said he did not know where Bates was, that he (Third) had phoned

Bates and was unable to get in contact with him. As if this was a satisfactory answer, the trial began as I was reflecting how a matter that affected the future of my livelihood was in the hands of only three people and one of them was not present, and no excuse of why he was not there was given.

Under examination from Bruce Downey, McGrady testified about his background with APD. He had last been employed by the city on 10 February 2013. He had retired as chief of police, a position he had held for three years. He had succeeded Chief John Dryden in 2010. McGrady had "come up through the ranks," from patrolman to sergeant, lieutenant, captain, and then chief. He served a total of just under thirty years.

I think it worthy to note how precise Chief McGrady was with his positions at the department and the specific dates of his time when he was chief. Every officer I have ever known that has attained rank, especially high rank, has fond memories and fairly accurate dates of those occurrences. This will stand in stark contrast with the "faulty" memory of Chief Denham concerning what dates he held what rank in his later testimony.

McGrady admitted he knew me during his tenure and that I was a member of an organization known as the League of the South. This was common knowledge throughout the department and the city government and had been for years.

McGrady testified that he did not know "a lot" about the beliefs and positions of the League of the South. "I knew they were, I guess, a limited federal government type of league, but that's about as far as it went."

Chief McGrady may not have had "a lot" of understanding about the beliefs and positions of the League as they stood from 2009-2013, but he was a member of the administration when I was investigated and cleared in 2009, and he was chief of police and presided over the promotional interview board in April 2010 when I was asked multiple questions about it (as was Shane Denham, who asked most of those questions).

Under questioning from city attorney Bruce Downey, McGrady testified about my promotions. "Was Mr. Doggrell's membership in the League of the South a factor that you considered with regards to his promotion?" asked Downey.

LM: "No, sir."

BD: "Why not?"

LM: "It didn't affect his job performance or the police department."

McGrady then testified that at no time during his tenure was he aware of any incidences where my membership or participation in the League affected my abilities to perform my duties as a peace officer.

Then Downey asked this: "Did you have any reason during your tenure as chief of police to believe that Mr. Doggrell had associated his membership in the League of the South with his position with the Anniston Police Department?"

At this my attorney interjected: "I'm going to object. It's misleading. It states facts that are not in evidence. It would be the same as him asking Chief McGrady did you know that Chief Doggrell beat his wife. It's an improper question.

{Twice here, Mr. Shinbaum erroneously refers to me as "Chief" instead of "Lieutenant." I think it was just words running over themselves and a mistake.}

As would become her custom throughout the trial, board attorney Trudie Phillips overruled our objection, as she would sustain those of the city. Shinbaum continued nevertheless: "More specifically, it assumes that Chief Doggrell associated his position as a police officer with the League of the South."

MS. PHILLIPS: "Overruled. He can answer the question."

BD: "Do you recall the question, Chief? It was, in essence, did you have any reason to believe during your tenure as police chief that Mr. Doggrell had associated his membership with the League of the South with his position as an officer of the Anniston Police Department?"

LM: "No, sir."

BD: "Are you aware of any incidences during your tenure as chief of police where Mr. Doggrell's membership or association with the League of the South brought criticism or affected negatively on the Anniston Police Department?"

LM: "No, sir."

The city was attempting to lay the groundwork here to claim that I "associated" my membership in the League with my position as a police officer in the speech I gave in June 2013 in Wetumpka, AL. I believe we do an adequate job of refuting that claim in later testimony, so I will not go into details here.

BD: "Do you recall any instances where you discussed the League of the South with Mr. Doggrell?"

LM: "Yes, sir."

BD: "When did this occur?"

LM: "It was after an interview, or after a promotional interview; I'm not sure which one."

BD: "Was it during your term as police chief?"

LM: "Yes, sir."

This conversation occurred in late June or early July of 2012. In June, I was the sergeant for the Investigative Division and was a candidate for promotion to lieutenant. I had participated in the interview, which was conducted by Chief McGrady, Captain Denham, and Captain Wilburn.

BD: "What do you recall discussing with Mr. Doggrell?"

LM: "He came in the office and asked me if there was any questions that I needed to ask him about the League and his association with it; I told him no. As long as it didn't affect his job performance or reflect badly on the police department, we wouldn't discuss it."

Downey then showed a clip from my speech where I referenced this conversation and subsequently asked McGrady, "Did you view the portion of this speech where he discussed communications — where he discussed the relationship between the Anniston Police Department and the League of the South?"

Nowhere in that clip, and nowhere in the entire speech or question-and-answer session immediately following it (both of which, taken together, lasts over an hour) did I mention any kind of "relationship" between the League and the Anniston Police Department. This was a blatant misrepresentation by the city. The only instance in the entire speech where I made any reference whatsoever to APD was in the twelfth minute when I merely stated I worked there. I immediately followed that up with the words, "Which, I'll go ahead and go on record. Nothing I say here today is necessarily the views of the Anniston Police Department. I speak only as an individual and not an employee of that agency."

Downey then played a portion of the speech when I recounted McGrady's comment to me that "we pretty much think like you do." Then Downey asked, "Is it true, Chief, that during your tenure as police chief, as chief of police, that the Anniston Police Department was very supportive of Mr. Doggrell's participation or membership in the League of the South?

Shinbaum objected: "I am going to object to that statement. That is not what was said on the tape and it's taking what was said on the tape out of context."

That was a great objection. Phillips did not sustain the objection (she appeared very remiss to go against the city), but it did result in Downey asking a different question.

BD: "Chief McGrady, was the department, during your tenure, very supportive of Mr. Doggrell's membership in the League of the South?"

LM: "No."

BD: "Was the department supportive at all of his membership in the League of the South?"

LM: "Not that I'm aware of."

At no point in my life have I ever tried to put forth the idea that APD was supportive of the League of the South. However, the fact that they allowed me to participate and be a member, and even be the chairman of a local chapter, told me that (prior to, during, and after Chief McGrady's tenure as police chief) they were supportive of me exercising my constitutional rights by my participation and membership in the League. This was why I was cleared in the investigation of 2009 and this position was related to me multiple times by multiple supervisors from 2009-2015.

BD: "I'm going to play you another clip from Mr. Doggrell's speech in June of 2013."

Here the city played the portion of the question-and-answer portion of my speech where I recounted the private conversation with McGrady in his office.

BD: "Chief, were you the chief of police in 2012, which would have been the year prior to this speech?"

LM: "Yes."

BD: "Did Mr. Doggrell — do you have any recollection of Mr. Doggrell ever stating to you anything relating to him not being willing to sell out his position with the League of the South as it being something he strongly believed in and that if it came down to it he would choose the League?"

LM: "No."

This is true. I never said that directly to Chief McGrady. I said it during the speech, and I meant it when I said it.

BD: "Is that something that you would expect to recall?"

LM: "Yes. That's something I would recall."

BD: "Why is it something you would recall?"

LM: "Because that would have been a red flag. That would have shown me that his loyalty was more to an organization rather than to the police department."

No, what that showed was that my principles and convictions about matters of faith are stronger than any attachments to a job, as it should be with any man.

BD: "Did you at any time tell Mr. Doggrell that we pretty much think like you do?"

LM: "No."

He told me exactly that. If he was thinking that Downey was asking if he ever stated that in relation to the positions of the League of the South, particularly, I can see where the chief would have answered in the negative here.

CROSS EXAMINATION

My attorney, Kenneth Shinbaum, began with questions about the video of the 2013 speech.

KS: "Now, did you view the whole video?"

LM: "No, I did not... I didn't watch the entire video."

McGrady testified that he watched a part of the video at his residence after he had been sent a link to it by Chief Denham.

KS: "Okay. How did you know — the parts that you watched, were they at the beginning, the end, or what?"

LM: "From the beginning to probably—I probably watched two thirds of it."

KS: "Two thirds, okay. Now this portion that was referenced on the screen, that was during a question session, am I correct? Somebody asked him a question?"

LM: "I have no idea... I wasn't taking notes. I was just watching."

Answers like this make me wonder why Chief McGrady did not take the time to view the speech in its entirety, and on his own, rather than in whatever fashion it was presented to him. Context and presentation (also known as "spin") have a lot to do with how something can be interpreted.

KS: "Now, did you see the part of the video where Mr. Doggrell states that he is not here to speak as a police officer for the Anniston Police Department?"

LM: "Yes, sir."

KS: "And did you see the part where he said that he does not speak for the police department of the City of Anniston?"

LM: "Yes, sir."

KS: "...Did somebody just send you some clips of the video?"

LM: "No, sir; sent me the whole video."

KS: "Okay. But the whole video would speak for itself and exactly what was said, am I correct?"

LM: "If you watch the whole video?"

KS: "Yes."

LM: "I'm sure it would."

Watch the whole video? *Before* judging it? What a novel concept.

Then a short series of questions led to what I considered a huge concession from McGrady about what my intentions may have been.

KS: "Okay. Now, do you know who posted the video?"

LM: "I have no idea."

KS: "Okay. Now, do you know when this video was done?"

LM: "I've been told, but I didn't — I don't know for sure, no, sir."

KS: "Now, if this video was done in June or July of 2013, you would not have been police chief at that time, am I correct?"

LM: "Correct."

KS: "Okay. And when Mr. Doggrell mentioned anything about someone being supportive on that tape, you don't know what he was referring to, supportive about what?"

LM: "I assumed it was supportive of the views of the League of the South."

KS: "Okay. Could it have been supportive of his — allowing him to participate in such an organization?"

LM: "Could have been."

Shinbaum then asked about the 2009 internal investigation of me and my involvement with the League of the South.

KS: "…Now, were you aware of any investigation that was done of Mr. Doggrell and his membership in the League of the South back in 2009?"

LM: "After the fact… The captain that conducted the investigation filled me in on it."

KS: "And who was that captain?"

LM: "Richard Smith."

KS: "And what did he refer you — say about it to you?"

LM: "Said that he was directed by the chief to conduct an investigation on Josh's membership in the League of the South and basically determine if it was an extremist group or not and he conducted the investigation and found that it wasn't… Now he checked with ROCIC and FBI and I believe that's where he got his information from."

KS: "And the FBI is the Federal Bureau of Investigation?"

LM: "Yes, sir."

KS: "And what is ROCIC?"

LM: "It's Regional Organized Crime Information Center. It's national, but our regional office is in Nashville."

KS: "Okay. And who runs that organization?"

LM: "I'm not real sure. I believe it falls under the government, too; it's contribution based. They basically work the — our office works the southeast. They are there if you need any help on equipment or anything like that, surveillance stuff, stuff like that."

KS: "Okay. And is that an organization that the Anniston Police Department relies on information from?"

LM: "Yes, sir, one of them."

KS: "And is the FBI an organization that Anniston Police Department relies on information from?"

LM: "Yes, sir."

KS: "And those are both, to your understanding, Federal agencies?"

LM: "Don't quote me on the ROCIC, but I believe they are."

KS: "Now, does the Anniston Police Department rely on the Southern Poverty Law Center as a source of information?"

LM: "No, sir. They didn't when I was there."

KS: "Now, did Mr. Doggrell, while he was a member of the — while you were with the Anniston Police Department, did he ever hide the fact that he belonged to the League of the South?"

LM: "No, sir."

KS: "...While you were a member of the Anniston Police Department, did you ever have any problems with the League of the South?"

LM: "No."

KS: "Was there violent activities you ever heard of by the League of the South while you were with the Anniston Police Department?"

LM: "No, sir; not that I have heard of."

KS: "Now... while you were the chief of police, did you believe that Mr. Doggrell had a constitutional right to belong to the League of the South?"

Bruce Downey sprang from his chair: "Object to the question. It calls for a legal conclusion. He is here as chief of police, not as a legal expert."

The city most certainly did not want Chief McGrady to answer this question. Based on his testimony to this point, in particular about the 2009 investigation of me, the answer should be obvious.

KS: "I will restate it. While you were chief of police, whether or not Mr. Doggrell did, in fact, have a constitutional right to be a member of the League of the South, did you believe that he had the right to belong to the League of the South?"

Downey: "I object to the question. Relevance. What the chief of police's opinions as the scope of constitutional rights are irrelevant to this proceeding."

Trudie Phillips: "Sustained."

KS: "It goes to an issue of support."

Phillips: "Still sustained."

KS: "Now, was there any reason why you — did you ever ask Mr. Doggrell to resign his membership with the League of the South?"

LM: "No."

KS: "Why not?"

LM: "It wasn't affecting his job performance or the reputation of the police department."

KS: "Now, while you were chief of police, did any officers of the police department express any problem to you about Mr. Doggrell being a member of the League of the South?"

LM: "No, sir."

Interesting — out of the hundreds of officers I worked with at APD, many of them black, homosexual, or of various ethnic backgrounds, NOT ONE ever expressed a problem with it to the chief.

Shinbaum then asked McGrady about specifics of the private conversation I had with him in his office in the summer of 2012.

KS: "...To the best of your memory, what do you recall that you did say?"

LM: "I don't remember a lot of the conversation other than the fact that he came in and asked me if we wanted to — if there was any questions I needed to ask him and I told him no. And then I remember him mentioning the League of the South and [I] told him that was not, you know, considered in the promotion as long as it didn't affect his job performance or the reputation of the department."

KS: "Okay. And with respect to Lt. Doggrell — well, with respect to whatever position he was at that time, you were — with respect to his membership in the League of the South, you had no objections?"

LM: "No, sir."

This should be emphasized: Chief McGrady testified that he knew about my League membership, that I never tried to hide it, that we had at least one conversation about it when he was the chief of police where I offered to answer any questions about it, that he had no questions about it, and that he had no objections to my membership in it.

KS: "Okay. And could you understand there why Lt. Doggrell might think that you were supportive of him?"

LM: "Because I didn't have any objections?"

KS: "Right."

LM: "Yes, sir. I can see that."

KS: "No further questions."

7.

THE TESTIMONY OF
CHIEF SHANE DENHAM

"The result of it [the previous internal affairs investigation] was no action was taken against Officer Doggrell."

26 August 2015

"HAVE YOU EVER ATTENDED BIBLE study with Mr. Doggrell?" asked my attorney, Kenneth Shinbaum.

"I don't think I have," was the quick response of Chief Shane Denham.

We were inside the Anniston, Alabama, old municipal courtroom. Denham was in the middle of cross-examination in the civil service appeal of my termination from the Anniston Police Department.

Shinbaum stopped and looked directly at Denham. I was seated at the defendant's table, and was also staring incredulously at the police chief. Shinbaum studied our notes to assure himself of the facts. Then he looked back at Denham and asked, "You do not recall inviting Lieutenant Doggrell to attend a weekly men's Bible study class at your church in the fall of 2013?" I leaned in, awaiting the answer...

* * *

Disappointment is a powerful emotion. The fear of disappointment combined with the desire to impress is great motivation. When I reflect on my life and the many dark, unwise, and sinful decisions I've made, the inappropriate behavior I have displayed and the hurtful comments I have uttered at times, I believe the lack of fear in disappointing my Lord was apparent.

Playing varsity football, I worked hard to please my coaches and teammates. I did not want to let them down or disappoint them. In the occupations I have held, I have striven to be dependable, trustworthy, punctual, dedicated — to not disappoint.

All four Gospels of Christ detail Simon Peter's denial of his Lord between the arrest and trial of Jesus. But it is in Luke's Gospel that we are given the vision, upon the predicted third denial, of Jesus as He "turned, and looked upon Peter. And Peter remembered the word of the Lord, how He had said unto him, 'Before the cock crow, thou shalt deny Me thrice.' And Peter went out, and wept bitterly." (Luke 22:61-62). The look from his Lord had to be one of disappointment, and it was extremely painful to Peter when he realized what he had done.

As a child, the fear of disappointing my father was a motivating factor in many areas of my life. The desire to make him proud of me also drove me. That carried into adulthood, and into my vocation as a peace officer. I followed in his footsteps, where he had established a reputation in Calhoun County, Alabama, of being one of the best cops there ever was. I had big shoes to fill.

In my career, I had the pleasure of serving subordinate to some fine leaders. I also had the displeasure to serve under some lousy ones. Both examples helped me and were learning experiences I used to craft my own leadership style once I was placed in greater roles of authority.

The former chiefs of Anniston that I served under were John Dryden and Layton McGrady. I maintain a high level of respect and admiration for both of those men. Shane Denham was promoted in the winter of 2013, after McGrady's retirement. Denham and I had not worked closely together but developed a working relationship I would describe as cordial and professional.

In the spring of 2013, my family and I were actively involved in our church. I was coming to grips with the weaknesses of my Christian living and putting forth renewed effort to put that house in order. In September, my oldest son was saved and baptized. I began teaching Sunday school and Bible studies again. I came under conviction regarding the consistency of my walk and better using my vocation as a ministering field.

That same September, I approached Chief Denham about beginning and leading a Bible study for the police department. He gave his permission and allowed me to use the briefing room for it. We discussed a few particulars, including the difficulty in planning a time for such a meeting. When you work at a place where the hours of service coverage are 24/7, it is impossible to make the meeting available for everyone.

About that same time, Chief Denham invited me to a Bible study that was beginning at his church in east Anniston. I accepted his invitation. The study was for men, and it was scheduled to meet once a week during the midday meal hour. I had never been to this church before, so Denham also agreed to meet me in the parking lot on the first day and escort me inside. That first day, we entered the church together and sat beside each other during the study. Just prior to that first meeting, Denham gave me a copy of the book used for the study. It was titled, *The True Measure of a Man*.

In the weeks to come, Denham missed a few of the meetings. I made most of them, including at least one or two that occurred on my off days. There were several more after the first meeting that he and I both attended.

As I was preparing for my trial defense in Montgomery throughout the summer of 2015, Shinbaum and I discussed questions we were going to ask the witnesses. We both agreed that using these two issues, the inauguration of a department Bible study led by me with the approval of Denham, and the invitation to accompany him to a Bible study at his own church, could, in effect, turn Denham into a positive character witness for me. Consider: The city's prosecution in this matter depended on casting me as some kind of "racist," who held "prejudicial" and "divisive" views. The Southern Poverty Law Center had already smeared me in their attack piece that precipitated this ordeal. City manager Brian Johnson fired me 48 hours after that publication. Chief Denham had known me for nine years and was my chief. Just what kind of person did he really think I was?

In attempting to anticipate his response, I figured he would acknowledge these two issues and probably try to downplay them. He could have said he invited several employees to his church — and he may have. But I did not know of any others and he and I were the only police officers I observed who attended throughout the entire series of meetings. I thought he may have tried to say it was his outreach to me. Maybe it could be spun that I was such a deviant he thought I needed more exposure to the Word (and I would not contest I am in constant need of more exposure). Of course, that might be hard to sell considering he allowed me to *lead* a Bible study at the department during the same time frame.

Many things went through my head when I contemplated what his response would be. But never did I anticipate what he actually did say.

* * *

Kenneth Shinbaum (**KS**): "Have you ever attended Bible study with Mr. Doggrell?"

Shane Denham (SD): "I don't think I have."

Remember, now, this study had been *less than two years prior* to this testimony. It was at *his church*. He gave me the study book. *We discussed its contents* as well as the issues raised by the book and the class. He met me there. He escorted me inside. *We sat together*. It was a weekly meeting that lasted two or three months. Yet, now he answers, "I don't think I have."

He must have misunderstood the question, I thought to myself. *He answered too quickly. He's under oath. Surely he realizes I could subpoena his fellow church members who were also attendees just to verify this? Surely he simply misunderstood the question. Had to be.*

Apparently, Mr. Shinbaum was thinking something similar. He paused, looked down at his notes, then looked back at Chief Denham and got specific. "You do not recall inviting Lieutenant Doggrell to attend a weekly men's Bible study class at your church in the fall of 2013?"

Here was Denham's answer in its entirety: "I remember he asked me for permission to do a Bible study at the police department and I recall that he did it a few times and there was only a couple of people participated. I don't think I ever participated in that, but I can't recall. Now I have — as a matter of fact, I actually took the city manager one time to a — it wasn't a Bible study, it was a — but it was at a church and it was a men's group. I may have invited him to that. I don't remember that I did, but I do remember one day when the city manager was riding with me when he was new, I had that on my schedule to do, had committed to be there, and actually took the city manager with me."

I was stunned.

Not only did he deny remembering inviting me and attending with me, but he took the opportunity to, first, belittle my efforts at initiating a Christian ministry among the police officers at our department; and second, to interject that, while he certainly did not recall taking the reprobate on trial that day to his church, he did take his boss, seated across the room at the other table, the star witness for the prosecution and the man who had terminated said reprobate, to such a group event.

Shane Denham did not bother to attend any of the Bible studies he approved that I conducted at the police department. So I am not sure how he would know what the attendance was. (It was more than "only a couple," but even if it had been only a couple, I read in Scripture that "where two or three are gathered together in my name, there am I in the midst of them." [Matthew 18:20] I think it shameful for any professing Christian to disparage a group of his Christian subordinates attempting to spread the Gospel, no matter their size. And why on earth would he even bring up the size in his answer, if not to disparage?)

Some may think it plausible that the chief's memory is so faulty that he honestly did not recall that invitation, giving me the book, discussing the issues, and attending those meetings with me. But consider: *That same month* of September in 2013, Brian Johnson assumed his position as city manager of Anniston. He would have been "new," as Denham described him in his above answer, and riding with Denham to see the city and familiarize himself with his new police chief. So, it would have been almost exactly the same time frame (two years) from that time to the time Denham stood under oath on 26 August 2015 and testified that, while he did not recall inviting or attending a Bible study at his church with *me*, he did vividly recall attending a similar meeting with his boss, Brian Johnson, who just happened to be the man who fired me and needed the chief to back up that decision. I guess it just seemed like a good time for Denham to throw that in.

The feeling of disappointment—that you have been let down someone you admired and respected—weighs heavily. Unfortunately, I have administered that feeling in my life. But never have I been on the receiving end of such disappointment like I was when sitting in that courtroom and staring at my police chief as he spoke these words. The sting was sharp.

THE CITY'S STRATEGY

The City of Anniston's prosecution strategy against me became apparent on the first day of the trial, 26 August 2015. They wanted to minimize, as much as possible, the city's prior knowledge of my membership and involvement in the League of the South and any beliefs that were actual policies of that organization. At the same time, they would take any and all sensational viewpoints they could find expressed by individual League members or associates and destroy me via guilt-by-association. This type of strategy should never hold up in a genuine court of law, but it was allowed in the Civil Service Board appeal hearing.

Denham was the second witness the city called following former Police Chief Layton McGrady. After establishing his credentials as chief, the first question city attorney Bruce Downey asked him was, "Are you aware that an article was published by the Southern Poverty Law Center [SPLC] on June 17th, 2015, in regards to Mr. Doggrell's membership in the League of the South?"

"I am."

Downey asked Denham if he knew, prior to the publication of the SPLC hit piece, if I was a League member. Denham said he knew I "had been a member at some point." When asked if he was aware of the "beliefs and positions" of the League prior to the article, he responded, "Not really." There ensued a back-and-forth where the picture was painted that the chief of police, who had been a member of the administration during the city investigation that cleared me for my League activity in 2009, really did not bother to familiarize himself with the beliefs and positions of what the SPLC had long deemed a "hate group."

Following that investigation in the spring of 2009, then-Lieutenant Denham took considerable time to ask me about the League and my beliefs during a promotional interview for a sergeant position in April 2010. Two years later, then-Captain Denham and I also had a conversation about my League membership in his office in the summer of 2012.

During cross-examination, my attorney, Kenneth Shinbaum, asked Denham about that 2009 investigation, the file of which the city refused to produce for the hearing despite our request of it. "Do you remember an investigation being done on, I guess, Officer Doggrell, or whatever position he was in in 2009, in approximately 2009, with respect to his membership in the League of the South?"

"I was aware that one had been done, yes."

"And how did you become aware of that?"

"I think through our local newspaper here — they wrote some articles on it back in 2009. I think that's how I became aware of it."

This was confusing to me. Denham admitted that he knew I had been previously investigated by the city for my League membership. He was in an administrative position at the time. Yet he said he learned of it through...reading the local paper?

Shinbaum asked, "And as a result of that, what was the result of that investigation?"

Denham responded, "The result of it was no action was taken against Officer Doggrell."

One of the more prevalent questions I have been asked since this all went down has been: How can they fire you for something which they cleared you of six years earlier? Strange, is it not?

Shinbaum pressed forward: "Now when was the first time Officer Doggrell was asked not to belong to the League of the South?"

"I don't know that he was ever asked that. You would have to ask him. **I never asked him not to.**" (No one ever asked me that.)

"When was the first time Lieutenant Doggrell was reprimanded with respect to anything he did with respect to the League of the South?"

"I am not aware of any reprimands regarding League of the South." (There were none).

Shinbaum asked how long Denham had known me. He said he had known me since I started working there (nine years). "Have you ever known Officer Doggrell or Josh Doggrell ever to say anything that was racially offensive?"

"No, I haven't."

Shinbaum then asked about the 2009 investigative file on me that the city refused to produce. Denham said, "I am trying to remember some of the stuff that was in the 2009 file, which I reviewed once this all happened... And it seems to me that the League hasn't really changed much since then as far as their core belief as a secessionist group and as a pro-white group as far as their — what they publicly put out there on their [web]page in 2013 to 2009."

So, according to the chief, the League itself had not "really changed that much." Yet, I was cleared in 2009...and fired in 2015.

In the aftermath of my termination, following the city's 48-hour "investigation" from 17-19 June 2015, city authorities began a whirlwind of after-the-fact attempts at justification. In the middle of this, City Manager Brian Johnson announced that the city would be instituting a new policy to prohibit city employees from being involved in "hate groups." One question I never heard answered was just how the city was going to define a "hate group." The main question I had was why a new policy was needed. I had just been fired for this, so you would think the city would have already had such a policy. But if one was needed, then what, exactly, had been the policy I violated?

During this same aftermath, Chief Denham testified that a "questionnaire" was distributed to all the police officers in the department requiring each to list every single organization of which he or she was a member. He said it was "part of our internal affairs investigation." I guess this was the city's attempt to drive out all officers who belonged to any one of the thousands of organizations that the SPLC would call a "hate group." This provided the following interesting discourse:

Denham described, "We asked them to list all groups that they could come up with in their memory, whether it was good, bad, or indifferent; anything they were a dues-paying member to, a civic club, anything, to include the FOP [Fraternal Order of Police]."

"And if an officer did belong to a group that might be considered to be inflammatory," my attorney asked, "what was your plan then?"

"We would have to address that situation on a case-by-case basis." (Based on how the city handled this situation, I figure the question the chief would have to ask himself here would not, necessarily, be whether or not an officer had a constitutional right to belong to that particular organization, but whether or not the professional protesters, local race baiters, or the SPLC would object).

Shinbaum asked, "Would that be potentially asking them as to whether or not they would be willing to resign from the club?"

"That would be one option that I could use," Denham agreed.

Shinbaum then turned, looked at Denham, pointed at me, and asked what should have been the obvious follow-up question: **"And you never asked Josh Doggrell to resign from the League of the South, did you?"**

"No," responded the chief.

Later, Shinbaum asked about events during all the time Denham had been in a supervisory position over me. "Now, during the time you were Josh Doggrell's supervisor, do you know of any instance where he treated anyone unfairly?"

"No."

"During your time as Josh Doggrell's supervisor, did you ever know of any time where Josh Doggrell showed prejudice against anyone?"

94

"If he did, I wasn't aware of it."

"During your time as Josh Doggrell's supervisor, did you ever see him display any violence toward anyone other than what was required within his duties as a police officer?"

"No, sir."

"During your time as Josh Doggrell's supervisor, were there ever any complaints of Josh Doggrell using excessive force?"

"I am not aware of any."

"During your time as Josh Doggrell's supervisor, was there any time that anyone ever accused Josh Doggrell of unfairly arresting them?"

"Not that I'm aware of, no."

"Since you have been a supervisor of Josh Doggrell, have you ever seen him act in a prejudicial manner toward any citizens of the United States?"

"No."

THE CHARGE OF GIVING AN UNAPPROVED SPEECH

One of the four city/department policies the city accused me of violating was giving a speech in my capacity as a police officer without the permission of the chief. The speech in question was one given on 21 June 2013 in Elmore County, Alabama. Never mind that I had given scores of speeches at League events — most of them in Anniston and Oxford — before, during, and after I was cleared by the city in the 2009 investigation. Not once did I obtain permission from any police chief in any of those speeches, because I was not giving them *in my official capacity* as an officer nor was the speech on behalf of the department. That was the requirement of the policy.

In the Elmore County speech, I mentioned the Anniston Police Department *once* in a speech that lasted over an hour. It occurred in the twelfth minute, when I offered as partial proof that I knew about local police matters due to the fact that I was an officer at the Anniston Police Department; and I immediately followed with this disclaimer: **"Which, I'll go ahead and go on record. Nothing I say here today is necessarily the views of the Anniston Police Department. I speak only as an individual and not an employee of that agency."** Shinbaum asked Denham about that disclaimer.

"...did you see where Josh Doggrell stated that he was not there in his capacity as a police officer of the City of Anniston?"

Denham said, "I saw his disclaimer, which was no good as far as I was concerned because he had already identified himself as an Anniston police officer. And that was the entire reason why he was there — to speak on issues that regarded police officers and [he] identified the City of Anniston, [he] also identified another lieutenant in attendance. So that disclaimer to me meant nothing."

This was the same bizarre spin that the city manager would give in his later testimony. The city was accusing me of falsely associating the views of the League of the South with the Anniston Police Department. Yet, the only time I mentioned the department was in the twelfth minute, when I gave a disclaimer so no one would confuse me with trying to make that very assumption. The spin from City Manager Brian Johnson, now carried out by his police chief (and contrary to that chief's view that he stated to me on 17 June in his office), was that, because I had given such a disclaimer, in which I *mentioned* the Anniston Police Department (how else was I to give a disclaimer?), the disclaimer was no good...because the very fact I gave a disclaimer made the disclaimer null and void. Try to wrap your head around that logic without inducing a headache.

Shinbaum asked for clarification from the chief on when approval would be needed for giving a speech of any kind. "What I'm saying," replied the chief, "is if you are going to make a speech, **any**

speech, it makes no difference, really, you have to get permission from the chief of police for the reasons...we can't afford to let the reputation of the department and the integrity of the department — we need to know what that speech is going to be about, if it's about a controversial issue or any issue. That way we can make a determination because, as I stated earlier, the reputation of the department is much more important that any individual's rights to make any speech."

In that answer, Chief Denham stated that, as far as he is concerned, an officer must get his permission before making "*any speech*" so that he can safeguard the "reputation of the department" considering "controversial" issues. That is **NOT** what the policy stated. In its entirety, the policy reads:

"All employees giving speeches, lectures, etc., or conducting public relations programs on or off duty on behalf of the police department must obtain prior approval from the chief of police. A memorandum giving the date, time, and circumstances of the event is to be forwarded to the chief of police in order that a record of such activities can be maintained."

I submit that my disclaimer made it *clear* that I was not in violation of this policy.

Since I was a Sunday school teacher and could be seen as "giving speeches" many Sundays throughout the year, I directed Shinbaum to ask if permission was needed in those occasions, as well.

"So, now... if he is speaking as a Sunday school teacher and he happens to have mentioned that he is with the Anniston Police Department, does he need to get the approval of the chief first?"

"In my opinion, no, because that's a religious protection."

Well. That last statement goes against the "any speech" prohibition he mentioned earlier. And, along with certain religious protections, there are also *political* protections for all citizens. Alabama law 17-1-4 states, in part, "No person in the employment of any city...shall be denied the right to participate in city, county, or state political activities to the same extent as any other citizen of the State of Alabama..." Also: "All persons in the employment of any city, county, or state shall have the right to publicly support issues of public welfare, circulate petitions..." And, perhaps most importantly, subsection (c) reads: "**When off duty, out of uniform, and acting as a private citizen, no law enforcement officer, firefighter, or peace officer shall be prohibited from engaging in city, county, or state political activity** or denied the right to refrain from engaging in political activity so long as there is compliance with this section."

Did Chief Denham think his prohibitions were above the law?

The Charge Of "Harassment" Through Social Media

Denham was asked about the charge that I used social media to "harass" people. He dodged with a likely scripted answer: "In reference to the city harassment policy, that question would be better directed to the human resources director because that's her job." When pressed, Denham admitted he had read a substantial amount of my posting on Facebook, "stuff about anti-federal government type stuff..." He admitted having conversations with me about my stated opinions.

Shinbaum then asked, "Did you ever say, hey, it would be best for the Anniston Police Department if you don't post that?"

"**I never saw anything that rose to the level that I needed to address or it would have been addressed,** " Denham replied.

Note here, that I was on trial for "harassment" through social media, and Shane Denham just testified that he never saw "anything that rose to the level that I needed to address or it would have been addressed." Hmm...

Shinbaum continued: "Now, has Josh Doggrell ever been disciplined for the use of social media?"

"I don't think so." (I never was).

Denham then went on to explain what a problem social media had been at the department, and about how it had been abused and been the cause of memos, changed policy, and discipline upon misuse by one officer, in particular. But, yet, he "never saw anything that rose to the level that I needed to address or it would have been addressed" regarding *my* use of social media. At least one officer was disciplined for misusing social media, but I never was. Yet... suddenly in June 2015 I was fired for it.

Shinbaum attempted to question the chief about officers (in particular, Nick Bowles) who had actually been disciplined for misusing social media and he began to answer but was interrupted by an objection from Downey that it was not relevant. This was sustained. Shinbaum remarked that the relevance was that *I* was now being charged with "harassment" via social media, even though I had never been disciplined for it and the chief did not consider that it "rose to the level" that needed to be addressed. It seemed relevant to me.

THE "EVIDENCE" PRESENTED

During Denham's testimony, the city entered nine pieces of "evidence" into the record. These articles were not made available to me beforehand (another matter of procedure that would never have been allowed in a formal court of law). They were also not shown to me in the internal affairs interview I participated in on 18 June, therefore a reasonable conclusion would be that *the city itself was not aware of these articles when they fired me*, but discovered them in the two months *between* the firing and the appeal hearing, when they were desperately trying to come up with a legitimate reason for terminating me in the first place.

This reasonable conclusion would be verified by then-Captain Nick Bowles in federal depositions in October 2016, when Bowles admitted in his testimony that these nine articles of "evidence" were not discovered by the city at the time of my termination.

The nine exhibits allowed entry into evidence by the city consisted of writings of other people and various pictures and memes posted on social media. *Not a single piece of "evidence" was anything I had ever written or produced or shared and not a single piece of "evidence" was part of official policy of the League of the South.* Some of the exhibits were writings of League President, **Dr. Michael Hill.** A few were photos unknown individuals had posted to a League website or social media, and at least one photo's original source could never be established. Most of these exhibits were things I had never seen. **It is worth emphasizing: All of the "evidence" presented against me by the city on this day were exhibits that I did not produce, much of which I personally disagreed with, and much of which I had never even seen.**

Now, it would seem superfluous to mention what should be obvious here, but the person on trial was *me* —not Michael Hill and not various people throughout the world (that I may or may not even know) who posted miscellaneous photos on an internet site. **A question every citizen should consider is: If this type of loose guilt-by-association persecution could be successfully carried out in this situation, who among us is safe if the hounds of the cultural Marxism decide to pounce?**

Police officers: Did you lose your constitutional rights when you took the oath? Government employees: Should you be able to publicly endorse a political candidate or discuss your faith with a co-worker?

There comes times in life when someone who holds a position of great power and authority has an opportunity to rise above the noise of the crowd, to decide an issue on its merit, to avoid the howls of the wolves of opportunistic professional protesters and those attacking the institution and individuals he presides over, to stand up for his people in the face of political correctness and to stand up to an officious, unscrupulous, arrogant, impulsive city manager who, I believe, held very little regard for the employees or citizens of the city. It was an opportunity, simply put, to do the right thing.

And Shane Denham failed.

8.

The Testimony of
HR Director Bersheba Austin

"Now, this thing with the Confederate battle flag, it means different things to different people, am I correct?"

15 September 2015

ONE MAN'S "FREEDOM FIGHTER" is another man's "terrorist." Compassionate interest intended by some may be taken as pesky, meddlesome interjection by others. A "patriot" to one cause is often seen as a "traitor" to the other side. And images...symbols... can be different things to different people.

In the spring of 2013, the issue of "gay marriage" was, again, making its rounds across the State of Alabama. In the world of social media, an image of a mathematical equal sign was being used by the proponents of a change in laws to allow people of the same gender to enter into a relationship of wedlock recognized by government. I came down against this latest abomination from pop culture on Biblical grounds, as God's word and the laws of nature prohibit such a practice. I also believed that the vast majority of my fellow Alabamians were against this idea and, constitutionally, this was a matter for the individual States.

As a counter to the equal sign, many opponents of this move who were supporters of traditional and Biblical marriage began to adopt a mathematical non-equal sign as a profile picture on social media. I was among those who did this.

I thought the image was appropriate to the situation and the issue at hand. The idea of "gay marriage" was not "equal" to traditional and Biblical marriage in either the eyes of God, the citizens of Alabama, or the civil law of the State of Alabama. Furthermore, I am not an egalitarian. It is against reality. I believe in the equality of individuals before the law, but not in any kind of inherent equality insofar as it relates to how human beings are created and how God blesses individuals (and groups in some instances) with unique abilities and special talents, along with particular weaknesses, that make them obviously "unequal" to other people.

In 1 Corinthians 12, the Apostle Paul writes of the body of Christ being comprised of many members, each bestowed with particular gifts not given to others, so that the members are dependent upon one another. Being different is okay. It is nothing to be ashamed of nor denied.

This seems like common sense to many, but we live in a world that continuously wants to deny such things are reality. Among examples I have often explained to friends and family is if God created me "equal" to everyone else, then I should be able to throw a football like a professional quarterback and the same could tie me in a spelling contest. In 21st Century America, such obvious conclusions are often considered "hateful."

Never did I realize that this "unequal" image and others' interpretation of it would consume so much time two years later during a civil service trial appealing my termination from the City of Anniston.

Following the testimonies of the current and immediate past police chiefs of the city on 26 August 2015, the second and longest day of the trial occurred on 15 September 2015. The original date and venue were changed from the council chambers at city hall to the new municipal courtroom at the Justin Sollohub Justice Center across the street. The explanation given to me was an expectation of a larger crowd.

This change in venue was another direct violation of State law, which governs the rules and procedures of the Anniston civil service system. Alabama code 45-8A-22.06 mandates that "All meetings of the board shall be held in the city hall." There are absolutely no exceptions given.

The first witness called by the city that day was Bersheba Austin (who, for the purposes of upcoming context, was a black female). Austin was the director of Human Resources for the city. I had known Ms. Austin throughout the entirety of my career at Anniston. She was a personnel specialist when I began and conducted my in-processing work upon my hire. Over the years, we saw each other and interacted on a regular basis regarding personnel matters. Our meetings and correspondence were always cordial. Never, prior to the trial, had she ever mentioned a word of disagreement or concern about my religious or political views.

Moreover, a few days after City Manager Brian Johnson announced my termination on 19 June 2015, I spoke on the phone to Austin to find out where I stood regarding health insurance for my family. During that conversation, Austin told me that she was not one to "jump on the bandwagon" on these types of things, and that she based her opinion of someone on her own experiences and interactions with that person. Therefore, she said, she had no problem with me whatsoever.

In light of that pronouncement, and what she testified to two-and-a-half months later, I can only conclude one of two things occurred: a) Austin flatly lied to me on the phone; or, b) after our conversation and before her testimony, Austin was shown images and/or content from my personal Facebook account and she decided (or was coached, or "persuaded") that she did, in fact, have a problem with me. I think the latter option is much more probable. If so, it demonstrates one more in a series of examples where the "justification" for my termination was decided *after* it was carried out.

All following quotations in this chapter are taken from the official written transcript of the trial.

After Austin was sworn in, City Attorney Bruce Downey asked Ms. Austin when she became the Human Resources Director for the City of Anniston. "June 2014." Prior to that, she was "personnel specialist." She had been employed with the city for "a total of fifteen" years at the time of her testimony on 15 September 2015.

As HR Director, she described her duties as handling "in-processing, procedures for new hires, keeping up to date with personnel policies and procedures, making advisement and recommendations to the city manager when necessary with regards to disciplinary actions that come from the department directors." She agreed with Downey that "application of the [personnel and procedure manual] policy" was "within the scope of [her] duties."

Then the attention was focused on the social media policy, one of the four policies I was accused of violating and had never been used (to my knowledge) against any city employee before this occurrence.

Downey asked Austin to summarize the policy regarding city employees' use of social media. "To summarize that policy, city employees are to be mindful of their activity on social media to ensure that their activity on social media doesn't interfere with their position with the city or potentially violate other personnel policies even though the activity takes place off duty."

Downey then led Austin to make a connection between the social media policy and the city's "harassment" policy, which Austin said were "activities that violate an employee's federal protected rights, including race."

"How did the city become aware of Mr. Doggrell's social media activity?" asked Downey.

"After the article hit the news media outlets by Southern Poverty Law, the city actually began to look into — began to take a look at Mr. Doggrell's public Facebook profile."

Austin then went on to say that this "look" uncovered publicly available "activity" that violated the city's policy against "harassment." Downey then entered into the record the city's "Exhibit 10," the first of ten "exhibits" that was actually something *I* wrote, produced, or submitted in any form.

The image was one that I would spend a considerable amount of time speaking about during my own cross-examination. It was a digital photograph of a mathematical not-equal sign. According to her testimony at this time, Austin claimed her interpretation of this mathematical symbol was that "it appears to be an image that portrays that blacks are not equal." She later said, "I mean, that image is intimidating."

At no time during her testimony under Downey did either address the large amount of commentary that accompanied this copy of one of my many Facebook "profile photos." It would seem reasonable to conclude that that conversation may have shed light upon the issue by providing clarifying context. Downey chose to ignore all of it completely. My attorney, on his cross-examination of Austin, did not.

"Now," said my attorney, Kenneth Shinbaum, "let's look at Exhibit 10." Shinbaum then read from the comments immediately to the right of the image. "And, there is some typing on the side of it. And what...does it say... '[Doggrell wrote] some of those of my perspective have countered with the inequal sign. Let me ask you, what message do you think those with the equal sign are trying to send?'... And then the next part says, 'Jennifer Walker [wrote]: Well, the sign is in support of gay marriage. It started with the federal government involvement in possibly repealing Prop 8 in California. It means basically that one supports gay marriage,' does it not?"

"Yes," Austin agreed, "that's what it says."

107

"That's April 5, 2013," Shinbaum continued reading. "Then, 'Josh Doggrell: I see. Well, all the more reason to have this one then.' Is that correct?"

"Yes," Austin agreed.

Shinbaum read more of the accompanying comments and continued. "Now, on this non-equal sign, the only thing I see really being discussed — I don't see race ever used. I see gay marriage; is that correct?"

"That's correct," Austin agreed.

"Now," said Shinbaum, "are you aware that in April of 2013 that gay marriages were not allowed in the State of Alabama?"

"Yes."

"As a matter of fact, I think it wasn't until sometime later this year — in the past couple of months or few months that the Supreme Court came out with a decision on gay marriage; am I correct?"

"Correct."

"So...in 2013 in Alabama, gay marriage was not equal?"

Austin's reply: "In some people — in their minds, no, it was not."

"Well," Shinbaum added, "in the State of Alabama government's mind it was not equal in April of 2013; am I correct?"

"Correct," Austin agreed.

The city attorney also entered "Exhibit 11," which was a collage of various Facebook profile photos I had had over the years (none of which were ever considered a problem until the SPLC hit piece on 17 June 2015 and the accompanying "public outcry.") Downey asked Austin why "the city" (in which he seems to really mean Bersheba Austin) found those particular pictures in violation of the "harassment" policy.

She answered, "Several images with the Confederate flag are on this photo album in addition to one picture that has a Confederate flag on it with Nathan Bedford Forrest's picture on it." She said those pictures "speak for themselves. You know, Nathan Bedford Forrest, which was [sic] the founder of the KKK, that's an effective photo."

The following points should be made regarding Austin's statement: The Confederate Battle Flag has been, since its creation, a State-sanctioned emblem. It flew over our State capitol dome for decades during the 20th century. It flew on capitol grounds surrounding the Confederate war memorial for decades, including the day I was fired. It is still, currently, on the shoulder patch of every Alabama State Trooper and on the door of every Trooper patrol vehicle. It is a primary feature of the State-sanctioned Coat of Arms. Our State flag is patterned after it. It was on display inside the Old House Chambers of our capitol. To many, it is a proud symbol of our heritage as Alabamians and Southerners, and, being State-sanctioned, should not automatically be seen as intended to "harass" or "intimidate." Bersheba Austin may be the HR director for the City of Anniston, but she is not endowed with any special authority to determine what is and is not offensive for an entire city, much less a State.

A second point: Nathan Bedford Forrest was a fantastic Confederate general and perhaps the greatest military soldier ever produced by the State of Tennessee, and one of *the* greatest *ever*, but he was NOT the "founder" of the Ku Klux Klan. One might think if Austin was going to make the kind of interpretations and accusations that she did, she might have placed a priority on knowing what she was talking about.

Under cross-examination, Shinbaum referred to the fact that I, and other employees of the city, had displayed private vehicle paraphernalia with images of Confederate flags. Austin claimed to have no knowledge of that.

"Has the City of Anniston ever told anyone you were not to display a Confederate flag, Confederate battle flag, anywhere?" asked Shinbaum.

"Not that I'm aware of."

"Now, this thing with the Confederate battle flag, it means different things to different people, am I correct?"

"Correct," Austin agreed.

"You may view it as racial, others may view it as Southern pride or Southern heritage; am I correct?"

"Correct."

Shinbaum addressed the image of General Forrest. "And are you aware that he was a Confederate general?"

"I'm aware of that," Austin said.

Shinbaum cut to the chase. "Has any employee of the City of Anniston ever come up to you and reported to you that Josh Doggrell has a Confederate flag on his Facebook page and it offends them and asked to have something done about it?"

"An employee has not come to me with that complaint."

"Okay. Has *anyone* come to you with that complaint?"

"No. That is offensive to *me*."

"...And did *you* ever ask Josh Doggrell to remove it from his Facebook page?"

"I have not had that conversation with him, sir."

Shinbaum then made a great point similar to the one made when he was asking Chief Denham about the list of organizations each officer had to submit for examination after I was fired. He had then asked if a group deemed potentially "controversial" was discovered, if asking that employee to leave the group was one option to resolving the situation. Denham agreed that it was, and then agreed that he never asked me to leave the League of the South. Presently, Shinbaum asked HR Director Bersheba Austin, "Now, if the City of Anniston — if an employee feels that another employee has done something that may be harassment and reports it to the Department of Human Resources, what's the Department of Human Resources do?"

"Start an investigation of the complaint."

"And is it supposed to make aware the person who allegedly harassed — to interview that person?"

"Yes."

"Is it also to notify them that whatever he did, that somebody else considers it to be harassment?"

"Yes."

"And the purpose for that is so the person may not do that again; correct?"

"Correct."

Shinbaum looked at Austin and pointed at me. "Did anybody ever contact Josh Doggrell in this case and say, hey, don't post that on your Facebook page? You were the person here, [the] Human Resources Director — [did you ever say] don't post it, it offends me?"

"You said during the course of this?"

"Yes."

"I have not..."

"Did you ever ask anybody to inform Josh Doggrell of that?"

"I have not asked anyone."

Austin went on to say that any city employee displaying a Confederate flag in miscellaneous methods could be subject to disciplinary action if a complaint was filed by someone who was "offended." Probing this rationale, Shinbaum asked, "Is displaying the [Christian] cross harassment to people that are not Christian?"

"It could potentially be considered harassment to someone who is not Christian."

"So... If an employee exhibits the cross on their Facebook page and it offends another employee of the City of Anniston, the employee posting the cross on their Facebook page may be in violation of the City of Anniston's policy?"

"Potentially," Austin answered.

Never on Facebook did I ever identify myself as an Anniston Police Officer. Never did I discuss any proceedings or anything at all about the Anniston Police Department. I used images and content that I found pertinent to issues and topics being discussed among myself and people who had agreed to be participants on my Facebook page. I did this as a Christian whose duty it is to spread the Gospel and as a concerned citizen wishing to advocate for what I believed were issues important to the betterment of my city, State, and country.

Anyone writing or talking about such things is bound to "offend" someone. As Ms. Austin testified, even the display of the Christian cross (and presumably, her own first name, with its Christian origins) may "potentially" violate the City of Anniston's "harassment" policy. And an employee could be terminated for such a display without any prior warning. Under this rationale, no one targeted has constitutional rights of freedom of speech if the government deems it so. The city can (and did, in my case) fire someone for unrelated reasons, and if justification after the fact is needed, someone from the city can simply come forward and say that something the employee said, wrote, wore, displayed, etc., "offended" them.

All of this... in "The Land of the Free."

09.

THE TESTIMONY OF
CITY MANAGER BRIAN JOHNSON

"Where does it stop...? This line of thinking, it can be used against anyone who has different views from others..."

15 September 2015

IT IS MY FIRM BELIEF that things would be much better if Christian men got angry more often. I believe my beloved Southland, and all of Christendom, would not be in the mess it is in today if men displayed such anger more often. I am not talking about vengeance, which the Lord claims as His own. I am talking about righteous anger about worldly injustice — the kind of anger needed by men to set things right. It is the kind of anger required to preserve those things that are worthwhile and sustain civilizations. It is the kind of anger mandatory for a culture to survive under attack and the kind of fury needed to defend against the forces of evil.

On 17 September 2015, I was in the middle of undergoing hours of cross-examination from City Attorney Bruce Downey in my civil service appeal trial regarding my termination as a police officer with the City of Anniston. I was answering a question about my inability to get an opportunity to speak to City Manager Brian

Johnson before he fired me. I looked over the table at Johnson and pointed my finger at him. "It would have been wonderful to have the opportunity to talk to Brian Johnson, this man that fired me, and [to have] sat down with him face-to-face...and had a conversation. And I asked for that and he didn't grant me that. He was too busy trying to rush in here [city hall] and get to his press conference."

Downey then said, "You appear to have a fairly aggressive look on your face right now."

"Sir, my eighteen-and-half year career has been taken from me."

An aggressive look? A louder tone? Was I... angry?

Absolutely, I was angry. For what my family had been put through by the city, I was angry. For my picture being splashed across the newspapers and news programs, and my name being slandered, I was angry. For the police chief that decided between 17 June (when he told me he argued with Johnson about even putting me on administrative leave) and his testimony on 26 August that standing up for me was going to cause him too much difficulty, I was angry. For all the people I had worked with for so many years who were being cowed by the city into public silence, I was angry. For the loss of a vocation I loved, I was angry. And I had cold, burning, righteous anger at the official who had taken my livelihood away to appease the politically correct crowd, the man who I judged held little regard for my hometown other than that which he could use to feed his ego and pad his resume for his next job in another town.

In the time since, I have learned to forgive through the grace and mercy of a faithful God. But forgiving is not forgetting. And the anger still smolders.

Yes, I was an angry man. Would to God we had more angry men today.

* * *

Anniston, Alabama, City Manager Brian Johnson was the man who fired me on 19 June 2015. To this day, we have never had a one-on-one conversation. He did not speak to me in the 48-hour "investigation" preceding my termination, despite my request to speak to him.

All the following quotes are from the official and legal transcript of my trial.

Johnson took the stand in the late morning of 15 September 2015 in the municipal courtroom of the Justin Sollohub Justice Center in Anniston. After being sworn in, he identified himself for the record by name and position. He listed his general responsibilities as chief executive officer of the municipality, which included "ultimate responsibility for the supervision of those persons within the administrative service of the city..."

JOHNSON'S CALL FROM THE SOUTHERN POVERTY LAW CENTER RESULTS IN INACTION AND NO OFFICIAL INVESTIGATION

City attorney Bruce Downey, serving as city prosecutor, asked Johnson when he first learned that I was a member of the League of the South. "The first I ever heard of that was from a phone call [in May 2015] of an individual who identified himself as being with the Southern Poverty Law Center..." Johnson said he had "never heard of the League of the South prior to that." He related that when he received the call, he was expecting it because he had already been apprised by Police Chief Shane Denham of the similar call Denham had received earlier in the day.

Johnson said he asked the caller from the Southern Poverty Law Center (SPLC) what their characterization was of this organization about which he knew nothing. "They had just characterized it as a hate group and it was on their hate watch list of organizations they were watching."

Led in further questioning by Downey, Johnson then emphasized that he drew no conclusions simply based on the phone call from the SPLC because their information "needed to be corroborated internally by city staff..." Much like Chief Denham in his earlier testimony, Johnson stressed that the caller was "pushing me" about what it was he was going to do about this information. Johnson testified that he told the caller, "...I'm not an attorney or, you know, a personnel specialist, but I don't believe that the city can do anything based merely on someone's membership in an organization."

Johnson said the "first thing" he did following that phone conversation was to speak with Chief Denham about it. He asked Denham if he knew of my affiliation with the League and was there any disciplinary actions in my personnel file regarding it. Obviously, Johnson knew Denham knew of my affiliation because Johnson had just testified that he had been expecting the call from the SPLC because Denham had received the same call and given him a heads-up.

Johnson testified that he then had a conversation with the Human Resources Director, Bersheba Austin, about the city's policies regarding employees' memberships in "hate organizations or the like."

Johnson then detailed why he delayed in having a meeting with Downey about the situation. He said that "the day or two after that phone call I ended up leaving for a week on vacation and had been previously scheduled to come back for two days and then leave for another four for another conference I was speaking at." So, however seriously Johnson may have taken these "allegations" from the SPLC, *he did not deem it necessary to consult with the city attorney about it for at least two weeks.* He spoke to Denham and Austin and directed them to "look into" the matter and "paint for me the context that we were in..."

Based on his own testimony, as well as that of former Chief Layton McGrady and others, Denham would have told Johnson in that initial conversation that he and the entire department knew about my membership in the League, had, in fact, known about it for years, and that I had been investigated and cleared by the city six years prior to that. I find it highly probable that Denham would have included this information in his phone call warning Johnson about the pending call from the SPLC, making Johnson's claim that he had never heard of the League of the South prior to the SPLC call unbelievable.

Another point to consider: In his testimony, Lt. Nick Bowles (the head of Internal Affairs at the time and the lead investigator into this matter) testified that he received the same information from the SPLC in May 2015 (the same time as Johnson and Denham). Bowles, like most of my colleagues, had known about my League membership for years. Bowles even attended the inaugural meeting of the chapter I founded in Anniston in March 2009. In Bowles's own testimony later that same day (15 September 2015), he testified that, after receiving the information from the SPLC in May, he watched the entirety of the video of the speech I gave in Elmore County in June 2013. He then consulted with Chief Denham about it that same day, did nothing further, and did not open an investigation *because he was not told to do so*. ***He said he was not told to open an investigation until about three weeks later, on 17 June 2015, immediately after the SPLC published their attack piece.*** Despite Johnson's claims that the SPLC intervention into this matter was not the reason for his decision to terminate me, the fact is that the city sat on this "information" for three weeks and did absolutely nothing until after the SPLC's article. In fact, I was told by Lt. Bowles and my immediate supervisor, Captain Greg Feazell, both of whom had viewed the video of the speech, that they found nothing wrong with it. Only three hours after the SPLC publication, I was placed on administrative leave and, a mere forty-eight hours later, I was fired by Johnson.

THREE WEEKS LATER,
A LEFTIST ATTACK PIECE CHANGES THINGS

After that initial phone call from the SPLC, Johnson testified that "the next significant event was the publication of the article." He claimed that the article contained "a number of things that had not been even conveyed to me during the telephone conversation..." Johnson went on to say those things were that there were two Anniston police officers that were League members instead of just one, that I had given a speech that was published on YouTube, that I had insinuated that the police chief endorsed the League's views, and that I had "identified" myself as being employed as an Anniston police officer.

Johnson said that after the SPLC article, he "convened a meeting of some of my senior staff" to discuss "what's the word out—you know, how is the community reacting to this..." *I cannot emphasize the following enough, and I strongly expressed it to Chief Denham in his office the morning I was fired: "Community outrage" should have no bearing on the right or wrong of any situation, as "community outrage" is susceptible to political grandstanding, "squeaky wheels," race hustlers, and professional protesters and agitators. Either I had done something wrong, or I had not — but "community outrage" was irrelevant to that consideration.* As an example, if "community outraged" was the gauge of right and wrong, Officer Darren Wilson would have been convicted of murder in the aftermath of defending himself in Ferguson, Missouri, rather than having been exonerated by a grand jury. I told Denham that, if the city caved, it was leaving the constitutional rights of its employees at the mercy of the whim of the feelings of professional protesters and citizens with a contrary viewpoint.

Johnson testified that "subsequent to that meeting...we needed to open up a full-blown Internal Affairs investigation..." Again, this decision was *not* made in the weeks after the police department's command staff had viewed the video of my speech, nor in the weeks after Denham and Johnson had received the phone calls from the SPLC, nor in the years 2009-2015 when the city knew of my League membership... but *only after* the publication of the SPLC attack piece.

JOHNSON'S CONCLUSION
THAT A DISCLAIMER INVALIDATES ITSELF

Next, Johnson made a bizarre conclusion. One of the policies I was accused of violating was giving a speech "in my capacity" as an officer without the approval of the chief of police, even though I gave a full disclaimer in that speech that I was, in fact, not speaking on behalf of the city or the department. City Attorney Downey asked him "did you consider Mr. Doggrell's speech in 2013 at the League of the South annual conference to be one that was in his capacity as an Anniston police officer?"

Johnson's conclusion: "Well, ultimately, yes, because despite when, you know, saying, oh, I'm not giving it in the capacity as a police officer, by virtue of saying that, immediately everybody knows that you are. And so, you know, you can't undo that."

And there you have it, folks. According to City Manager Brian Johnson, giving a disclaimer that you are not giving a speech in your capacity as a city employee is invalid because... by giving the disclaimer you are identifying yourself as a city employee. So... giving a disclaimer automatically invalidates the disclaimer. This was one of the numerous times during the proceedings when I sat in my chair at the defense table, stunned at the idiotic statements being made.

Next, we had the admission by the city manager (corroborated by the internal affairs lieutenant and the police chief) that the reason he made the decision to fire me was due, not to merit or the right and wrong of the situation, but to the "public outcry" with which he was dealing.

How sad the state of national affairs regarding police activity had become played a large part in how Johnson mishandled this situation. This was evidenced, in part, by the unusual step of the city manager holding a Friday afternoon press conference on the day of the firing to publicly announce it (and publicly shame me in the process). My reputation received irreparable damage at the hands of Johnson, Denham, and the city council members involved in order to attempt to appease the hounds of political correctness. Johnson put it this way in his testimony when asked by Downey why he chose to hold such a press conference:

"Well, because of this—the spotlight that was put on this, if we did not do that there was, you know, there was that risk that we were going to go into the weekend with people not knowing what the decision was. And, you know, I believe the term 'powder keg' came up a number of times within the community. We were afraid if we did not make it very clear to all the media outlets and let them send it out, that we could have a situation over the weekend, a Ferguson-like situation."

Downey asked, "The city, then, feared that the community could become hostile if actions were not taken?"

"Absolutely," Johnson answered. "Absolutely. Including some individuals who, you know, to a degree contacted me directly and were endorsing that very thing."

PLEASE DO NOT MISS THIS! We see the critical role that the professional protesters, race hustlers, rioters, and criminal malcontents in places like Ferguson, Baltimore, *et al*, played in a decision with huge implications on me and my family — a decision that should have been based on the merits of the policy issues and constitutional rights in question.

CROSS EXAMINATION

Defense attorney Kenneth Shinbaum's first question to City Manager Brian Johnson was when Johnson had first viewed the entirety of the 2013 speech I had given. "I don't know. A couple of weeks ago." (That would have been a couple of weeks prior to his 15 September 2015 testimony, or, about a month and a half *after* he fired me for it.)

Shinbaum then challenged Johnson's disclaimer theory. "Now...did you view the video where Mr. Doggrell states that he is not there to speak on behalf of the City of Anniston Police Department?"

"Yes."

"But you say that in itself means that he *is* speaking on behalf of the Anniston Police Department?"

"No. It's just that he identified—that identifies him as an Anniston police officer so anything he then says subsequent to that, you know, is done in the context of who his employer is and what his profession is."

Shinbaum then entered into the record, as our first exhibit, the city's own personnel policy and procedure as it related to social media in order to draw a parallel between giving a speech and posting on social media. Shinbaum had Johnson read it:

"Identify your views as your own. If you identify yourself as a city employee, it should be clear that the views expressed are not those of the city. In fact, unless your job duties with the city entail posting on social media regarding city business, employees are prohibited from posting anything that implies or indicates that they are posting in their official capacity as an employee or representative of the city."

Shinbaum addressed the parallel: "Would that apply if somebody is speaking at an event that — a person, a city employee, that they should let the audience know that the views that they are speaking about are not those of the city?"

Johnson clearly wanted to dodge this parallel. "I can only comment on what it says there about social media." Shinbaum pressed the matter.

"...[I]t sounds to me like...you are...saying by him saying it's *not* the views of the city, you are saying he *is* saying it is the views of the city."

"I didn't say that."

"Well, that's what you said with the YouTube video where Mr. Doggrell stated that he is not speaking on behalf of the City of Anniston; you stated that implicates that he is speaking on behalf of the City of Anniston."

CLEARED BY THE 2009 INTERNAL AFFAIRS INVESTIGATION

Shinbaum addressed the fact that the city had previously investigated me for my affiliation with the League of the South in 2009.

"Now, in 2009 the city did investigate the fact that Josh Doggrell was forming a chapter of the League of the South...is that correct?"

"That's my understanding."

"And Josh Doggrell was a police officer at the time; is that correct?"

"That's my understanding."

"And further, Josh Doggrell had been identified in the newspaper [*The Anniston Star*] as forming...a local chapter of the League of the South at that time; is that correct?"

"I believe that is my understanding..."

Johnson said he was not sure of the details of what occurred in that investigation. Shinbaum asked, "Isn't it true that Josh Doggrell was investigated by the police department in 2009 concerning his forming a local chapter and he was not terminated, he was not told to leave the League of the South, or not to form the chapter?"

"I can't speak on behalf of what was in that Internal Affairs investigation. I haven't seen it."

I find Johnson's claim that he had not seen the file of my previous investigation extremely hard to believe.

Shinbaum, considering Human Resources director Bersheba Austin's testimony earlier that morning, asked if the city had any policy about an employee displaying the Confederate battle flag. "Not that I'm aware of," Johnson answered.

"Why not?"

"I can't speak on why it has not been in there."

"Does the City of Anniston presently have that policy?"

"Specific to that image, no."

So, Ms. Austin testified that she found it "offensive" that my Facebook profile contained images of the Confederate battle flag, and her testimony was used to support my termination, but there was no policy on its display whatsoever.

DOGGRELL'S PERSONNEL FILE

Shinbaum asked Johnson if he ever reviewed my personnel file.

"I did not."

"Did you ever ask anybody about what was in his personnel file?"

"I did."

"Who did you ask?"

"Both my HR director [Austin] and police chief.

"And what did they say was in there?"

"I'm assuming you mean disciplinary action..."

"Disciplinary actions."

"That where was none." (In a news account, Johnson described my record as "without blemish.")

Shinbaum asked Johnson, "prior to this investigation...had you ever heard of any complaints about Josh Doggrell?"

"I'd never heard his name before."

"Were there employees of the City of Anniston that were interviewed that said they had any problems with Josh Doggrell?"

"Not that I'm aware of."

JOHNSON AND THE CITY COUNCIL BREAK STATE LAW

Shinbaum went on to question Johnson about conversations he had had with city councilmen. Before the trial, we had filed a complaint with the State attorney general's office regarding the criminal violation of council members by interfering with the executive's decision to terminate my employment. Perhaps based on this allegation, Johnson claimed to have had no such conversations with Councilman Reddick.

"Did you have any conferences with Councilman Reddick... regarding this matter?" Shinbaum asked.

"I did not. I did not speak to Councilman Reddick, Council-woman Harris, or Councilman Jenkins through this entire time, not one word."

Not one word, he said. Later that day, Reddick took the stand and unequivocally contradicted this testimony. At that time, Shinbaum asked Reddick, "Did you ever inform the city manager that your community wanted Josh Doggrell off the police force?"

Reddick responded, "In a way, I would say yes. I never went to him and said we want Josh Doggrell off the police department; that's not what I said."

"What did you say?"

"I told him— I said the community was upset, they were scared, they were angry, but I never at any time told the city manager what to or not to do."

"Did you ever say something needed to be done?"

"Something did need to be done, yes."

Shinbaum asked Reddick why something "needed to be done" in June of 2015 when the city knew I was a League member as far back as 2009.

"Well, as I understand it," Reddick replied, "he was cleared of that, so I would assume the city believed that it was an erroneous accusation is what I would believe. Considering there was an investigation... if there is an investigation and he was cleared, to me as a public official, I would have to assume that whoever did that investigation cleared him."

Now back to Johnson on the stand. Shinbaum asked him about the 2009 investigation in which I was cleared of wrongdoing. "Well, was there an Internal Affairs investigation that did not find anything wrong with what he was doing?"

"Yes, but that's not the point. The point is he discussed it with the public."

Next, Shinbaum asked Johnson if he had seen *any of* the city's first nine exhibits entered prior to firing me. He testified that he had seen *none* of them, only that they had been "reported" to him by other people.

Shinbaum referenced our exhibit E-02, which was my personnel file. "To this date have you looked at Mr. Doggrell's personnel file?"

"I have not," Johnson answered. Apparently, he concluded that all my previous years of service and conduct on the job were irrelevant to the consideration of terminating my employment on 19 June 2015.

Shinbaum asked Johnson if he had ever read the "Core Values" of the League or the "Frequently Asked Questions." These serve as actual policy of the League of the South, and not opinions or positions of various individual members. "I have not," he answered.

DOES COMMUNITY "PERCEPTION" DETERMINE THE MERITS OF A SITUATION?

Several questions centered on Johnson's assertion that the community "perception" of an organization plays an important part of the determination of whether or not that organization is acceptable for city employees. "...[C]an a police officer be a member of the Tea Party?" Shinbaum asked.

"If it doesn't bring into question their ability to objectively provide law enforcement service."

"There are a lot of people with the perception that the Tea Party has racist views. Does that mean that a police officer cannot be a member of the Tea Party?"

Johnson was clearly flustered with this logic. "I'm not going — we are— I'm not going to comment on individual groups. What matters is the public — how the public reacts to this."

Shinbaum pressed. "If the public has the reaction that Republicans have racist views towards people from Mexico because they have — one of their candidates [later President Trump] referred to them as 'anchor babies' and another one that's saying, well, some of these children, that their parents are not legal aliens of the South, but they are warning the United States that they should not be considered to be citizens. Would you consider that as being racially divisive?"

"I'm not going to —"

At this point City Attorney Downey stepped in to save Johnson from being caught in the snare of his own "Perception Doctrine," by making one of his (now routine) irrelevance objections which was promptly and robotically sustained by board attorney Trudie Phillips. Shinbaum went on to make his point: *"Where does it stop on it? This line of thinking, it can be used against anyone who has different views from others that people are going to say, oh, they have — they may be a hate group, or they may have racist thinking and..."*

Where does it stop, indeed?

Phillips now stepped in to save Johnson by repeating her most-used phrase of the trial. "The objection is sustained."

Shinbaum ended his questioning, and Downey had no questions for Johnson. My assumption is that Downey wanted Johnson off the stand as quickly as possible.

Here is what I took from Brian Johnson's testimony. Johnson received the information that I was a member of the League of the South three weeks prior to the SPLC's attack piece on me and decided to take no action other than to ask the police chief and the HR director to "look into it." I hold resolutely that, had the SPLC column not been published, and the small group of racial agitators not howled after it, I would have continued working at the City of Anniston Police Department until I retired. Johnson did not consider the merits of the accusations here, he only reacted like a coward when confronted with the professional protesters and the liberal media. The city (i.e., Johnson) made the decision to fire me on 17 June 2015 in order to attempt to satisfy the hounds of political correctness, then spent the next several months scavenging for reasons to validate it.

Johnson made the decision to fire me without even speaking to me (despite my request to speak to him), without even viewing the video of the speech in question, and without even looking at my personnel file. Politics *drove* his decision. And, sadly, the command staff at APD (minus myself, of course) went right along with it.

Johnson was a habitual and pathological liar and megalomaniac. After he was appointed city manager in September 2013 and began his quest to dismantle the civil service system, I predicted to anyone that would listen that he would be gone within five years, that he would lie and say anything he felt furthered his agendas, that he was using us and our city to pad his resume for his next position, and that he cared nothing for the city, its citizens, and its employees. Guess what? In October 2016, Johnson left Anniston to accept a job in Georgia.

After getting Johnson off the stand, the city rested their case. Now it was time for us to offer our defense.

10.

THE CHARACTER WITNESSES

"[He treated us] fair and equal all the way across the board."

15 September 2015

THE VARIOUS NEWS ACCOUNTS covering the situation in the immediate aftermath of my firing ranged from slanted to vicious. My advice from the attorney I initially contacted was to remain completely silent. I now consider this a major mistake on my part, because it allowed the city to set the narrative in the media and convince the public that their decision was justified, and I was some kind of monster. I feel my silence facilitated that. During the almost-daily barrage of negative press, I phoned an editor at the local newspaper to contradict an untruth that had appeared in their digital edition (I wanted to attempt to have it corrected before it went to print), and he seemed surprised at my account of the fabrications of the city's version. The particular untruth I called his attention to was corrected for the print edition the following day.

The general impression the public received through City Manager Brian Johnson and the command staff of the police department contained several untruths. It was implied that my affiliation with the League of the South was a discovery — that I had been "outed," so to speak. The truth is the city knew about my involvement since the time I was hired in April of 2006, when I discussed it in my hiring interview, listed it on my application, and in my polygraph (the written report of the polygraph was produced by the city for depositions in October of 2016, but it was not for the appeal trial in the summer of 2015. Draw your own conclusion.) There was also an internal investigation performed on me by the city in the spring of 2009, in which I was cleared of any wrongdoing and told I was within my constitutional rights to be a member of the League and chairman of the local chapter. (The record of this investigation was withheld by the city, and they refused to produce it in my appeal trial. Draw your own conclusion.)

The heavy implication by the Southern Poverty Law Center and the local race hustlers and professional protesters in Anniston was that I was a "racist." I confess that in modern America the epithet "racist" has become so puzzling with its wide range of definitions that I never know how to respond to the accusation. I have heard the liberal view that anyone born white is automatically "racist." It would be hard to argue with such "logic." The underlying accusations were that I hated black people, was a white supremacist, and treated people unfairly because they were not white. All of this is untrue.

Our team felt we needed to produce several character witnesses to refute the slander and libel that resulted in the severe character assassination perpetuated by the city. Our final determinations and subpoenas resulted in the testimonies of Officer Tiffany Taylor (my only black subordinate at the time of my firing), Sergeant Matthew Delozier (one of my subordinates when I was a uniform lieutenant in 2013-2014), Lieutenant Phillip Smith (my direct supervisor in 2006-2008 and my partner as sergeant on a patrol shift in 2010-2011), Captain Greg Feazell (my immediate supervisor at the time of my termination), Lieutenant Justin Sanford (whom I had worked with as a peer and supervised), and Mrs. Debbie Rooks (a clerk with approximately thirty years of service with the department whom I worked with in the administrative division).

In their formal charges, the city alleged that I had acted in a "prejudicial, divisive, or offensive manner." Therefore, we asked each of these people with whom I had actually worked if they had observed such behavior from me.

I believe it pertinent to note that the city produced zero witnesses to attack my character or job performance.

The first to take the stand after the city had rested their case on the morning of 15 September 2015 was retired Police Chief John Dryden.

POLICE CHIEF JOHN DRYDEN

As he would testify, John Dryden had known me since I was born. He worked closely with my father in the 1970s and '80s with the Anniston Police Department and their Special Duty Unit, which centered on vice and narcotics. Dryden is a native Annistonian, graduated from Anniston High School, and became a resident of my home community of Saks.

When I began my career as a Calhoun County deputy sheriff, then-Captain Dryden assisted me with shooting lessons. We were members of the local Fraternal Order of Police together, and he was police chief when I was hired as an Anniston peace officer in April 2006. He retired from that position in January 2010 after over thirty years of service to the citizens of Anniston. Ironically, he was *my* subordinate upon my termination in June 2015. He was then working as a part-time inmate work supervisor, which fell under my authority as assistant administrative commander. One of the most uncomfortable things I have ever done was to perform an annual job evaluation on one of the greatest peace officers Calhoun County has ever had. I felt plain silly.

All quotes are taken from the official transcript of the trial.

On the stand, Shinbaum asked Dryden "How do you know Mr. Doggrell?"

"I have known him all his life. I worked with his father and I worked with him."

Shinbaum asked about his tenure as chief, and Dryden confirmed it was from May 2002 to January 2010. "Now," asked Shinbaum, "what type of employee was Josh Doggrell during your tenure?"

"Above average."

"And did you ever have any problems with him?"

"No, sir."

DRYDEN'S MISSING LETTER

"Now, do you recall a city investigation in 2009 into Lt. Doggrell's affiliation with the League of the South?"

"Vaguely. I don't remember all the circumstances."

"Now you would have been the chief at that time; is that correct?"

"Correct."

"And what were the results of that investigation?"

"I would have to review the paperwork, but I would remember any action that was taken, so, evidently there was not enough evidence for any action to be taken or [further] investigation to be conducted."

"Now, how did it come to your attention about any need for an investigation with respect to Josh Doggrell and the League of the South in 2009?"

"There was a complaint filed," Dryden answered, "and that's what I meant reference to as far as any action taken."

"And who was the complaint filed by?"

"I would have to review the file. I was just [reminded] of that yesterday."

Shinbaum asked Dryden if the person who filed the complaint in 2009 knew that I was a member of the League. "I suppose. I would have to review the complaint. I mean, that's been almost seven years ago."

"But it would be a fact that the Anniston Police Department knew of Josh Doggrell's affiliation with the League of the South back in 2009?"

"Like I said, I would have to review it, but if the complaint was filed and we looked into it, I would say yes."

When I heard this, I was a little confused. I would have thought Dryden would have been more informative about this investigation. I reconciled, at the time, that as chief this incident would not have been near as important to him as it was to me then. And while it was the only time I had been under any sort of "internal investigation" when it occurred, he probably dealt with them on a fairly consistent basis.

What I learned over a year later, during depositions for the federal case, was that *Dryden had written a letter that could be described as a summary of that very investigation*. It was addressed and delivered to a local citizen. In 2016, City Attorney Bruce Downey finally elected to release that document to us. His explanation was that, since it was released to a member of the public it could have been widely disseminated by that same citizen and was, therefore, classified as public information. Why Downey did not come to this same rationale when we requested the file of the internal investigation for the 2015 trial is left to the reader's own conclusion. When reading this letter over a year later, it is my belief that when Dryden testified that he "would have to review the paperwork" and he "would have to review the file," (*four different times he stressed the need to review the file*) he may have been attempting to get the file—or at least that letter—into the trial. We could not press the issue at the time because, of course, we did not even know the letter existed...because the city refused to release it or any part of the file to us.

When my attorney and I finally received a copy of the letter in the fall of 2016, one year after the conclusion of my appeal trial, here is what we found.

The memorandum is addressed to "Elder Thomas G. Long, Sr." I do not know who this is, but it appears he is the person who lodged an initial complaint against me after two *Anniston Star* articles and local television stations in late March 2009 carried stories about the beginning of a local chapter of the League of the South in Anniston. Both *Star* articles identified me as the chairman and quoted me.

The subject of the letter is clearly stated to be "Request for investigation: League of the South" and is from Dryden in both his capacity as police chief and interim city manager, the city being without a full-time city manager at that particular time.

The first paragraph seems to indicate that Long was most concerned with whether or not an "elected or public official" was in attendance at our inaugural meeting at the Western Sizzlin' in Anniston on 26 March 2009. I seem to recall there being a rumor that Gene Robinson, who was then mayor of Anniston, was at the meeting. He was not, and I do not recall any elected official being at that meeting. There were approximately 30-40 people there, and several police officers were present, including Nick Bowles, who served as the primary internal affairs investigator for the city in the 2015 investigation against me. He would go on to become police chief of the City of Anniston a few years later.

The third paragraph affirms that there was a member of the police department who was a member of the League. It further states I was interviewed and gave a statement. That statement, of course, and all other information from the file of that investigation, was not turned over by the city for the trial against me six years later.

Dryden wrote, "He in no way affiliated his employment with the city to his membership with this organization." In the federal depositions in October 2016, the city keyed on this sentence to attempt to say that I had affiliated my employment with the city with my League membership in the Wetumpka speech of 2013, which is untrue. In the first of only two brief times, I mentioned my employment with the city in that speech, I gave a clear disclaimer that I in no way was speaking on behalf of the city, but in my individual capacity as a citizen. It should be noted that during several League meetings that occurred in Anniston in 2009 and 2010, I spoke of my vocation as a peace officer, and it was commonly known to attendees that I was a peace officer in that town. Obviously, it was known to the person who filed this complaint, even though I do not know him. It was also known to the many people who commented about it under the articles in the newspaper's online version.

Dryden wrote that I acted **"as a concerned citizen based on his beliefs, which is one of his constitutional rights."** I believe he was right about that then, and that my rights were violated six years later by a different police chief (Shane Denham) and a different city manager (Brian Johnson).

Dryden also wrote that **"He is a dedicated professional police officer that has never shown any radical action in his duties as a police officer. He took an oath of office to enforce all documented laws and constitutions and that has never been questioned since his career in law enforcement began."** Nothing in this regard had changed from 2009-2015, and the city was unable to dig up anything to present at trial to the contrary.

In the fourth paragraph, Dryden made the distinction that separates the League, as it stood throughout my membership in it, from organizations that are commonly prohibited from membership to a government employee: **"There is no evidence to show that anyone in this organization in question has** violated any laws, statutes, procedures, rules or regulations that pertain to a city employee, elected official or citizen." This remained the case through 2015.

Dryden concludes by noting that there was no active intelligence, civil, or criminal cases documented in relation to the League.

And then he wrote these revealing sentences about the leftist, Marxist, disreputable group that got the ball rolling on my firing with their character-assassination hit piece published on 17 June 2015: "**From past experience with the Southern Poverty Law Center [SPLC], this group can label anyone anything. Their last label of this organization was in the year 2000.**"

This indicates that Dryden was familiar with the SPLC, their treacherous ways, their vast "labeling," and their far-left tendencies. He also pointed out that they first "labeled" the League of the South a "hate group" nine years prior to this request for an investigation. This does not begin to mention the thousands of other organizations and people they have smeared with that label over the years.

Dryden's summary: "**This investigation has revealed no violations of any kind that action could be taken on.**"

Again, this memorandum, deemed public knowledge by the city a year later, was suppressed by the city during the appeal trial of my termination in the summer of 2015. As was the entire file of the internal investigation that cleared me of any wrongdoing, despite our multiple requests for it. To this day they refuse to release it. Why? The answer should be obvious. **The city's whole case falls apart when evidence is brought to light that they cleared me of something that they then fired me for immediately after the publication of an SPLC article.**

I have always admired John Dryden as a man, an officer, and a leader. This letter revealed about him what I already knew — that he was a man of integrity and fairness, and a leader who respected the religious and constitutional rights of his subordinates. How I wished he was still the police chief in 2015.

One cannot help but wonder... What else is in that file the City of Anniston took such painstaking efforts to hide?

Back on the stand on 15 September 2015, Shinbaum asked Dryden, "Did you ever inform him that he should not form a local chapter of the League of the South?"

"No, sir."

Shinbaum asked questions about my duties as jail administrator in 2014 and 2015. "And did you ever have any complaints about the way Josh Doggrell performed his job as a police officer or as the jail administrator?"

"No, sir."

"Did you ever see Josh Doggrell on the job ever do anything that was racially based?"

"No, sir."

"Ever hear of it?"

"No, sir."

"Did you ever hear of Josh Doggrell ever treating anybody unfairly?"

"No, sir."

"Did the citizen — other than the citizen that made a complaint about Josh Doggrell being a member of the League of the South back in 2009 — did any other citizens of the City of Anniston ever have any complaints concerning Josh Doggrell?"

"Not to my knowledge."

Unlike most of the city's witnesses, Dryden knew me and, I feel, knew my heart. He knew my service and the caliber of my work. He knew my love for the job. He knew and could testify to my fairness to the citizens. He knew of my affiliation with the League of the South. To a good extent, he knew of my religious and political convictions regarding the relationship of government-to-citizen. I felt he was exceedingly more qualified than *any* of the city's witnesses to testify on these matters.

Shinbaum had no further questions for Chief Dryden. The city had none whatsoever.

OFFICER TIFFANY TAYLOR

How difficult was it to have a logical conversation about the issue of race in 21st-century America? In the words of columnist Aaron Wolf, we live among a "carnival of ignorance...a generation of young white adults taught to hate their ancestors and view all history through the lens of Critical Race Theory... [where] the past is only a tool for manipulating the masses in the name of Progress, which translates into Power..."

What passes today for "pop culture" teaches us that "Tolerance" is among the highest virtues (unless you're tolerating the truly conservative), that "Multiculturalism" is to be strictly adhered to (unless it includes Western Civilization or Southern culture), that all races are equal and worthy of celebration (except for the white race), and that everyone has a right to pay homage to their heritage without outside interference (unless that heritage is Christian and/or European). More appropriately, this is not "pop culture," but the practice of political correctness; even more accurately, it is Cultural Marxism expanded and on steroids. And, in the spring and summer of 2015, this poison infiltrated the highest ranks of the municipal government of my hometown, Anniston, Alabama.

The second character witness we called to the stand was Officer Tiffany Taylor, the only black subordinate of mine at the time of my firing.

I first met Taylor in the spring of 2013 when our sons were on the same little-league baseball team in my home community of Saks in north Anniston. We were casual acquaintances as a result and our conversations were always cordial and pleasant. Later that year, she became employed at the Anniston Police Department as a corrections officer at the municipal jail (it should be noted I had no influence in her employment). At the time, I was serving as a shift lieutenant in the Uniform Division. She and I had very little interaction.

In July of 2014, I was transferred to the Administrative Division. My main responsibility was oversight and administration of the municipal jail, which meant all corrections sergeants and officers fell under my supervision. Taylor was on first shift and our working relationship grew. Together, with our fellow officers, we performed the many duties of detention, including the care and control of the inmates as well as servicing inmate family members, bail bondsmen, court officials, and other citizens.

Taylor was an ideal employee. She was dependable. Her attendance was impeccable. She was professional, even-tempered, and consistent. She was hard-working, intelligent, cautious, safe, stern yet compassionate. I do not say this because of her race, her gender, whatever her religious or political views may be, or what she testified on this occasion. She was, quite simply, one of the best workers I have ever been associated within the detention field.

My reason for phoning Taylor in July 2015 and asking her to testify (I did not have to ask, I could have just subpoenaed her, but thought that imprudent) had less to do with that and much more to do with the fact that she was a black female. I was being painted by the city, by the local newspaper, and by local race-baiting professional protesters (most of whom had never had even so much as a conversation with me) as being a racist monster. So, I needed someone who actually knew me to testify under oath to the contrary. This was someone who actually had a working relationship with me and could testify about my work performance and supervision. And the most important reason I phoned Taylor and asked her to do this, an action that we both knew could possibly have severe negative repercussions for her as a city employee, was that I had no doubt that if she took the stand she would tell the truth.

"Fair and Equal All the Way Across the Board"

"Now, do you know Josh Doggrell?" asked my attorney, Kenneth Shinbaum, after Taylor had been sworn in and answered preliminaries.

"Yes."

"Did you know Josh Doggrell before you joined...the City of Anniston as an employee?

"Yes... [through] Saks Youth Sports."

"...have you ever worked with Josh Doggrell?"

"Yes."

"In what position?"

"Corrections officer... [he was my] Lieutenant."

The time of this was stipulated to be from July of 2014 to June of 2015.

"Now," Shinbaum continued, "in the time that you have known Lt. Doggrell, have you ever seen or heard him behave in what you would describe as a prejudicial, divisive, or offensive manner?"

"No."

"Would you describe what type of supervisor Lt. Doggrell was and how he treated his subordinates?"

"I mean, fair and equal all the way across the board."

"Did you ever see Lt. Doggrell interact with inmates?"

"Yes."

"And did you ever see Lt. Doggrell mistreat any inmate?"

"No."

"Did you ever see Josh Doggrell interact with members of the public?"

"As far as outside? Yes."

"Did you — how did Josh Doggrell treat members of the public?

"Pretty much the same."

"Was he always courteous?"

"Yes."

Shinbaum asked a very important question: "Did you ever feel that Lt. Doggrell ever treated you any differently from any other subordinate or employee because of your race?"

"No."

"Were there subordinates under Josh Doggrell that were both white and African American?"

"Yes."

"Were there any employees of any other race besides African American or Caucasian?"

"No."

"No further questions."

Unlike most of our character witnesses, the city had questions for Officer Taylor. **I think it is of extreme importance to consider the consequences of this line of questioning on the freedoms individuals are supposed to have in this country.** I will elaborate on that further below.

City Attorney Bruce Downey asked Taylor, "Did you know at any time when you were working with Mr. Doggrell, he was a member of the League of the South?"

"No."

True — the issue of our political positions never became relevant between Taylor and me while discharging our duties.

"Did you subsequently learn that he was?"

"Yes."

"And did you after learning make any effort to understand what the beliefs, positions, and statements were of that organization?"

"Yes."

"And did you, in that effort, find any of those beliefs, positions, and statements to be offensive to you?"

"Somewhat, yes."

"...Nothing further. Thank you."

And that was it. The city's stance was that, subsequent to my firing, Taylor had researched the League of the South and found that some of their "beliefs, positions, and statements" were "*somewhat*" offensive to her.

Well, stop the presses! You know, if Officer Taylor — or just about any other city employee — had had their religious, political, or cultural opinions scrutinized as were mine, I imagine there would be any number of other city employees — including *me* — who would find at least *some* of those opinions "somewhat" offensive. *And, keep in mind, these were not necessarily my beliefs, but beliefs of other people with whom I just happened to have an association.* What did this prove, exactly? Based on her previous testimony, it should prove that individuals are not robots, and they are different, and they come from various backgrounds and hold differing opinions on a myriad of issues. *Should this really surprise anyone?* And yet, she and I were both professional enough to not let those opinions and positions interfere with our ability to carry out our duties as officers and perform our jobs well.

Both in this trial and in the federal depositions in the fall of 2016, our side made it a priority to point out that this level of scrutiny and guilt-by-association would make it *impossible* for anyone to hold a position in any level of government.

To the reader: Consider your affiliations. Consider your church, your fraternal organizations, your reading subscriptions, your voting records, your political party affiliations, etc. ... Might there be something there with which someone might find "*somewhat*" offensive? Should this mean that you are unfit to serve in your capacity in whatever job you hold?

Shinbaum redirected. "Now... did you ever speak to Josh Doggrell about his membership in the League of the South?"

"No," Taylor replied.

"Did you ever ask him what his views were?"

"No."

"...did Josh Doggrell ever publish anything that you were concerned about?"

"No."

"No further questions."

Officer Taylor found some of the "beliefs, positions, and statements" of *one* organization to which I affiliated with to be "somewhat" offensive to her. Guess what? I find some of those same statements of some League members to be offensive to me, too. I find some opinions of my fellow Christians and Southerners to be offensive to me. I find some statements of some of my fellow church members to be disagreeable to me. I often exchanged in debates with my fellow members of the Fraternal Order of Police

(FOP) in which I found their views to be misguided or offensive. I often found myself at odds with my colleagues of the Anniston Police Department regarding policy and behavior. I have supported political candidates who were/are members of the Republican Party, all the while finding many "beliefs, positions, and statements" of that party to be particularly offensive to me. *YET*, at no time have I ever called for anyone to be excommunicated from my church. I never stood up at an FOP meeting and demanded that a member be thrown out of the organization. I never considered not voting for a candidate I believed in who affiliated with the Republican Party simply because that party, or individual members of it, put forth positions or statements with which I disagreed. AND I never went to city hall and made an entreaty that an officer lose his or her vocation because he or she affiliated with someone who held views that were "somewhat" offensive to me.

Examine yourself, citizens. If this line of scrutiny can be used to justify someone losing his job, being blackballed from his lifetime vocation, and ruining his reputation regardless of how he conducted himself or performed his duties, I ask you: **Who among us is safe?**

SERGEANT MATTHEW DELOZIER

The prosecution's strategy of putting Michael Hill on trial and convicting me was reinforced by their cross-examination of Hill. But we went forth with our remaining character witnesses because we were hopeful an appeal judge and fellow citizens would one day find merit in them.

These witnesses all testified the afternoon of 15 September 2015 at the Justin Sollohub Justice Center in Anniston, Alabama. Two of the three Civil Service Board members were present. One, George Bates, was again unexplainably absent and heard none of the afternoon witnesses, although he still voted against me three days later.

All quotations are directly from the official trial transcript, which is public record.

Matthew Delozier had retired from the Anniston Police Department by the time of my trial and was working as an officer at Pell City Police Department. Incidentally, Pell City was one of the many departments at which I applied following my termination. As an entry-level applicant with eighteen years' experience, I passed their physical fitness requirements and never received a call for an interview.

Delozier was a shift sergeant and my direct subordinate when I was a shift lieutenant in 2013-14. As he was to testify, he did not necessarily enjoy working under me. But he agreed to testify for me when he saw what the city had done to me and my family. I am thankful for his truthfulness and courage.

I believe Delozier's testimony was very valuable for our defense. First, it was from someone with whom I worked extensively for several years, as a peer and as a supervisor. Secondly, we were not very close, so our relationship was strictly professional. He was not "covering" for me. His testimony also proved that my Southern nationalism views and my affiliation with the League of the South was open knowledge throughout city government, despite the feigned surprise of Brian Johnson. I was not "outed." As has been proven, I was investigated and cleared for my membership and activities by the same municipal government six years prior.

My attorney, Kenneth Shinbaum, asked Delozier, "In all the time that you have known Lieutenant Doggrell, have you ever seen or heard him carry out his duties in what you would describe as a prejudicial, divisive, or offensive manner?

"No, sir. Always professional."

"Would you describe the type of supervisor Lt. Doggrell was and how he treated his subordinates?"

.

"He was very by the book, wanted it done 100 percent from you, wanted it done right and by the book. And he was always fair with the subordinates. But if you messed up, he was very firm with you. He treated everybody fair and equal and expected the same out of everybody."

"Did he ever give you an evaluation that was less than favorable?"

"Yes, sir. The last two evaluations I got were from him and they were less than favorable, but it was, you know, it was stuff I needed to improve on and needed corrections."

"Now did you see Lieutenant Doggrell interact with members of the public?"

"Yes, sir."

"Did you ever see him mistreat any of them?"

"No, sir."

"How would he treat members of the public?"

"He treated them with respect, and he always looked at himself as a public servant, so he was out there for the people. He was always more than fair and respectful and always professional."

"Did you ever see Lt. Doggrell treat anybody different because of the color of their skin?"

"No, sir."

"Did you know that Lt. Doggrell was a member of an organization called the League of the South?"

"Yes, sir. I think most of us did. I was aware he was a member of that... I think most people at the police department knew he was a member of this group."

"And why do you say that?"

"It was just — it wasn't hid. It was pretty much — seemed to be common knowledge. It wasn't something that was spoke of all the time, but most people that knew him knew he was involved in this group."

"...Did you see any negative impact on any of the other peace officers?"

"No, sir."

"Did anyone ever complain about the fact that he was a member of the League of the South?"

"No, sir."

"Now, did you ever see Lt. Doggrell conduct bible studies?"

"Yes, sir. He had started a bible study at the police department and I was able to attend the first one and it was only about five of us there..."

"And did he invite — encourage all the employees of the police department, black or white, to attend the bible studies?"

"Yes, sir. It was an open invitation for anybody that wanted to come."

"Now, can you describe what it was like to work under Lt. Doggrell?"

"Probably a little stressful for me. He is very organized, by the book. I am kind of disorganized and just get the job done. So we didn't always see eye to eye on things because he wanted — he wanted it done right, 110 percent, and it always — maybe sometimes put a little stress on me because that wasn't always how I would do some things."

"Did Mr. Doggrell have a League of the South sticker on his car?"

"Yes, sir. I believe he has got one on this vehicle and the previous truck he drove he had one."

"Did he drive that truck to work every day?"

"Yes, sir."

"And so, it was no secret he was a member of the League of the South?"

"No, sir."

"...Did anybody [from the city] ever inform the police officers that they should not have a Confederate flag emblem on their car?"

"No, sir, not to my knowledge."

"No further questions."

The city prosecutor had no questions for Matthew Delozier.

LIEUTENANT PHILLIP SMITH

Phillip Smith was the first person to welcome me when I stepped into the Anniston Police Department on my first day of work on 17 April 2006 and the only one to wish me well on my way out on my last day.

Phillip was my sergeant and immediate supervisor when I first started as a patrolman with Anniston. After my first promotion we served as partner-sergeants on a patrol shift. More importantly, we became friends. And I do not use that word flippantly. He offered to help in the midst of this ordeal and he has actually stayed in touch since I left. Very few have done either.

The reason for the line of questioning we took with Phillip is that the city's stance was that I was unfit to be a police officer based on the howlings of the local mob (professional protesters, race hustlers/pimps, and wolves of political correctness). Phillip supervised me, answered calls from the public about me, evaluated me, etc. We thought it would be beneficial and make sense to have testimony from people who actually knew me and worked with me rather than surrender my fitness for the job to the rantings of people at press conferences that had never even spoken to me (radical notion, I know).

To the best of my recollection, Phillip was the only person who contacted me directly that was still employed as an officer at APD and expressed a *desire* to testify on my behalf at my civil service appeal trial. He was a lieutenant with a lot to lose (and nothing to gain) from the command staff for testifying on my behalf, yet...he took the stand and was sworn in the afternoon of 15 September 2015.

* * *

My attorney, Kenneth Shinbaum, began: "Now in all your time that you have known Lieutenant Doggrell, have you ever heard him carry out his duties in what you would describe as a prejudicial, divisive, or offensive manner?"

"No."

"Have you ever had an opportunity to observe...how Lieutenant Doggrell treats subordinates?"

"Yes."

"And how does he treat subordinates?

"Fair."

"Have you ever seen Lieutenant Doggrell...treat members of the public with disrespect?"

"No. He treats everybody — everybody I have seen him interact with has been in a very respectful manner."

"Have you ever — has anyone ever complained to you about anything that Mr. Doggrell may have done that was racially offensive?"

"No."

"Have you ever seen him discriminate against anybody?"

"No."

"Do you know that he — did you ever learn that he was a member of the League of the South?"

"Yes, sir."

"How did you learn that?"

"During conversation."

"Was the common knowledge around the police department that Mr. Doggrell was a member of the League of the South?"

"As far as I know it was, yes."

"Do you know if he was ever told not to be a member of the League of the South?"

"I do not."

"Has anyone ever complained to you that Josh Doggrell treated them differently because of their race?"

"No, sir."

"Has anyone ever come to you with any complaints as to Josh Doggrell ever using excessive force against anyone?"

"No, sir."

"Have you ever heard of any complaints from the public concerning Josh Doggrell?"

"None that I can remember."

"No further questions."

The city had no questions for this character witness.

MRS. DEBBIE ROOKS

After being told I was going to be on administrative leave "for at least a month" by Chief Denham on 17 June 2015, I spent the rest of that Wednesday afternoon trying to scurry about and tie up loose ends of my responsibilities. The atmosphere around the halls of the department had that surreal, dreamlike quality that tenseness often brings. Whispers turned to awkward silence when I rounded a corner.

I remember passing Lt. Clint Parris in the hall. Clint and I had known each other since before I came to the city. We hung out at Fraternal Order of Police meetings when I was still a county deputy. We both made investigator on the same day (28 March 2008) and worked cases together for years. In 2011 and 2012, I was his sergeant in investigations. In 2013 and 2014, I was his lieutenant when he was a patrol sergeant. In 2014, I picked him up at his house and took him to a men's Bible study and fellowship at my pastor's house. One week before I was fired, I shared with Clint one of the countless (probably hundreds) meal breaks we had together. I told him several times that I considered him a friend as well as a colleague. When I passed him in the hall that day, he wouldn't even look me in the eye. I have not seen or spoken to him since.

Political correctness is a disease that rots a man from the inside.

That Wednesday I walked into the Records Division I could feel the eyes peering from down-turned heads. Except for Debbie Rooks. She stood from her chair, looked at me, and said, "Are they not going to back you on this?"

"I guess we'll see," I said. I discovered the answer pretty quick.

Following my termination, I immediately began attempting to get a copy of my personnel file, something which I had obtained for subordinates before and something to which all personnel have a right. My file was a record of what kind of employee I was, so I thought that would play an important role in determining the merits of my firing (silly me — merit has no place in the ridiculous world of political correctness). My immediate supervisor, Captain Greg Feazell, managed to weasel his way into shifting the responsibility to Internal Affairs Lt. Nick Bowles.

After realizing Feazell was not going to procure the file, I text messaged Nick on 25 June 2015 asking for it. He replied, "Ok. I'm not at work today. I'll get to it when I get back and holler at you." I thanked him. Four days passed with no word. I wrote back on 29 June. He replied, "Unfortunately, I have been told not to release that to you."

"Who told you that?" I asked.

"Down the chain to me. I'm not 100% sure who made the final call."

"Interesting," I answered. I could see where this was going. The city knew how damning my file, with its record of performance evaluations, merits, commendations, and promotions would be to their case that I was, all of a sudden, unfit for the position.

The next day Bowles messaged me back that the chief had relented and I could pick up a copy at the front desk. (I assume I was no longer welcome inside the halls where I had, until the week before, worked for years.)

Alas, on 30 June, I picked up my file (which had been gutted of all commendations) from Mrs. Debbie Rooks in the Records Division. She and I had been very cordial for years. She had worked there 32 years, which means she worked with my father when he was still an officer there in the 1980s. She was always kind, sweet, and funny. It was then that she volunteered to testify for me at my appeal trial:

Attorney Kenneth Shinbaum: "Now, do you know Josh Doggrell?"

Debbie Rooks: "Yes."

"How do you know Josh Doggrell?"

"Worked with him."

"And why did you ever have to work with him?"

"Well, I didn't work directly. You know, he, with the police department, came through records."

"Now, in all the time that you have known Lt. Doggrell, have you ever seen or heard him carry out his duties in what you would describe as a prejudicial, divisive, or offensive manner?"

"No."

"Did you ever see Lt. Doggrell interact with members of the public?"

"Yes."

"Did you ever see Lt. Doggrell mistreat any of the members of the public?"

"No."

"How did he treat them?"

"Good."

"Would he treat them with respect?"

"Yes."

"Did you know that Lt. Doggrell was a member of an organization called the League of the South?"

"No."

"Now, did you ever see Lt. Doggrell ever treat anybody differently based on their race?"

"No."

"Could you describe what kind of public servant Mr. Doggrell was?"

"Nice, very respectful, very polite; never heard him raise his voice to any person that came up."

Mrs. Rooks saw me interact with several people in the lobby of the police department, where I would be taking reports, complaints, returning property, signing citations, etc.

"No further questions."

The city nor the civil service board had any questions for Mrs. Rooks and she was excused.

LIEUTENANT JUSTIN SANFORD

After nine years as a Calhoun County deputy sheriff, I accepted a position as a patrolman with the Anniston Police Department in April 2006. One of the officers on the shift I was assigned was Justin Sanford. Over the next nine years, we became friends as well as colleagues. We often visited each other's house. We went on trips together and spent a considerable amount of time together. We communicated regularly by text messaging. He knew me pretty well, which is why we called him as a character witness.

After I was fired, my relationship with Sanford ended. He called me one month later, in July. I invited him over and he said he was going to come visit me soon (not in a city vehicle, he assured me). He never did, and he has not contacted me in all the years since then. **One of the positive things about going through character assassination and public shaming is it gives great clarity about who your friends really are.**

* * *

Justin Sanford was sworn in at 4:20 pm on the afternoon of 15 September 2015 in the Justin Sollohub Justice Center in Anniston, Alabama. He began his testimony by identifying himself, his position at Anniston Police Department (lieutenant), his duration there (ten years), and how long he had known me ("approximately ten years").

Attorney Kenneth Shinbaum (**KS**): "Now, in all your times that you have known Lieutenant Doggrell, have you ever seen or heard him carry out his duties in a way that you would describe as being prejudicial, divisive, or in an offensive manner?"

Justin Sanford (**JS**): "No, sir."

This was the same question we had asked multiple witnesses, to peers, subordinates, clerks, jail officers, supervisors, etc. In other words, from people who actually knew me and worked with me over a period of years — not the professional protesters and race hustlers calling for my termination in June 2015. From these witnesses, we received a "no" answer every single time.

KS: "Has Lt. Doggrell ever supervised you during this time period with the Anniston Police Department?"

JS: "Yes, sir."

KS: "How would you describe Lt. Doggrell as a supervisor?"

JS: "He was very thorough and fair."

KS: "Did he treat everyone the same regardless of their race?"

JS: "Yes."

KS: "Did you ever see Lt. Doggrell interact with members of the public?"

JS: "I did."

KS: "Did you ever see him mistreat members of the public?"

JS: "No, I did not."

KS: "How would he treat members of the public?"

JS: "He was very courteous and very professional."

KS: "Did you know that Lt. Doggrell was a member of an organization called the League of the South?"

JS: "I did."

KS: "How did you know that?"

JS: "He told me he was a member."

KS: "How long had you known that?"

JS: "I don't recall how long."

KS: "Now, in all your time as a colleague of his on the Anniston Police Department, did you ever see his affiliation create a negative impact on how he performed his duties as a peace officer?"

JS: "I did not."

KS: "No further questions."

The city and the civil service board members (the two present — *George Bates was once again mysteriously absent for the entirety of this testimony*) said they had no questions for Sanford.

CAPTAIN GREG FEAZELL

The City of Anniston used a speech I had given two years in the past (which someone had posted to YouTube) to fire me in 2015. But the chief of police, the command staff, internal affairs, and my supervisor at the Anniston Police Department were all aware of the speech and viewed it weeks before the firing. The chief thought it did not even warrant an investigation at the time and only "suggested" to my supervisor that he might want to view the speech "in case something came up" so he "would be familiar with it." So, the speech, deemed worthy of termination by the city only *after* the Southern Poverty Law Center published a hit piece and local agitators began their game of political correctness, was, when viewed absent the hoopla, determined to be no big deal.

My direct supervisor, Captain Greg Feazell, was administered the oath and took the witness stand on the afternoon of 15 September 2015.

After being sworn in, Greg Feazell began answering questions from my attorney, Kenneth Shinbaum. He stipulated his name, his position with the Anniston Police Department at that time (captain — commander of the Administrative Division), that he knew me, and that he served as my immediate supervisor from July 2014 to the day City Manager Brian Johnson fired me via press conference on 19 June 2015.

One of our overall strategies was to put forth the record of my job performance during my years of service with Anniston, as we firmly believed *that* should be the basis of the justification of my termination, rather than the liberal views of the local professional protesters and race hustlers who disagreed with my religious and political views.

JOB PERFORMANCE: "ALWAYS PROFESSIONAL"

Shinbaum: "Now, did you ever do an annual evaluation of Mr. Doggrell?"

"I would have to see his file to see if I ever completed one..."

This is interesting. By virtue of the chain-of-command structure, I was the only police officer that was a direct subordinate of Captain Feazell. Yet, he claimed he could not even remember the only evaluation on an officer that he completed that year. So, we showed it to him. Looking at it, his memory seemed to come back to him and he said he recognized it.

"That's an evaluation I did that covered the period from 1/25/14 to 1/25/15."

"And how would you describe that evaluation?"

"He rated satisfactory in all categories."

"Were there any negatives?"

"No."

"Did you make any comments?"

"I did, but I can't read them."

Perhaps Feazell had forgotten to take his spectacles to the stand with him?

Shinbaum: "Let me go over some of them. I believe it says — it looks like 'Lieutenant Doggrell' and then [says] something 'in a very professional manner.'"

Feazell, suddenly recovering his abilities to recall *and* read now, replied, "It says 'performs his duties in a very professional manner.'"

"Now, in all your time you have known Lt. Doggrell, have you ever seen or heard him carry out his duties in what you would describe as a prejudicial, divisive, or offensive manner?"

"No."

"Now...would you describe what type of supervisor Lt. Doggrell was and how he treated his subordinates."

"He supervised the jail staff, corrections officers, as well as the inmate detail supervisors. And as I indicated on his evaluation, he always handled everything in a professional manner."

"Now, being over the jail staff, there was both African American and Caucasian employees that he supervised, is that correct?"

"Correct."

"Did he ever treat any of them differently because of their race?"

"Not that I saw."

"Did any of the people that he supervised ever complain to you about Lt. Doggrell treating them differently because of their race?"

"No."

Shinbaum asked Feazell to describe my duties regarding being jail administrator, and he detailed them, including overseeing and resolving inmate grievances about correction officers. As a result, I interacted with a large number of inmates.

"Did the inmates have any grievances against Mr. Doggrell?"

"I didn't receive any."

THE SPEECH — NO BIG DEAL?

"Now, did you know that Lt. Doggrell was a member of an organization called League of the South?"

"I didn't know until all this surfaced."

At this point, allow me to remind the reader from previous testimony, I had been a member of the League throughout my police career, had two local newspaper articles written about the fact that I was chairman of the Anniston chapter, had been investigated by the city for it and cleared of any wrongdoing, drove a pickup truck to work every day with a sticker on the back window with a Confederate flag and the words "League of the South" on it, and Feazell was a member of the APD command staff and my immediate supervisor. Yet, here he testifies that he did not know I was a member prior to the "public outcry" of June 2015.

Shinbaum: "You never heard that before?"

"I knew he was a member of a group. I didn't know the name of it, you know, or what it was about or anything like that."

This despite conversations we had about it.

"Although you knew he was a member of the group, did you ever see where his being a member of the group affected his — created a negative impact on how he performed his duties as a peace officer?"

"No."

Shinbaum then asked Feazell about the speech I gave in Wetumpka on 21 June 2013 to the national conference of the League of the South. This speech was used by the city as justification for firing me. The speech had been placed on YouTube (not by me) and the Southern Poverty Law Center (SPLC) had sent it to Chief Shane Denham in May 2015. As he testified, Denham, his captains, internal affairs, and others all viewed the speech. One day in late May or early June, I walked into Feazell's office, and he was in the process of watching it on his computer. I asked him what he thought of it. He asked me what a "scoundrel" was and laughed. (That was how I referred to the then-county sheriff in the speech). He went on to say that, although he did not agree with everything I believed, he saw nothing wrong with the speech and believed it was my right to engage in political activity of that sort.

Shinbaum: "In June of 2015, prior to Lt. Doggrell being placed on administrative leave on June 17th, did you have an occasion to view the speech in question that he gave on June 21, 2013?"

"The chief told me about it. He suggested I might want to look at it in case anything came up that I would be familiar with it. I started to watch it but I got called away for some other duties. I never did watch the entire thing."

I found something in this above testimony incredibly interesting. Note that he said the chief "suggested" he watch it "in case anything came up..." Based on Denham's and Lt. Nick Bowles's (the primary investigator in the 2015 internal investigation) testimonies, they both immediately watched the video in May when the SPLC first sent it to them. So, presumably, Denham had already watched the speech when he "suggested" that my supervisor also watch it, so he could be "familiar with it...in case anything came up..." Put this with Lt. Bowles's testimony that, in spite of watching and being aware of this speech in May 2015, he was not directed to even begin an investigation until 17 June 2015, AFTER the SPLC character-assassination hit piece was published on the SPLC website and sent out. All this evidence proves that, had it not been for the SPLC's article, I would have never even been investigated for a second time by the city, much less fired. My termination was not based on job performance, but thought crimes as defined by the leftist, Marxist group known as the Southern Poverty Law Center.

Shinbaum: "About how much of it did you watch?"

"I don't know. I watched part in just a few minutes, then I had to leave and go handle duties. I came back, it was still playing on my computer. I think I sat down maybe a couple of minutes and then I didn't watch hardly any of it all, to tell you the truth."

Let me ask the reader this: Considering that the city declared this speech a matter worthy of terminating my career, does it seem odd that the chief, the captains, the internal affairs lieutenant, and my supervisor all watched at least part, if not all, of this speech prior to the SPLC article — and apparently did not even consider it a big deal? Not one of them told me there was anything wrong with the speech and the only ones to offer any comment at all on it (Bowles and Feazell) both told me they saw nothing wrong with it regarding policy.

Shinbaum: "With respect to what you did watch, did you find anything wrong with it?"

"No; not that I saw."

"And who told you to watch the video?"

"The chief recommended I watch it. He didn't give me an order to watch it. He just said you may want to look at this if you have time."

Wow. Again — not until after the SPLC article, apparently, did this become a big deal. Then, it was an issue worth ending my career. Before, it was not even worth the chief making sure my supervisor watched it. He just "recommended" it — "He just said you may want to look at this if you have time." And, apparently, Feazell did not take the time to watch the whole thing. It does not sound too pressing, does it?

"Was that in early June?"

"That was — I don't recall the exact date. It was around the time all this surfaced and came to light."

I don't know what "surfaced and came to light," unless he was referring to the SPLC article. As was repeatedly proven throughout the trial, the city's knowledge of my political activities was widespread.

Shinbaum had no further questions. And the city had no questions. But one of the three civil service board members (only two were present for Feazell's testimony, as member George Bates missed Feazell's and most of the others and was asleep or incoherent when he was actually present) did.

Randy Third: "Do you know if anybody ever told Josh one way or the other, any of his colleagues said, Josh, this is going to come back to bite you in the rear or anything like that?"

Feazell: "I don't know."

He didn't know, meaning clearly he had never done so as my immediate supervisor, and he knew of no one who did. Because there were none. As a matter of fact, I was investigated in 2009, cleared of any wrongdoing, and told I was within my constitutional rights.

Based on this question, Shinbaum redirected:

"Did you ever mention to him that it would be best if he didn't belong to the League of the South?"

"No."

"How long has Chief Denham been over you?"

"I was promoted to captain in June of 2014."

"And Chief Denham was over you in June of 2014?"

"Yes."

"From June of 2014 through May of 2015, did Chief Denham ever discuss with you saying, listen, it would be better if Josh Doggrell was not a member of the League of the South?"

"No."

"No further questions."

* * *

Leaders are supposed to be advocates and defenders of their people when under unwarranted attack. The chief of police, his captains, and internal affairs did not see anything about the speech or my religious and political activities that even deserved an investigation in the spring of 2015. But, the SPLC went after me, City Manager Brian Johnson was intimidated and cowed to them and the local mob, and so, suddenly, what was no big deal was transformed into an offense worthy of immediate termination.

Greg Feazell was among the command staff that told me, verbally and in writing, what a fine job I was doing for years. They wrote me commendations and promoted me twice. They investigated me for my religious and political activity in 2009 and told me I was good to go. Then the mob descended. And they threw me to the wolves.

11.

THE TESTIMONY OF DR. MICHAEL HILL

"I would feel a responsibility to help him even if he disowned me as a friend and a compatriot."

DR. J. MICHAEL HILL can, I believe, be described as a "lightning-rod" figure in contemporary America. He possesses the ability to attract both vehement criticism and fierce loyalty — at times from the same source.

In the late morning of 15 September 2015, he was called to the stand in the municipal courtroom of the Justin Sollohub Justice Center in Anniston, Alabama, to testify in the civil service appeal trial of my termination from the City of Anniston. All quoted remarks are taken directly from the official transcript of the trial, which is public record.

I first met Dr. Hill in the fall semester of my freshman year (1995) at the University of Alabama. The occasion was a meeting of the campus chapter of The Southern League (a name changed circa 2000 to The League of the South). Prior to moving to Tuscaloosa, I had never heard of the League. It had only been founded the previous year by Hill and other intellectual Southern partisans.

Dr. Hill was an impressive figure to me. He was tall and stout, with piercing eyes and a gentlemanly demeanor and a professorial voice. He seemed a natural leader and firmly devoted to the South. For many years, I looked up to him.

I had expressed my reservations and disagreements to **Dr.** Hill and other members about what I perceived as a new direction within the League that began occurring around the spring and summer of 2013. **Dr.** Hill and I had much written correspondence about this, and in late December of 2014, I requested and arranged a meeting with him that included a younger friend of mine, Marshall Rawson, a League member from Georgia who shared my concerns. We met in Cullman, AL, and had a conversation that lasted several hours in which he listened to our concerns. This would be testified about by **Dr.** Hill at the trial.

In the preparatory meetings I had with my counsel, Kenneth Shinbaum, and his staff at his office in Montgomery during the summer of 2015, we discussed subpoenaing **Dr.** Hill. I elected not to, because I did not feel this was really about *him* — it was about *me*, my affiliation with the League, and whether or not that affiliation had affected my job performance. It was during the first day of trial in August we would learn that the city chose to pursue a different course. **During the first day, it was clear that the city intended to put Dr. Michael Hill on trial and convict me for his alleged "crimes."** I will give the city credit — they did an excellent job of making a case that **Dr.** Michael Hill would be ill-suited to be a peace officer in the City of Anniston (I think even he would agree with that). The only problem was...Josh Doggrell was the one who was *supposed* to be on trial.

In light of this, Shinbaum and I made the decision to subpoena Hill for the next day of testimony in September. If the city was going to put him on trial and make me pay for it, we could use him in our defense.

Shortly after this decision, I had a phone conversation with **Dr.** Hill about the expectation of receiving a subpoena. He expressed willingness and a desire to help. I explained to him how the city's "evidence" thus far had largely been his writings and quotes. "Maybe," he said, "it will do you good if they see me walk in without horns and a tail."

ORGANIZATIONAL POLICY VERSUS INDIVIDUAL OPINIONS

"Do you know Lieutenant Josh Doggrell?" my attorney, Kenneth Shinbaum, asked **Dr.** Hill.

"Yes, I do... [we first met] roughly twenty years ago when he was a student of mine at the University of Alabama."

Dr. Hill went on to certify that he was the national president of the League of the South.

Shinbaum addressed the League's "Core Beliefs Statement," which we had entered as Exhibit E-3. **Our intent was to present how one could be a member of an organization and adhere to its policies or platform without being assumed to be responsible for contrary beliefs of individual members within that organization.**

Dr. Hill said, "This is our Core Beliefs Statement... I actually helped write those and our Board of Directors passed them... it basically is there to give our members and prospective members some kind of general idea about what it is that we believe as an organization and on what principles we operate."

Shinbaum asked, "...is the League of the South...an organization [where] just one person decides all the rules, or how is the Core Beliefs Statement determined?"

"Well, the Core Beliefs Statement was written by a committee, and it was then submitted to the Board of Directors, who looked it over and made suggestions, returned to committee, the committee redid it. And when it was in final form, the Board of Directors approved it as an official document and position of the League of the South."

Dr. Hill then explained that no one, *including himself*, could unilaterally change the Core Beliefs. To be amended, they would have to go back through the committee process.

Shinbaum showed Hill Exhibit E-4, the League's published "Frequently Asked Questions (FAQ)" form. Hill described that that process also went through the Board of Directors before being formally approved and adopted for usage. As with the Core Beliefs, any changes would have to be approved by the Board.

Several questions came from the Core Beliefs. "Would you say the League of the South reveres the tenets of the historic Christian faith and acknowledges supremacy over man-made laws and opinions — is that correct?"

"Yes. We stand by all of these."

Shinbaum directed Hill's attention to the portion in the FAQ "regarding blacks in the South... What is the answer?"

Dr. Hill read from the document:

> "**The League of the South disavows a spirit of malice and extends an offer of goodwill and cooperation to Southern blacks in areas where we can work together as Christians to make life better for all people in the South. We affirm that, while historically the interests of Southern blacks and whites have been, in part, antagonistic, true constitutional government would provide protection to all law-abiding citizens, not just to government-sponsored victim groups.**"

Shinbaum asked Dr. Hill about my lack of activity in recent times with the League. Hill said he had not seen me at any League functions that year (2015). He agreed that for at least the past one or two years I would accurately be described as a "mere member."

"Josh Was Right About That."

There was an exchange about the large Christian influence in the League. Shinbaum asked, "Has Josh Doggrell ever expressed anything to you that he may have had some problems with certain people [who] may have been starting to speak up — that he felt they weren't exhibiting true Christian values?"

"Yes. Last year he came to me [this would have been the aforementioned meeting in Cullman in December 2014] and expressed some concern about some people in the League that I had placed in positions of some authority, about the fact that they were not behaving like Christians and that some of the rhetoric that was on our Facebook page in particular was not something that we could point to Christian aspects of the League and say we are following you here. And Josh was right about that. He met with me and another fellow...and I went and made corrections... and tried to put a stop to it. So, yes, he was concerned about that."

"Now, has Josh ever mentioned to you that he...may have been considering dropping out of the League of the South?"

"Well, he did talk to me about this possibility if this trend continued because Josh is a good, Christian young man. He had certainly legitimate concerns, I think, looking back on it. So, yes, he had mentioned that to me and I took it seriously because I have known Josh for twenty years and known him to be a good, Christian young man. I knew if he had concerns about it, they were worth listening to."

Gun Rights

"Do you know if Josh is a supporter of gun rights?" asked Shinbaum.

"From all I know, he is a supporter of gun rights."

"Were you present when he gave a speech in June of 2013, I believe, in Wetumpka?"

"Yes, I was there. That was the 2013 League of the South national conference... I asked Josh to speak."

"During that speech did he speak for gun rights?"

"Well, I would have to do this only from memory. I have heard lots of speeches. And I think... I do recall that he did mention gun rights in the speech... I know that he and I both are supporters of gun rights."

"...And are there members of the League of the South that may be weary of police officers?"

"Yes, there are quite a few. I think the proliferation of videos on the internet, Facebook, and other social media of police misbehavior which, of course, are the ones that get put online, have caused some members of our group to be what I would consider to be a little hypercritical of police officers in general. I have tried to tell our members that that's not worthy of making a condemnatory decision about all police officers on. I come from a family that has law enforcement... And even though I'm not one myself, I do have sympathy for them..."

The point here was that the primary subject of my speech of June 2013 was gun rights and the role of peace officers and citizens regarding those rights. This speech was used by the city as justification for firing me. The city was painting me as a "racist," even though the subject of race was never even discussed in the entirety of the one-hour-plus speech.

"THOSE ARE MY PERSONAL VIEWS"

Shinbaum ventured into the recent posts and Twitter "tweets" published by **Dr.** Hill and entered by the city as "evidence" and how they related to the League as a whole.

"...with respect to posts, are all the posts that you ever do to the website or to the Facebook — are they the views of the League of the South?"

"Well, not on my personal Twitter or Facebook pages. The only thing that might be construed to be that is if I make a link to something that is on the League website on my personal Twitter account, but it will merely be a link that somebody can click on. If I make actual commentary on Twitter, it's my personal commentary."

"And is your personal commentary also the views of the League of the South?"

"No, not necessarily... my opinions that I write on both of these social media are oftentimes merely my own personal opinions that have not been vetted by the League board of the League staff or any other official body of the organization."

Shinbaum presented the city's Exhibits 5, 6, 7, 8, and 9 — all "tweets" from **Dr.** Hill's personal account. "And are these all Twitters of yours?"

"They are."

"And are those the views of the League of the South?"

"Those are my personal views."

Shinbaum then presented the city's Exhibits 1, 2, and 3 — all internet posts from **Dr.** Hill. Hill confirmed that he published or posted all three. Shinbaum asked, "Does that necessarily mean that it's the view of the League of the South?" **Dr.** Hill explained that, no, none of those publishings had been approved by the Board, all three were merely articles or comments he posted as his personal opinions, and they were not necessarily the views of the League.

Hill went further. "I would venture to say that there would be some members even of the Board and of my staff who may take issue with some issues brought up in these and [there] certainly would be rank and file members and State officers who might as well..."

Shinbaum then presented the city's Exhibit 4 — what I refer to as the "mystery exhibit" due to *no one* being able to ascertain from where it came. **Dr.** Hill said he was unfamiliar with it and it had never been approved to be on the League's internet sites. **The fact that the city entered this mysterious, inflammatory picture without an established source as "evidence" against me is something I considered revelatory regarding their desperation to justify, after the fact, Brian Johnson's decision to fire me.**

CROSS EXAMINATION

Throughout his cross-examination, city attorney Bruce Downey attempted to get **Dr.** Hill to say that his personal views could be considered League policy (although there existed clear and written League policy). Hill refused to concede to this.

Downey asked Hill whether "a person who is devoutly committed to your beliefs can be entrusted with the awesome power which is that of a law enforcement officer?" Hill responded that he believed that were "public and private domains men are able to exist in at the same time" and he used as an example his eighteen years as a professor at Stillman College (a primarily black college in Tuscaloosa), five of which he was also president of the League.

Downey presented Hill with many writings Hill had made on social media. He presented material that even Downey admitted was only "a couple of months old," even though it had been three months since I had been fired. Shinbaum objected, but by this point it was clear that if Shinbaum objected, board attorney Trudie Phillips would overrule him; if Downey objected, Phillips would sustain him.

Downey asked Hill about the misgivings I had taken to **Dr.** Hill about League matters, but Downey pointed out that I had not registered misgivings about the writings from 2015. On redirect, Shinbaum brought up the fact that the last time Hill had spoken to me was 2014, and asked Hill why he thought I had not asked him about the 2015 writings. "Because they had not been written yet."

Yes, just like I could not have had an opinion on anything at the time of my firing which was done or printed after it, and just like I could not have had an opinion on things of which I had not seen or was not aware of, I could not express misgivings to Dr. Hill about things which were going to occur in the future. The fact is I was fired for something, and the city went out looking for what that "something" was after they fired me. That, my friends, displays a mockery of "justice" that occurred in Anniston, Alabama.

Downey made an issue that the League had undertaken a fundraising effort to assist me in paying my exorbitant legal fees. He asked if Hill knew if I was still a member (I was not). I believe Downey was trying to create the impression that, since **Dr.** Hill was spearheading an effort to raise money for me, we must be pretty tight and, therefore, agree with each other on most issues.

On redirect, Shinbaum asked, "Even if Josh Doggrell is not still a dues-paying member, would you still feel a responsibility to defend [him]?"

I feel Hill's reply to this is worth quoting in its entirety:

"Yes, sir. Josh Doggrell could stand up and say that he disagreed with me on everything that I said and that he was never going to speak to me again and I would still help him because of his dedication, of his friendship with me from the time that he was a student and I was his professor, and also for the fact that he agreed to speak at something that we put on and that's what got him in trouble. I would feel a responsibility to help him even if he disowned me as a friend and a compatriot."

Shinbaum then asked, "Do you know if Josh Doggrell has ever treated anybody differently because of their race?"

"No. From what I understand, he has an exemplary record and that's why I brought up earlier that a man has a public sphere and a private sphere, and an honorable man can get along well in both."

Shinbaum asked if the League advocated following the laws (Hill said they did) and whether or not the League had ever condoned or been involved in any illegal activity (it had not). Downey did not challenge this, and **Dr.** Hill was excused from the stand.

The testimony of Michael Hill consumed 75 pages of transcript and lasted for over two hours. He was on the stand longer than anyone except me.

CONCLUSION

I do not regret the twenty years in which I was a member of the League of the South. The Core Beliefs that were still League policy at the time of my termination are beliefs which I still hold and defend today. I do regret the direction the League has taken recently. I know a lot of former members who feel the same way.

What I regret most is the cowardice of the city leaders of Anniston. Brian Johnson fired me without even speaking to me because of the political heat he faced over two days from people who are professional protesters and race pimps. Police Chief Shane Denham took the easy way out and stood behind Johnson, going against what he told me he would do when first contacted by the SPLC in May 2015, because it was convenient. Merit, and right versus wrong had nothing to do with the decision. Political correctness had everything to do with it. Thus, I was fired for something I had been cleared of by the same entity six years before.

12.

THE TESTIMONY OF LT. NICK BOWLES

"There was nothing on the video...unless I missed something... I didn't see anything in there inflammatory..."

15 September 2015

WHEN THE CITY OF ANNISTON began their second internal affairs investigation of me on 17 June 2015, Lt. Nick Bowles was assigned lead investigator by Chief Denham. Bowles interviewed me the morning of 19 June (see Chapter Five). That afternoon was when Denham appeared with city councilmen and the city manager to announce my termination.

At the time, the chief and command staff of the Anniston Police Department were well aware of my Christian faith, my belief in Southern nationalism, my pride in my Southern ancestry, and my longtime affiliation with the League of the South. They had already investigated me for that affiliation in 2009, when I had been cleared of any wrongdoing and told I was within my constitutional rights.

The Southern Poverty Law Center (SPLC), a crooked, neo-Marxist organization that continues to come under intense scrutiny for their activities and methods, began calling Chief Denham about me on 28 May 2015. He spoke to me that day. They sent him a video of a speech I gave on 21 June 2013 in Wetumpka, AL. Denham and Bowles both watched the video and Bowles reported to me their conclusion that there were no policy violations, and I was within my rights. As Bowles testified, and is recounted below, **twenty days then passed with nothing else done. An investigation was not even opened.**

Then, on 17 June 2015, the SPLC published a hit piece on their website and sent it to *The Anniston Star*, our hometown newspaper. *Only then* did Denham direct Bowles to open another investigation, with a wimpy city manager breathing down his neck and the local mob of race hustlers and professional protesters beginning to call and make demands. Immediately, I was placed on administrative leave. A few hours later, there was a shooting at a black church in Charleston, South Carolina, that received extensive press attention and as has become custom, all things Confederate were subjected to scapegoat scrutiny. That was Wednesday evening. I spent a total of one full calendar day on administrative leave. On Friday afternoon, Denham appeared at a televised press conference with city councilmen and the city manager to announce my firing. With the accompanying stigma and character assassination in which I was smeared, it effectively ended my nineteen-year career.

City Suppresses 2009 Investigation

After being sworn in the afternoon of 15 September 2015, at the Justin Sollohub Justice Center and having his name and credentials stipulated, Nick Bowles verified that he was the Anniston Police Department lieutenant who was assigned to Training and Inspections, which encompassed the Internal Affairs Unit. Thus, he was at the head of the second internal affairs investigation of me that commenced on 17 June 2015, and resulted in my termination 48 hours later.

Under questioning from my attorney, Kenneth Shinbaum, Bowles testified that he knew me as a police officer and, prior to that, as a "casual acquaintance" through the Fraternal Order of Police. He said we had worked in the Investigations Division together. He said he knew that I was a member of the League of the South as early as 2008, which was true. Bowles was very upfront about being an atheist. He and I had multiple discussions about religion, politics, and culture. We discussed my plans to begin a local League chapter in Anniston in 2008. He was supportive, inquisitive, curious, and attended the inaugural meeting in March 2009.

Kenneth Shinbaum (**KS**): "Did you ever see him do anything that would make you feel that he treats people of different races differently?"

Nick Bowles (**NB**): "Not that I saw."

Bowles was asked about the 2009 internal investigation that the city conducted on me, in which I was cleared of any wrongdoing and told I was within my constitutional rights to engage in such religious and political activity. This investigative file was suppressed by the city for the 2015 appeal trial, and as soon as Shinbaum began asking about it, City Attorney Bruce Downey objected, and the civil service board attorney, Trudie Phillips, sustained.

KS: "As a result of that 2009 investigation, was any action taken against Mr. Doggrell?"

NB: "Not that I'm aware."

Shinbaum asked if any recommendations were made to me at the conclusion of that investigation. Downey again objected. This caused a heated exchange between the attorneys, as Shinbaum was trying to get it on the record that I had already been cleared by the city for something that they were now using to fire me.

KS: "I'm looking for the results of the investigation. That's very important in this case."

Downey: "We will stipulate and it's well established that no disciplinary action was taken subsequent to the 2009 investigation."

KS: "Will you stipulate that after the 2009 investigation that there was no action taken against Josh Doggrell and no further recommendation made to him to leave the League of the South?"

Downey: "That's beyond what's undisputed."

KS: "Well, if there was a recommendation made for him to leave the League of the South, *we need to know it now!*"

Downey: "I'm not a witness, Mr. Shinbaum."

KS: "Well, I am trying to ask the witness here if recommendation —"

Downey: "I am asserting for the record the privilege that he not be compelled to testify to any contents of an internal investigation file."

KS: "We need to know the results and what the recommendations — whether or not Josh Doggrell was ever informed or asked to leave the League of the South."

Phillips: "I will sustain the objection as to recommendation."

THE SPEECH AND THE TIMELINE

A large part of the allegations the city leveled against me in an attempt to justify their firing was a speech I had made on 21 June 2013 in Wetumpka, Alabama, at the national conference of the League of the South. Someone uploaded the video to YouTube. In May of 2015 the Southern Poverty Law Center sent a link to that speech, their own leftist commentary, and a short inflammatory video they had created to Chief Denham. He viewed the speech, as did Bowles...

NB: "I viewed that video on May 28th [2015]."

KS: "...What was the reason you viewed it on May 28th?"

NB: "Chief Denham came in my office and told me that he had gotten an email from someone — I'm sorry. A phone call from someone with the SPLC and that Josh had made this speech in 2013. He forwarded me the emails and with a link to the speech and I watched it from there."

KS: "...Now, did you subsequently report to Chief Denham after viewing it?"

NB: "We talked about it, yes, sir...same day. I watched the entire video."

A credit to Bowles: Unlike past witnesses Shane Denham, Leyton McGrady, Brian Johnson, Greg Feazell, and others, he actually watched the *entire* video.

That same day, 28 May 2015, I learned that the SPLC was attempting to smear me and the department when Chief Denham came to my office, closed the door, and told me they had called him. He said they asked if he knew I was a League member and he said he told them he did. He said the female on the phone was very belligerent, demanding to know "what I was going to do about it." Then he asked me about the speech and if there was anything he needed to "worry about." I told him there was nothing, that the speech was mainly about gun rights and the police-citizen relationship. I said he could watch the video and ask me about anything on it. He did watch the video, and *he never asked me anything. In fact, we did not discuss it again until twenty days later, when the SPLC published their attack piece against me online.*

After that workday of 28 May, I was running on the treadmill in the department workout room when Bowles came in and asked to talk to me in the hall. I followed him there. He said he had just begun watching the video of the speech. He asked me if he was going to see anything controversial. "What do you mean, Nick? What is it you're afraid to find?" He specifically asked me if I had said "the word 'nigger' or anything like that?"

"Hell, no," I answered. "There is nothing like that out there." I told him no one could supply anything like that because it didn't exist. I told him that in that particular speech, the subject of race was not even addressed. I then asked him if he would watch the video and call me with his impressions afterward. He agreed. The entirety of the speech and the question-and-answer session that followed (in which the issue of race never even surfaced) was about seventy minutes. A couple of hours later, Bowles called me. By this time, I was home. I remember taking the call in the bathroom. How I wish I would have recorded it. Nick told me he and the chief had watched the speech, discussed it, concluded that no policies had been violated, and that he, Nick, had contacted the SPLC representative and told her that and that I was within my rights.

Here is how Bowles responded during the trial...

KS: "So, now, did you ever discuss your viewing of that tape with Josh Doggrell?"

NB: "I did."

KS: "Did you ever tell Josh Doggrell that you did not find any policy violations after viewing it?"

NB: "I don't believe I said those exact words, no, sir."

KS: "What words did you say?"

NB: "The way it was put to me — the way we were being led to believe [by the SPLC] was that there was something over the top in the video. So chief wanted me to watch it for any, lack of a better word, smoking gun. So that's what I watched it for, and I didn't see anything over the top, egregious, as far as race or anything like that in the speech itself."

KS: "Now, did Josh Doggrell in that speech talk about gun rights?"

NB: "He did."

KS: "Did he talk about how police officers were individuals that are out there to help people?"

NB: "He did."

KS: "Did you see a part in there where Josh Doggrell stated that he was not speaking on behalf of the Anniston Police Department?"

NB: "After he had identified himself as an Anniston police officer, he did say that."

Denham, Johnson, and Bowles tried to make a point that, by identifying myself as an Anniston police officer, that somehow contributed to invalidating the disclaimer that I was not speaking on behalf of the city. Question: Why would I need to declare such a disclaimer if it was not known that I was an employee of the city? If I had not been a city employee, why on earth would I have felt the need to tell people that I did not speak on its behalf?

KS: "Now, do you recall telling — calling Josh Doggrell on the phone the evening of viewing the speech and telling him that you had spoken to Chief Denham and the chief concluded he had violated no policies?"

NB: "No. I don't remember those specific words. I did call him, though."

KS: "Did the chief ever tell you that after he viewed it what he thought about it?"

NB: "I don't specifically remember the conversation...We were looking for something major and egregious in the video and we did not see that."

Note that Bowles testified that he and the chief found nothing "major and egregious in the video" but that speech was still used to terminate my career.

What followed was very important. It proved the city did absolutely nothing about the SPLC allegations from the time the APD command staff viewed the video until twenty days later when the SPLC published their hit piece. **If I had said or done anything in that speech that would warrant disciplinary action, especially being fired, would I not have been further questioned about it and an investigation launched? Can anyone imagine the merit of an employee doing something that would warrant being fired, but the bosses waiting around to see if it made the news before taking any action?** Testimony such as the following shows that, had it not been for the SPLC's actions, I would never have been fired.

KS: "So, now that's May 28th; is that correct?"

NB: "To the best of my recollection, yes, sir."

KS: "Now, between May 31 and June 5th, did you do anything concerning investigating Josh Doggrell's involvement with the League of the South?"

NB: "I did not."

KS: "Between June 5 and June 9th, did you do anything to investigate Josh Doggrell's involvement with the League of the South?"

NB: "I did not."

KS: "So from May 31 through June 9th, you did not do anything to investigate Josh Doggrell's involvement with the League of the South, is that correct?"

NB: "That's correct."

KS: "Did you do anything to look further about his involvement given that speech?"

NB: "No."

KS: "Why not?"

NB: "I wasn't directed to."

KS: "When were you first directed to do any type of investigation?"

NB: "On the late afternoon of June 17th."

This should not be overlooked! Chief Denham and Lt. Bowles watched the video on 28 May. The same evening, Bowles called me and told me they found nothing to worry about. My captain, Greg Feazell, watched it and said he found nothing to worry about. Twenty days went by without another word being spoken to me about it. Bowles — the head of internal affairs — was not directed to do another thing about it. No investigation was even opened! We were back to business as usual...

Then, on 17 June, the SPLC published a yellow-journalism, character-assassination article about me and the speech. They created a video showing me speaking while images of a completely unrelated 1961 bus burning were inserted. The local news got a hold of it, the race baiters and professional protesters started their usual howling, and *ONLY THEN*, "on the late afternoon of June 17th," I was placed on administrative leave and fired 48 hours later.

THE SPLC, YELLOW JOURNALISM, FERGUSON

Shinbaum asked Bowles about that video clip the SPLC created and linked to their article.

KS: "Now, on June 17th, 2015, do you know if the Southern Poverty Law Center posted an article concerning Mr. Doggrell's involvement with the League of the South?"

NB: "Yes."

KS: "And did they also post a video?"

NB: "An edited video, yes."

KS: "An edited video. And what do you mean by an edited video?"

NB: "I believe it was three minutes of just excerpts from his hour-plus-long speech from the June 2013 speech."

KS: "... [Was there] editing of other videos that were taken at a completely different time?"

NB: "Correct."

KS: "Were some of those videos of police in Anniston beating people at the bus station back in the early 1960s?"

NB: "There was some older pictures that they [SPLC] were asserting police brutality, yes, sir."

KS: "And the City of Anniston Police Department is not saying that Josh Doggrell had anything to do with that?"

NB: "No, sir."

KS: "Was he even born then?"

NB: "I do not believe so."

KS: "Now, and in your opinion, was that editing done to inflame the public?"

NB: "Yes. I would say so."

Shinbaum asked Bowles about the SPLC as an organization.

KS: "Do you consider the Southern Poverty Law Center to be a reputable tool [in an investigation]?

NB: "I used to."

Shinbaum produced and directed Bowles to a transcript of his interview with me conducted on the morning of 19 June 2015.

KS: "[Bowles states] 'And I'm going to shoot you straight, man, you have been doing this job longer than me, and you were an investigator for about as long as I was.' And Josh answers 'uh-huh.' And then your next thing is you say, **'The city is reacting to the public reaction, that's why this is happening.'** Did you say that?"

NB: [Long pause] "Apparently so."

This was significant because the "public reaction" should have had no bearing on this issue. "Public reaction" does not determine whether an employee breaks policy. As I told the city multiple times, either I had violated policy, or I had not. The "public reaction," the outcry of the mob, the professional protesters, the race pimps — that should not have determined the issue. If that was what determined such issues, Officer Darren Wilson would have been indicted for killing Michael Brown in Ferguson, Missouri, less than a year earlier, where the "public reaction" resulted in thugs terrorizing the streets and burning the city down. But the grand jury no-billed Wilson because *he had done nothing wrong.* Here was Bowles admitting that the entire motivation for the city coming after me was due, not to my actions, but the "public reaction."

KS: "Go to page 52, all the way down to the bottom of the last question starting on line 22. And the question is, 'Well, like I said, I stopped reading (inaudible) — I get them and throw them in the garbage when they come in.'"

NB: "That's true."

KS: "What were you referring to?"

NB: "The intelligence reports."

KS: "From?"

NB: "SPLC."

KS: "Southern Poverty Law Center?"

NB: "Yes, sir."

KS: "Why would you throw them in the trash?"

NB: "Because it's right next to my mailbox. When I flip through it, if it doesn't have anything that interests me or that is for this surrounding area, it goes right in the garbage."

KS: "And I think Josh Doggrell says, 'good place for them.' **And then you say, 'Because I saw — it was just — it was the same ol', same ol', everything, and just the scare tactics, that's all that I personally saw it as.' Did you say that?**"

NB: "[Low] I did."

KS: "Huh?"

NB: "I did."

KS: "...Now, let's turn to page 102, start at line 6. And that's you speaking, is that correct?"

NB: "Apparently, yes."

KS: "Could you read line 6 through 16?"

NB: "[this is Bowles quoting Bowles] 'And there was nothing on the video that I saw, unless I missed something, and I didn't see anything in there inflammatory...'"

Bowles went on to testify that, although his investigation did not begin until "the late afternoon" of 17 June, right after the SPLC's article was published, it did not end until "the third week of July." That's right. I was fired on the second full day of the investigation... yet the investigation was not concluded until almost a month later. Bowles was shown at this trial and, later, at federal depositions in October 2016, the large amount of "exhibits" (that I had nothing to do with) the city produced on the first day of trial in August 2015 and the fact that these "exhibits" were not brought up in his interview with me on 19 June 2015. They were not brought up because the city had not even discovered them at that time. Yet, I was fired on that day. The timeline shows evidence that the city reached a quick conclusion to fire me to satisfy the hounds of political correctness, and then spent a month (and more, as further testimony would show) to desperately try to come up for reasons to justify it.

The city attorney, Bruce Downey, had only one question for Bowles, and that was if he knew if he was the only person investigating me for the city. He said he did not know. I imagine Downey was trying to say that someone else from the city may have seen these controversial "exhibits" prior to my firing. But, Bowles testified that he was referring to a questionnaire from Downey while interviewing me. And he stepped out of the room for a few minutes during the interview and came back with further questions. At that time, I asked him if Downey wanted him to ask me those, and he admitted that Downey was, in fact, watching the interview on video. (I've been around enough to know how this goes). If the city had any documents they thought were controversial at the time, Bowles would have presented them and asked me about them.

Regardless, I consider the "exhibits" to show what a desperate case the city had that the mountain of "exhibits" they presented against me were things which I had no part in producing, and most of which I had never before seen.

The testimony of Nick Bowles was more evidence that justice was not served in this situation, and that my career and my reputation were sacrificed on the altar of political correctness, more accurately known as Cultural Marxism.

13.

THE TESTIMONY OF
COUNCILMAN DAVID REDDICK

"It was like another Ferguson in Anniston."

WHEN THE SOUTHERN POVERTY LAW CENTER published a hit piece against me on their website on 17 June 2015, the Anniston city manager and city council began falling all over themselves trying to appease the professional protesters and race hustlers that began barking at their doors. Press conferences were held, Facebook posts were made, "tweets" were sent out... I doubt these numbskulls were aware of it, but besides being opportunists and/or cowards, *they were breaking Alabama State law and their own city policy concerning council members interfering with the administration of the city.*

What follows is a criminal complaint I sent to the Alabama Attorney General's Special Prosecutions Division in the fall of 2015. About a week after sending it, I received a letter from that office notifying me they were looking into the matter. When I called to follow-up about a month later, no one I spoke with claimed to have any idea what I was talking about. It appears my complaint had vanished. I was promised a call from a supervisor, which I never received.

* * *

Criminal Complaint

Date: 20 October 2015

To: Alabama Office of Attorney General (Special Prosecutions Division)

From: Josh Doggrell

Anniston, Alabama

Offense: COUNCIL NOT TO INTERFERE IN APPOINTMENTS OR REMOVALS —

Alabama statute 45-8A-23.059

Neither the council nor any of its members shall direct or request the appointment of any person to, or his or her removal from, office by the city manager or by any of his or her subordinates, or in any manner take part in the appointment or removal of officers and employees in the administrative service of the city. Except for the purpose of inquiry, the council and its members shall deal with the administrative service solely through the city manager and neither the council nor any member thereof shall give orders to any subordinates of the city manager, either publicly or privately. Any councilman violating the provisions of this section, or voting for a resolution or ordinance in violation of this section, shall be guilty of a misdemeanor and upon conviction thereof shall cease to be a councilman.

Dates of Occurrence: 17-25 June 2015

Offenders: Anniston Mayor Vaughn Stewart

Anniston Vice-Mayor Seyram Selase

Anniston Councilman David Reddick

Anniston Councilman Jay Jenkins

To whom it concerns,

I wish to file a criminal complaint against the above four public officials of the City of Anniston. I realize that, under normal circumstances, I would file an initial criminal complaint with a local police agency with jurisdiction (Calhoun County). However, these circumstances are not normal and I respectfully request an investigation and prosecution by the Alabama Attorney General's Office concerning this matter. Among other reasons, there is already a pending criminal case before the Calhoun County District Court involving the arrest of Councilman David Reddick on the charge of Harassment against an Anniston citizen. The usual prosecuting agency in that case would be the Calhoun County District Attorney's Office. However, that agency has recused itself, citing a conflict of interest due to its partnership with the City of Anniston in local crime fighting projects, and has deferred prosecution to your office.

Prior to 18 September 2015, I was employed as a police lieutenant with the City of Anniston Police Department (APD). I had been a member of the organization The League of the South for twenty years, which included the nine-plus I had served with APD. My membership and affiliation with this organization was common knowledge within the city government, as evidenced by, among other things, an internal investigation conducted by the city in the spring of 2009 and local media coverage of me beginning a local chapter that resulted in that investigation. The result of that investigation was that I was cleared of any wrongdoing— I had violated no laws, no policies, was within my civil and constitutional rights, and my affiliation had not negatively affected my job performance. This matter was also addressed at public hearings of the Anniston City Council since that time. At no time was I ever disciplined as a result of my League affiliation, nor was I ever asked to end my membership with the League. I had been told by the immediate past police chief in 2012 that my League affiliation would not be addressed again because doing so would open the city to the possibility of liability.

On 17 June 2015, the Southern Poverty Law Center (SPLC) published a "hit piece" against me on their "Hatewatch" blog on their website. The article was posted shortly before noon on that day. Roughly three hours later, I was notified by Chief Shane Denham that I was being placed on administrative leave pending a city investigation of the "allegations" made by the SPLC. Approximately 48 hours later, on the afternoon of 19 June 2015, my termination was announced at a press conference at Anniston City Hall. Present at the table with City Manager Brian Johnson were the four offenders in this complaint. All four spoke. The mayor was seated at the head of the table. The only council member not present was Millie Harris.

In the approximate 48 hours between me being placed on administrative leave and being fired at the press conference, it is my contention that the four offenders listed in this complaint violated Alabama statute 45-8A-23.059, the State law prohibiting the city council from interfering in the removal of an officer in the administrative service of the city.

One of the traditional justifications for the council-manager form of government for municipalities (the form Anniston chose to adopt) is that it reduces the political influence on personnel matters. The city manager is an appointed position, free from the need to be constantly campaigning for re-election. This allows the council the freedom to pursue their legislative duties and be the politicians that they are. More importantly, it protects the city employees from councilmen playing politics using the employees' livelihoods. That protection was not carried out in my situation.

Under the current city manager, the city has instituted a "City of Anniston Policies and Procedures Manual" that has been issued to every city employee. A section entitled "Relations With Members of the Council" is found beginning on the bottom portion of page 17. Detailed in that section is the fact that city policy regarding interactions between employees and members of the council is governed by the Civil Service Act, which is codified in Alabama law in Title 45-8A-22/23. Page 18 lays out the "Legalities and Consequences" of violating the law pertaining to the relationship between the council and employees. The manual states that the city's policy shall be to "adhere strictly to the provisions of the law..." It further states that **"[b]y design, it seems, the rules of interactions between the staff and Council pose more restrictions on the behavior of Councilmen than on employees."** The manual even quotes Alabama law 45-8A-23.059 in its entirety. It reads, in part...

"Neither the council nor any of its members shall direct or request the appointment of any person to, *or his or her removal from, office* by the city manager or by any of his or her subordinates, *or in any manner take part in the appointment or removal of officers and employees in the administrative service of the city...* any councilman violating the provisions of this section, or voting for a resolution or ordinance in violation

of this section, shall be guilty of a misdemeanor and upon conviction thereof shall cease to be a councilman [emphasis added]."

Now, the city council had enormous involvement in my removal. In the 48-hour "investigation" supposedly conducted, it seemed like three of the council members (Stewart, Selase, and Reddick) were almost knocking each other down to see how many news cameras and microphones each one could find. The following are just a few examples: On 17 June, Stewart used his Twitter account to write, "Like many of you, I was shocked yesterday by the allegations brought against two Anniston police officers. Rest assured, I am working hard to get to the bottom of it. Anniston has no tolerance for racism and hatred. Anniston has come a long way since bigots attacked a bus of Freedom Riders in 1961. We will continue to move forward, not backward." This quote was reported by multiple news sources. It is interesting to note that Stewart used the personal pronoun "I" to show how hard *he* was working "to get to the bottom of it." The problem is, this was not a matter for a council member. The State law prohibits him from participating "in any manner" in the removal of an officer. I also find it shameful that Stewart would use an episode of history from sixteen years before I was even born, and which was irrelevant to the issue at hand, to paint me in such a disgraceful and inaccurate light.

On 18 June, the local (and now defunct) Anniston chapter of the National Association for the Advancement of Colored People (NAACP) held a press conference at Anniston's city hall to address the issue. Councilmen Reddick and Selase were present in front of the cameras and microphones, constituting two of the handful of people in line. Selase and Reddick made comments at that press conference, as well as to multiple other news outlets, where they called for my termination, even though the above-referenced State law prohibits them, "*in any manner,*" from having anything to do with my removal. In particular, Reddick made multiple outrageous statements and falsehoods concerning me to multiple media outlets. For example, in coverage by, among others, WTVM.com on 17 June, Reddick was quoted as saying, "We will not allow police officers or anybody else come and be a part of hate groups, and protect and serve a city that's over 50 percent black." Here Reddick uses the term "hate group," as defined by the Southern Poverty Law Center— an organization that has no legal authority to declare such things. The SPLC is a leftist and highly opinionated political group that obviously has a liberal agenda. When Reddick includes himself in the decision-making process ("We will not allow...") he is inserting himself into a process which he is prohibited "*in any manner*" from entering. In the same news story, Selase was quoted as saying, "The City is taking these allegations very seriously.... We will keep the public informed." Notice, again, the use of "we."

These four council members were involved in the process that led to my removal from the beginning, even though they are prohibited from any involvement "*in any manner.*" Several news media sources, including wsfa.com, quoted Selase as saying, "We will look for an immediate remedy to this particular situation with these allegations...." The above cited State law mandates that "[e]xcept for the purpose of inquiry [a particular process involving thorough procedure that is spelled out elsewhere in the law and city policy], the council and its members shall deal with the administrative service solely through the city manager." Clearly, that did not occur in my situation.

Then there was the press conference on 19 June. The mayor was seated at the head of the table and presided over it! He said, "This city will not tolerate any kind of connection to racism and bigotry." The city manager, in his statements, commended the council for giving him guidance and allowing him to act quickly on the situation! He said he "convened my senior applicable staff that would be involved in something like this, the city attorney, the director of human resources, the police chief, specifically, as well as communicating with members of the legislative, policy-making branch to discuss the strategy going forward. The decision was made to put them on, um—for me to put them on administrative leave immediately and separate them from the situation, allow the city to initiate an investigation into these allegations, which we did so immediately."

Then Councilman Jenkins said, "It is unfortunate and disappointing that we have to deal with a situation like this in today's world. But we did handle it well, I am comfortable with that." Notice how many times Jenkins and other council members used the personal pronouns "we" or "I" as they explained their involvement with my termination. In their rush to satisfy the wolves of political correctness and to create the impression they were "handling the situation," four of the five council members—Stewart, Selase, Reddick, and Jenkins— BROKE THE LAW.

After I was terminated by the city manager (by press conference on 19 June, and officially by written notification on 25 June), I appealed the decision to the Anniston Civil Service Board on 2 July. On the first day of the hearing on 26 August, Chief Shane Denham testified. My attorney asked him about the various meetings he held with people during the 48-hour "investigation" conducted from 17-19 June. Under oath, the chief admitted that he held meetings during that time period that were attended by council members Stewart and Selase in which they both, individually, recommended to him that I be fired. The State law prohibits council members to involve themselves "*in any manner*" in the removal of an officer.

For the record, I wish to state that I certainly disagree with the characterization of The League of the South, myself (by implication), and many other of the groups the SPLC smears. As was covered at my civil service hearing, things have been written and said by various members with which I disagree and for which I should not be held accountable. This would be the same situation with any entity or organization to which one could belong. In accordance with my Christian beliefs, I do not "hate" anyone. During the testimony delivered by the many witnesses at my hearing, all that were questioned testified that they had never heard me utter a racist comment nor act in a prejudicial, offensive, or divisive manner.

It is my position that I have been a victim of character assassination by the Southern Poverty Law Center and the City of Anniston, particularly the four council members listed as offenders in this complaint. My reputation in the police field lies in shatters. The damage done to me and family has been irreparable. I have been unable to obtain employment in the field of my 19-year vocation due to the negative publicity surrounding this episode. I have been unemployed for four months. The issue of a reversal of the city's decision to fire me, along with constitutional issues of rights violations, are pending in Calhoun County Circuit Court.

My submission to the Alabama Attorney General's Office is that probable cause exists for the arrest and prosecution of the four offenders named in this complaint for violating the listed State law (which, again, was also part of the City of Anniston's own written policies and procedures).

The information contained herein has been limited to what I believe was necessary for an initial complaint and proof of probable cause. I wholeheartedly believe the complete evidence at my disposal and available to the Office of Attorney General will uphold a standard of proof beyond a reasonable doubt necessary for criminal conviction.

Sincerely,

Josh Doggrell

Anniston, Alabama

* * *

It was nearing 5:00 pm on 15 September 2015 by the time Councilman David Reddick was called to the stand and sworn in at the Justin Sollohub Justice Center.

Reddick stated his name, his position as a city councilman, and agreed that he was a past president of the local chapter of the National Association for the Advancement of Colored People (NAACP). There are many who view the NAACP as a controversial organization. I was fired for my affiliation with another such controversial organization. Yet, here was a city councilman who had been president of such an organization immediately prior to becoming a councilman and still was affiliated with it at the time. As a matter of fact, he had appeared (along with Councilman Selase) at the NAACP press conference one day after I was placed on administrative leave (and one day before I was fired) demanding that I be terminated for being a member of a "hate group," as designated by the Southern Poverty Law Center (SPLC).

198

Interestingly enough, the SPLC has, in the past, labeled the Nation of Islam (NOI), a "hate group." On the SPLC website, they state the Nation's "theology of innate black superiority over whites and the deeply racist, antisemitic and anti-LGBT rhetoric of its leaders have earned the NOI a prominent position in the ranks of organized hate." In 1993, the executive director of the NAACP, Benjamin Chavis, appeared at a press conference with NOI leader Louis Farrakhan and declared that the NAACP "stands with the Nation of Islam." A year later, the NAACP issued a statement of support for the NOI (http://articles.baltimoresun.com/1994-02-05/news/1994036073_1_farrakhan-muhammad-nation-of-islam).

Here is the point in all this: The city fired me for my affiliations with an organization that was deemed controversial (even though they had cleared me of any wrongdoing in my involvement and told me I was within my rights six years earlier through an internal investigation), using the tactic of guilt-by-association. "Exhibits" were presented by the city at my trial and used as evidence against me (most which were not discovered until after they fired me) that were not written by me, not endorsed by me, and many that were even unknown to me. The implication was that I could be held responsible for views simply because I was affiliated in some way with people who expressed such views.

However, here we have a city councilman (who was one of the loudest in publicly demanding that I be fired) who was not only affiliated, but was an immediate past president of an organization that had explicitly and publicly aligned itself with an organization (Nation of Islam) and its leader, Louis Farrakhan, a man who has screamed vitriolic, violent comments about Jews, Christians, whites, and just about anyone not black and a Muslim over the years. Moreover, the SPLC had labeled the Nation a "hate group." If the city was going to play guilt-by-association, was not David Reddick a prime target? Or, in a city consumed with political correctness, does one have to be a Christian, white, Southern police officer to be a target?

* * *

Attorney Kenneth Shinbaum (**KS**): "Have you ever held any office with the NAACP?"

David Reddick (**DR**): "Yes."

KS: "What office have you held?"

DR: "I was the president of the NAACP."

KS: "Which chapter?"

DR: "Anniston, Calhoun County, Number 5002."

KS: "And have you ever stated that you stand — that the NAACP stands with the Nation of Islam?"

DR: "No; not that I know of."

KS: "...Now, back on or about June 17th, 2015, did you provide ABC — local ABC channel 33/40 exclusively with correspondence between former Anniston Police Chief John Dryden, former City Attorney Cleophus Thomas, and former City Manager Don Hoyt?"

DR: "Yes."

KS: "What was that correspondence about?"

DR: "It was about a case that came up in 2009, as I recall, about a chapter of the League of the South being created in Anniston."

KS: "And was that concerning Josh Doggrell forming a chapter of the League of the South at that time?"

DR: "Yes."

This was interesting, since I was not allowed any access to the file of that internal investigation, and the city refused to present it when we subpoenaed it for court, yet Reddick provided "correspondence" about it to the news media.

KS: "And that was where it was brought to the attention of the city administration that there was a police officer, Josh Doggrell, that was forming a chapter of the League of the South; am I correct?"

DR: "Yes."

KS: "So the city knew about this, Josh Doggrell and his membership in the League of the South, back in 2009? Is that correct?"

DR: "I would have to assume. As I understand it, there was an investigation and when the investigation was over, the investigation cleared Mr. Doggrell, as I understand it."

And Reddick was correct about that.

KS: "...Where did you get the correspondence from between Anniston Police Chief John Dryden, former City Attorney Cleophus Thomas, and former City Manager Don Hoyt?"

DR: "It was emailed to the entire council."

KS: "It was emailed to the entire council?"

DR: "Yes, sir. It's public records."

I am no legal expert in these regards, but I highly doubt that emails from members of city government to council members are considered public records. And, again, the 2009 internal investigation was something the city refused to release to me or the civil service board for my trial.

KS: "When was that emailed to the entire council?"

DR: "I'm not — I don't have a date book in front of me. I don't have my email account in front of me."

KS: "Was it this year?"

DR: "I would assume so."

KS: "Was it back in June?"

DR: "I would assume so."

KS: "Who emailed it to the entire council?"

DR: "I don't have that info in front of me."

KS: "Now, were you at a meeting on…June 18th, 2015, at which time —"

DR: "I'm not sure. I don't have that in front of me."

KS: "…Have you ever notified the city manager of any problems the community had with Josh Doggrell?"

DR: "Yes."

KS: "When would you have done that?"

DR: "After the story broke, it *[sic]* was outrage in my community. It was the emotions of another — I can't recall any incidents, but it was — there were people angry, they were upset, they were scared. And my constituents were very upset because they were telling me they felt — how can they have a police department that allows people that are members of these organizations that have this personality that's prejudiced toward blacks, how can they — how can that police officer represent them? So, my constituents were upset, they were scared. They didn't know what to do. **It was like another Ferguson in Anniston. It had that feeling that it could break out at any moment.**"

Let us examine these last two statements. Reddick interjected the situation in Ferguson, Missouri, from the year before where a white police officer killed a black man named Michael Brown. I will refrain from going into the details of that incident, but remind the reader that a grand jury determined that the officer did nothing criminal, but was defending himself from a man who had just robbed a convenience store and assaulted the store employee. Despite that, a mob descended on the city streets and began looting, terrorizing, burning, destroying property, vandalizing, assaulting, and more or less raising immortal hell. And David Reddick was comparing these two situations and seemed to be threatening that the same reaction of mob mentality could take hold in Anniston if things did not go the way he thought they should.

As I told Chief Shane Denham hours before I was fired via press conference on 19 June 2015, the reaction of the mob should NOT be what determines the merits of a situation. Either I had done something wrong, or I had not (and I had not). But the mob of professional protesters and race hustlers such as David Reddick, who threaten to turn Anniston into "another Ferguson" should NOT be what ends careers, assassinates the characters of good men, ruins reputations, and dictates policies and guides the decisions of city leaders. Yet, that is exactly what happened.

KS: "With respect to that, did anybody ever mention to you what Josh Doggrell's record was as a police officer with the City of Anniston?"

DR: "I never discussed his record with anybody."

I mean, why would someone's record of his job performance have anything to do with his fitness for the job, right? For race hustlers, records are irrelevant when it comes to political correctness.

KS: "Did anybody ever mention to you that there was never any hint of any problems with Josh Doggrell as he performed his duties?"

DR: "I've had community people say they had problems with Josh Doggrell when he was an officer."

KS: "What 'community people'?"

DR: "Reverend Williams, one of the pastors, said he had to spend the night in jail. He had a confront— he had to deal with Doggrell. He said he didn't like the way he was talked to and treated by him. I had other members that had to deal with him on certain things that said they didn't like the way he dealt with them. But all of that is how they felt."

I have no idea who this "Reverend Williams" is, by the way. And it is common for "community people," if they are committing crimes, to dislike the treatment they receive from arresting officers.

KS: "Did they ever make any complaints about their treatment by Josh Doggrell?"

DR: "If I'm not mistaken, Rev. Williams did publicly."

KS: "Publicly? When publicly?"

DR: "After he was arrested and had to spend the night in jail and complained about how he had to sleep on the floor in the jail system and all that."

Again, I have no idea who this person is. If I ever actually arrested him, as arresting officer I would have had nothing to do with where he slept inside the jail. That would be a matter for the corrections officers. And I certainly would have recalled if this man "publicly" complained about me. My guess here is that Reddick either doesn't have his facts straight or is just lying.

KS: "Now—"

DR: "I also had a community member come to me who had a case that — she brought her case — it was identity theft and she said Doggrell was working her case, her identity theft case. And she said when certain names came up, he wouldn't even work with her. He wouldn't return her calls. He wouldn't talk to her. He was very rude when he dealt with her."

KS: "Did she ever file any complaints?"

DR: "I'm not sure. You can check the records."

Or maybe Reddick could have checked the records for these mystery people. I can't say whether I know this person or not, since a name was not supplied. And I worked a great deal of identity theft cases as an investigator.

KS: "Did you ever inform the city manager that your community wanted Josh Doggrell off the police force?"

DR: "In a way, I would say yes. I never went to him and said we want Josh Doggrell off the police department; that's not what I said."

KS: "What did you say?"

DR: "I told him — I said the community was upset, they were scared, they were angry, but I never at any time told the city manager what to or not to do."

KS: "Did you ever say 'something needed to be done'?"

DR: "Something did need to be done, yes."

"Something needs to be done" certainly sounds a lot like strongly suggesting that discipline should be imposed.

KS: "But this is not a problem that was first discovered in June of 2015. It had been known to the police department and the city as far back as June of 2009 or as far back as sometime in 2009, am I correct?"

DR: "What do you mean, this is not a problem? I don't understand."

KS: "I mean, the fact that Josh Doggrell was...a member of the League of the South had been known to the city as far back as 2009?"

DR: "Well, as I understand it, he was cleared of that, so I would assume that the city believed it was an erroneous accusation is what I would believe. Considering that there was an investigation in which I can't look at, I don't have access to that information. So, if there is an investigation and he was cleared, to me as a public official, I would have to assume that whoever did that investigation cleared him."

KS: "Well, would it surprise you Josh Doggrell did not make any secret of his being a member of the League of the South back between 2009 and 2014?"

DR: "Well, if I am surprised or not surprised, what does that have to do with anything? I don't understand."

Shinbaum had no further questions. The city only had one, where they asked if Reddick had resigned as NAACP president prior to taking his position as city councilman. He said he did. The attempted point was to create the impression he had given up any perceived controversial views or positions so that he could fairly carry out his duties as a public official. Any reasonable person knows that just because Reddick gave up that position, it did not necessarily impact his views or his thinking. The issue should be if a person, whatever his views, carries out his duties in a fair and impartial manner.

Regardless, the city had no policy about which groups an employee could or could not belong. Not only was I never asked to leave the League, but I was also, as Mr. Reddick testified, investigated and cleared.

In my internal affairs interview on the day I was fired, investigator Nick Bowles said, "The city is reacting to the public reaction, that's why this is happening." And he said, "It's cool to hate cops right now."

More specifically, it is cool to hate white cops now.

There is a successful strategy to tear down the Christian, Southern, white man today. Find a skeleton in a closet. If you cannot find one, put one there and "discover" it. Then blast it on the media. Make threats like if "something isn't done," we could have "another Ferguson" because "the community" is "upset" and "scared." Keep saying it over and over. With spineless "leadership" like what we had in Anniston, this is a winning strategy.

14.

THE DEFENDANT TAKES THE STAND

"I speak only as an individual and not an employee of that agency."

WE HAD BEEN GOING ALL DAY and it was now late in the evening. It was apparent that a second day of testimony would be required. Our side had subpoenaed all four city councilmen who had broken the law (as described in the previous chapter), but since the first one, David Reddick, had admitted of his illegal involvement in my termination, I felt the point had been sufficiently made. I was tired and ready to get it over with. I asked my attorney, Kenneth Shinbaum, to put me on the stand.

"I would like to call Josh Doggrell," he told the civil service board attorney, Trudie Phillips.

I had been waiting for this opportunity for three months.

Kenneth Shinbaum: "Could you please state your name?"

Josh Doggrell: "Joshua Emmett Doggrell."

Over what would stretch into two days (15 and 17 September 2015) I sat for hours on the stand at the municipal courtroom of the Justin Sollohub Justice Center and then the council chambers at city hall in Anniston, Alabama. The entirety of the testimony took up 170 pages of transcript, which is public record.

As I have written before, the day I was fired by the city manager I asked the police chief what policy I was supposed to have violated and he replied, "I don't know." It was six days after the press conference announcing my termination before I finally received in writing the policies I was alleged to have violated. For those six days, I was still on paid administrative leave, despite what City Manager Brian Johnson said at the press conference on 19 June. It is my firm belief that it took six days for the city to go through the deceptive brainstorming and mental sophistry necessary to decide which policies to try to use.

Shinbaum asked when I had joined the League of the South (1995). He asked when I began my police career (1997) and when was I hired at Anniston Police Department (2006). "...[W]hen you first started to work for them, were you a member of the League of the South?"

"I sure was."

"Did you ever try to keep that a secret?"

"No, sir. It was on my application and it was discussed at the interview in which I as hired."

We covered the facts that, not only had my membership been maintained throughout my years of service with the city, but three years after I was hired, while working as a caseworker in the investigative division, I became the chairman of a local chapter of the League in Anniston in 2009. We also stated the fact *The Anniston Star* had covered that inaugural meeting in columns published the day before and the day after the meeting. I testified that, largely as a result of that media exposure, I was the subject of an internal investigation conducted by the city in the Spring of that year and was cleared of any wrongdoing.

Shinbaum entered into evidence the Core Beliefs Statement and Frequently Asked Questions form from the League's website, which served as League policy at that time. He later directed my attention to the portion of the Core Beliefs that articulated the League's position regarding black people in the South. I read from that statement: "The League of the South disavows a spirit of malice and extends an offer of goodwill and cooperation to Southern blacks in areas where we can work together as Christians to make life better for all people in the South. We affirm that, while historically the interests of Southern blacks and whites have been, in part, antagonistic, true constitutional government would provide protection to all law-abiding citizens, not just to government-sponsored victim groups."

I supported that position then, and I support it now.

Throughout my affiliation with the League of the South, I met many fine people, particularly Christian pastors and friends. I also met people whom I despised and who held views with which I vehemently disagreed. At the trial, we entered into evidence the actual policies of the League itself at the time, all of which I agreed with in their entirety. Since I was being painted as a "racist," I thought the League policy toward black citizens was particularly appropriate:

Shinbaum also entered my personnel file and the city's policies and procedures manual.

We took the charges leveled against me one at a time.

CHARGE ONE:

The city centered their prosecution on a speech I gave at the League of the South national conference in Wetumpka, Alabama, on 21 June 2013 to allege that I had violated the Anniston Police Department policy (SOP) 400.020. We entered this policy into evidence (E-7) and it reads as follows:

> "All employees giving speeches, lectures, etc., or conducting public relations programs on or off duty on behalf of the police department must obtain prior approval from the chief of police. A memorandum giving the date, time, and circumstances of the event is to be forwarded to the chief of police in order that a record of such activities can be maintained."

By the time I gave that speech, I had been giving speeches — *with the city's knowledge* — at League events for four years. Most of those were in Anniston or Oxford. Never had it been suggested that I needed approval from the chief to give them, even though all my superiors including the chief knew about my affiliation, that I was chairman of the Anniston chapter, that I had already been investigated and cleared, and that my position as a police officer was well known in Anniston.

I was certainly not speaking "on behalf of the police department." As a matter of fact, the first time I mentioned my employment in that speech was in the twelfth minute (in spite of the city's accusation that I "began my speech" by announcing I was an APD officer) when I gave the disclaimer: *"Calhoun County has several police agencies. I work at Anniston, which I'll go ahead and go on record. Nothing I say here today is necessarily the views of the Anniston Police Department. I speak only as an individual and not an employee of that agency."*

I do not know how I could have made it any clearer that I was not speaking on behalf of the police department. On the day I was put on administrative leave, Chief Denham even conceded this fact to me. Yet, by the time he testified two months later he had gotten on board with the city attorney, who asserted that because I had a smile on my face when I said it, I must not have been serious. The city manager testified that, because I had made the disclaimer, I had brought attention to the matter and, thus, voided the disclaimer. In this convoluted logic, giving a disclaimer invalidates said disclaimer. And, if you have a smile on your face, that also invalidates a disclaimer. I know of no such precedence for this in the history of jurisprudence. Yet, in a kangaroo court in the City of Anniston it, apparently, held sway.

During the trial, we also presented the city's policy on social media activity as an example of why presenting a disclaimer was prudent. That policy was on pp. 58-59 of the city's personnel policies/procedures manual (entered into evidence as E-1). Under Roman numeral II, paragraph E ("social media best practices") it reads,

> "Identify your views as your own. If you identify yourself as a city employee, it should be clear that the views expressed are not those of the city. In fact, unless your job duties with the city entail posting on social media regarding city business, employees are prohibited from posting anything that implies or indicates that they are posting in their official capacity as an employee or representative of the city."

It would seem reasonable that restrictions concerning social media public commentary would also be applicable to verbal public commentary. I identified my views as my own. When I identified myself as a city employee, I immediately made "clear that the views expressed are not those of the city."

Therefore, since I was not giving the speech "on behalf of the police department," I did not need approval from the chief and did not violate this policy.

After making this point, Shinbaum asked questions about my history of promotions at the department, leading to my testimony that I had been promoted to sergeant one year after the completion of that 2009 internal investigation, and then to lieutenant three years later.

KS: "Did anybody ever come and say to you that, Josh, you know, this is putting a hardship on the police department and we would appreciate it if you disassociated yourself with the League of the South?

JD: "Never."

KS: "Did anybody ever say that to continue to be a member of this police force you have to leave the League of the South?"

JD: "Never."

Charge Two:

The city alleged I had violated Anniston Police Department policy (SOP) 500.090 (which we entered into evidence as E-8) "Associating With Undesirable Persons." It reads,

"Employees of the department are prohibited from associating in any manner whatsoever with known felons or persons of ill repute, except within the scope of official police duties."

The person the city deemed of "ill repute" was Michael Hill, the president of the League (although he was not deemed so in the city's investigation of me in 2009, even though he was specifically investigated). **Dr.** Hill is no "felon," and considering him a "person of ill repute" would be widely subjective, as would so many of the people with whom the average person "associates" daily. To my knowledge, he has never been arrested, never been involved with any kind of criminal activity, and never advocated criminal activity. His "crimes" were "thought crimes" as judged by the "thought police." He and I agree on some things, and we disagree on some things.

This policy is common to police departments, and has its origins in scandals involving officers getting mixed up in some type of criminal activity or vices such as gambling, drugs, and prostitution. In my nineteen-year career I never even heard of it being used. It would certainly seem to be more applicable to officers who spend their off nights and weekends drinking and cavorting at bars in the area among people with whom they deal with as law violators while on duty, yet I do not know of it being used that way in Anniston. Of course, again, I have never seen it used at all.

The city investigated me, my involvement with the League of the South, and my association with **Dr.** Hill in 2009. I was cleared and told I had not violated any policies and was within my rights. The issue was not brought up to me again from 2009-2015.

Did I "associate with people of ill repute"? I certainly do not think so. And, because of the city's own internal investigation of 2009, and their knowledge of my religious and political activities all the years I was there, they did not think so, either. I associate with a wide variety of people. Many of those people hold views with which I strongly disagree.

CHARGE THREE:

The city alleged that I violated their "harassment" policy regarding social media usage. This was applied to my personal Facebook page, which was in no way affiliated with my work and where I never identified myself as a police officer or a city employee in the six years I had been using it at that point. The *one* witness they provided who said they felt harassed was the human resources director, who admitted during testimony that not only had she never voiced disagreement with anything I had put on Facebook, but that *she had not even seen my Facebook page prior to me being fired!* She also testified that *no* city employee had ever contacted her about feeling harassed or threatened by my Facebook page. Under questioning from my attorney, she also testified that it was her belief that even religious symbols, such as the Christian cross, on Facebook might be considered "harassment" since certain city employees could find it offensive. Under this reasoning, (which violates constitutional rights, by the way) the city could use almost anything to justify a punitive action, including termination, against any employee.

The charge that I violated the city's harassment policy regarding social media usage is false. And the city's contention that they can be over-broad and vague in interpreting symbols, posts, and pictures that an employee uses outside of work and on their own social media accounts as "offensive" for punitive measures is unconstitutional.

CHARGE FOUR:

Finally, the city chose a "catch-all" policy to allege, "Conduct Unbecoming an Employee." It reads,

"Employees of the department shall not conduct themselves in a disorderly manner at any time, either on or off duty, or so conduct themselves in a manner unbecoming the conduct of an employee of the City of Anniston Police Department."

During testimony, we asked every witness who had ever worked with, under, and/or supervised me if they had ever seen me act in a disorderly manner. All answered negative. We asked every witness who testified that had seen the video of the speech in question if he thought I had acted in a "disorderly manner." All answered negative.

This leaves the accusation of conducting myself "in a manner unbecoming the conduct of an employee of the City of Anniston Police Department."

I certainly disagree with that charge, as well. And I think my best defense is the fact that I was a member of the League of the South since 1995 — two years before my police career began and eleven years before my employment with the City of Anniston began. I listed it on my application (which mysteriously disappeared from my personnel file before trial), I discussed it in my hiring interview, I discussed it during my polygraph hiring examination (which was documented and released by the city for federal depositions in October 2016, but was mysteriously absent during my civil service trial in the summer of 2015), I took off work to go to conferences every year, with their knowledge I began a local chapter in March 2009, and I was investigated and cleared by the city for my involvement in the Spring of 2009. If I was engaging in "conduct unbecoming an employee," the entire command staff of Anniston Police Department should have also been fired for condoning it all those years.

In my life, I have observed that the more intimately one gets to know another person, it becomes a certainty that one will find out something disagreeable about the other. One is bound to hold some viewpoint, some habit, some practice, contrary to the other's own viewpoints, habits, practices. Civilized people learn to live and let live to a large degree.

The man who routinely works on my air-conditioning unit is a Mormon. This is a religion with which I hold strongly different convictions on matters of faith. The doctor who performed surgery on my knee in 2022 is also a Mormon. One of my now retired work colleagues is a Mormon, yet I still consider him a friend who has shown me kindness and camaraderie for a number of years.

If it ever came to it, I could choose to separate these people from my lives. I could call on someone else to work on my air-conditioning unit. I could have found another doctor to perform surgery upon me. I could have informed my friend that our differences on matters of faith had reached a point where our friendship had been compromised.

At no point in my life have I ever considered being a part of an orchestrated effort to terminate someone's career and ruin his reputation because he does not think like I think he should think. But that is precisely what happened to me. That's the kind of business in which people and organizations like the Southern Poverty Law Center specialize.

Toward the end of my testimony, Shinbaum asked me, "Do you feel that you should be judged upon your actions in your nine-year career with the Anniston Police Department as opposed to what somebody has tweeted or facebooked or put on Facebook or on the League of the South website...which you have never seen?"

I replied, "**Dr.** Hill and I go way back, but we disagree on a lot and he knows that. I don't feel like I should have to answer for his personal opinions. And not only do I think I should be judged by the performance of my actions and my duties, but I think everybody should be judged by that regardless of their political views or affiliations. If they are within their rights, [if] they are not violating the laws and policies, and their job performance is not being affected by that, I think they all should be judged on their job performance and be judged by the people who know them like these men and women, black and white, who have come in here today [and testified] that know me. Not like Brian Johnson, with whom I never had a conversation..."

CONCLUSION

I believe in a court of law we adequately defended our position that the decision of the City of Anniston to fire me was not only erroneous, but criminal. We sought earthly vindication for that through the courts, to no avail. Such vindication would unexpectedly come through another branch of government years down the road.

Why was I fired? Because the Southern Poverty Law Center, that far-left-wing hate group, doesn't like me. They produced an attack article and video against me, which even my superiors at

216

the police department testified was done with the intention of inflaming public opinion. The SPLC routinely attacks those like me: Christian, Southern, white, conservative.

Due to the negative exposure over a course of 48 hours, the city manager and the police chief took the easy way out and sacrificed me and my family on the altar of political correctness.

I have made many mistakes in my life that I have taken up with God, but my firing and the assassination of my reputation and my vocation by the City of Anniston was not warranted. For those involved, may the Lord have mercy on your souls.

I decided to write about it for the curious and for those who do not base their judgments on media sound bites and salacious headlines. I write for the courageous, for those who will not bend a knee to political correctness.

I write for my children, so that when they get old enough to understand the wickedness they have been subjected to they can read this and better comprehend what the SPLC, the media, and the City of Anniston did to us.

I write for the encouragement of the Christians who read it, to share with them how our mighty God will preserve us through the trials and tribulations of life. Behold, He makes all things new...

Deo Vindice.

15.

CROSS EXAMINATION AND RACIST GOATS

"...life can actually flourish and things can be a lot better without the government having to hold your hand through it."

17 September 2015

WHEN I FINISHED GIVING TESTIMONY under direct questioning from my attorney on the evening of Tuesday, 15 September 2015, I was ready for the cross examination, as I was ready to have the whole hearing done. However, against my wishes, the civil service board attorney, Trudie Phillips, who was operating in a quasi-judicial role for the proceedings, granted the request of city prosecutor Bruce Downey to postpone cross examination for two days. My objection to this was denied.

Perhaps it had been a mistake to proceed with my testimony in the evening of what had been a long day. But I was anxious to be done with it and figured that if I testified the cross examination would immediately follow. Instead, we recessed at 6:30pm.

This gave Downey two days to review my testimony and prepare.

We met again at 3:00pm on Thursday, 17 September. All three board members in whose hands my fate rested decided to appear for this third and final day of the trial. Member George Bates, who missed the entirety of the first day, most witnesses from the second day, and the entirety of my direct testimony, graced us with his presence on this final day. Before falling asleep, he opened the hearing thusly:

"We will continue from yesterday and whatever order that we had on yesterday will continue today. Same rules apply…"

Now, we had not met at all the day prior, but since Bates had already demonstrated his disregard for justice, focus, interest, and proper procedure, it came as no surprise that his facts were off.

Downey began his questioning by referring to an image entered into evidence, a mathematical not-equal sign I had displayed on my Facebook page two years earlier. It did not take long for us to disagree.

BD: "Mr. Doggrell, you recognize that image?"

JD: "Yes, sir."

BD: "It was an image depicted on your public Facebook profile?"

JD: "Yes, sir."

BD: "You understand or do you understand that someone may take from that image the message that is intended to convey that whites and blacks are not equal?"

JD: "That is hard for me to understand."

BD: "You do see that it's a white not equal sign with a black background?"

JD: "I do see that the colors are white and black like the colors of a panda bear."

BD: "…So given that you had a white not equal sign and a black background, you find it hard to understand how someone might view that and take from it that it's intended to convey that whites are not equal to blacks?"

JD: "I find that an incredible leap beyond the bounds of reasonableness, especially when you couple it with the commentary that's right beside it."

Downey had seized on this image in an attempt to make a racial issue from something that was clearly not, as the commentary accompanying it revealed. The issue was the idea of same-sex "marriage." At that time the comments were posted (2013), many people in support of the legalization of this type of union were showing their support on social media through the display of the mathematical equal sign. One of the people involved in this particular printed conversation was an old friend from high school, Jennifer Walker.

BD: "Who is Jennifer Walker?"

JD: "She's a lady I went to high school with."

BD: "…I am going to show you what I have marked as City's Exhibit 16…does that reflect posts that were made to your Facebook profile?"

I had already reviewed the comments accompanying this photo, as it had already been raised in the testimony of Human Resources Director Bersheba Austin (see Chapter Nine). I had noticed that the comments made by Nick Bowles had been redacted. Bowles was the lead investigator of the city's internal investigation that led to my termination and, coincidentally, he went on to become the police chief a few years later.

JD: "It reflects more of the posts… I do see that Nick Bowles's comments [are] still excluded from this."

Downey clearly wanted to avoid that issue: "My question was does if reflect posts to your Facebook?"

JD: "It reflects partial commentary from the total, which is not included."

The incomplete "exhibit" was admitted into evidence.

BD: "Mr. Doggrell, could you read for us Jennifer Walker's post on April 4th, 2013, at 10:55 p.m.?"

JD: "She wrote, 'What does this mean? No equality?'"

BD: "Is it fair to say that Ms. Walker interpreted from the post that it was intended to mean that something was not equal to another?"

JD: "I don't know what Ms. Walker interpreted. She is asking a question."

BD: "...you find it divorced from reality that someone could also conclude from this image that it was meant to convey there is no equality between white and black?"

JD: "I said I thought that stretched the bounds of reasonableness when accompanied with the totality of the commentary which does not mention race at all, but does mention homosexual marriage a great deal."

On and on this went. Downey tried over and over to get me to say that I was intending to convey something racial with this mathematical image. That was untrue. The point of sharing the symbol was to declare my opposition with something my faith tells me is not only a sin, but an impossibility.

JD: "...As a Christian, I am against the concept of the legality of homosexual marriage. So, if people were using an equal sign to support that, it seemed perfectly logical to me to use an inequal sign to show my support for traditional marriage."

On and on this went.

CROSS EXAMINATION AND RACIST GOATS

JD: "... I believe you're trying to say that I chose this based on black and white racism and I am adamantly saying that never entered my mind."

BD: "What I'm saying is that you took an image that was intended to convey a message about homosexual marriage and I'm saying you adapted that image to a black background and a white not equal sign."

JD: "No, sir. That's not true. This image was not created by me. The colors were not chosen by me. I got it from someone who holds the same opinion about this marriage issue that I do, copied it and posted it. I did not adapt it in any way and I certainly did not put any thought whatsoever into the colors that were on it."

On and on this went. A couple of times I looked at my attorney, thinking surely we were past the point of an objection of "Asked and answered." But he was studying some papers he was holding.

BD: "... Help us understand. When you saw just this image, what about that image made you think about same sex marriage?"

JD: "I think I've explained that, but I will be happy to try to do that again."

BD: "Please do."

JD: "The debate in the spring of 2013, that continued well after that and continues to this day was about whether or not homosexual marriage should be legal. I am opposed to that as I was in the spring of 2013, and it was widely known and should be widely known by anybody who monitors social media at all that the equal sign was being used by people who supported homosexual marriage... Since my opinion to that is opposite of it, it seemed perfectly logical to choose a mathematical symbol that is the opposite of equal, which is the not equal sign."

BD: "I want to be clear. You did not create this image?"

JD: "I did not create this image."

BD: "You didn't choose the colors?"

JD: "Nor choose its colors, no, sir..."

BD: "But you just saw this image and just this image? Without the context that you just added, that you just saw this image and it said to you, you know what, that's telling me something about same sex marriage?"

JD: "That is true... I do not believe that homosexual marriage is equal spiritually to traditional heterosexual marriage..."

BD: "... Mr. Doggrell, when you said that it was not reasonable... for a person to conclude that this image had any connotation of race whatsoever, I am going to refer you to what was City's Exhibit 11 [this was a page of multiple images of profile pictures I had used on Facebook]. When you view that image [the not equal sign]... next to or among a photo containing Nathan Bedford Forrest standing in front of a Confederate flag, do you still think it is a stretch for someone to view that image and think, you know what, that's intended to convey a message about race?"

JD: "I do, because I would also think it would be in error to compare that to the images of Merle Haggard that I have here and Thomas Jefferson."

BD: "Merle Haggard – that picture of Merle Haggard in not a not equal sign in white in the black background, is it not?"

JD: "But it is among the same pictures that you just talked about. And if we are going to draw conclusions, then my goat Bubba is also a racist because he is right next to that not equal sign."

BD: "The not equal sign with the black background requires interpretation, do you agree with that at least? It's not a picture of a goat. It's intended to convey a message. You have admitted that you say it's intended to convey a message about homosexual marriage."

JD: "That is true and that's why I provided the commentary that I did with the picture."

On and on this went. I cannot recall just how long Bruce Downey asked me what amounted to the same question with me giving the same answer, but looking at the transcript now I can report that it started at the beginning of page 468 and was the only issue and line of questioning until the middle of page 482.

Downey finally shifted issues and questioned me about my membership and years of activity with the League of the South. We discussed several convictions I hold about my faith, Southern nationalism, and how a true constitutional republic should operate.

JD: "... Let me say also, Mr. Downey, those are the same views that I have had since 1995, the same views that were discussed when I was hired at Calhoun County Sheriff's Office in 1997, and the same views I had when I was hired at the Anniston Police Department and discussed with them in 2006, the same views I had when I was internally investigated by the Anniston Police Department in 2009, the same views I had when this matter was brought to the Anniston City Council in 2011 and 2012. Those views have not changed and it's been okay for eighteen years of my career."

There were exchanges about my years with the League, and about how much it meant to me for so long. However, I also recounted how the League had changed in recent years and how certain people with whom I shared many differences had taken a more vocal and pronounced position in the organization. I spoke about how I had told the chief and Lt. Bowles that I would not go so far as "denouncing" the League in order to save my job:

> "... after I said that's not going to happen, Lt. Bowles looked at me and said why not, why not just flush it if it means keeping your job; flush it, his words. And I said because that's not the right thing to do. I have known the pastors of this organization for

twenty years. I have got some – just because some people are saying some absolutely horrible things that have gotten a lot of attention, there are very good people that I have known that's within this organization; and, no, sir, I was not going to get up at a press conference and trash that organization and those people. I was not going to do that even if it meant saving my job. It would have been wonderful to have the opportunity to talk to Brian Johnson [at this point I pointed at Johnson], this man that fired me, and sat down face-to-face with him and had a conversation. And I asked for that and he didn't grant me that. He was too busy trying to rush in here and get to his press conference."

Downey paused and said, "You appear to have a fairly aggressive look on your face right now."

JD: "Sir, my eighteen and a half year career has been taken from me... If I had done something wrong, I would be here begging for mercy. I'm just asking for justice."

Downey moved on.

We discussed the years I had spent with the League, my respect for my heritage and love for the Southern people. We talked extensively about Michael Hill, since it was revealed strategy for the city to tar me with guilt-by-association. Downey spent a lot of time attempting to tie me with personal opinions of **Dr.** Hill.

Downey entered into evidence a photograph from years earlier of a group of men that included me and **Dr.** Hill and asked, "Michael Hill is featured squarely in the middle of the photograph, is he not?"

I had been awaiting this opportunity. "He is," I replied. "The point being to stress association. The man on the far left of this photograph, I don't even remember his name. He just happened to be in the room at the time. I haven't seen him since then, but am I also responsible for everything he has said since that time or before, or anybody else [in the photograph]? I don't think I'm responsible. How far does this authority go where I am responsible for what other people say and do that I may or may not have had a picture with? How far does that go, Mr. Downey?"

Downey entered another photograph from my Facebook account into evidence. This was from another League event. Among the group of people featured were me, **Dr.** Hill, and Anniston Police Department Lt. Wayne Brown. I attempted to get in front of this one without a question before Downey interrupted me. "Am I also responsible for everybody in this picture and whatever they –"

"Can we have the witness get in order, please, and answer questions and not try to intimidate and not badger?"

Board attorney Trudie Phillips, who served throughout the trial as a one-woman "Amen Corner" for Downey, interceded: "The witness is admonished to answer questions only."

Downey: "Do you recognize Michael Hill featured prominently – featured in this photograph as well?"

JD: *"Prominently?"*

Dr. Hill's face and partial torso could barely be seen from the back row in this one.

BD: "Featured in this photograph as well?"

JD: "Michael Hill is one of the many people in that photograph, yes, sir."

Downey mentioned that that photograph was one "of at least two" on my Facebook account that featured Hill. I pointed out that there were literally hundreds of photos on my account.

More guilt-by-association questions followed.

BD: "Mr. Doggrell, Michael Hill speaks for the League of the South, does he not?"

JD: "He is the president of the League of the South. Anything that would be official [League policy] would have to be approved by the board [of directors]."

BD: "So do you deny that he speaks for the League of the South?"

JD: "I don't think he speaks for the League of the South... just as Barack Obama is the president of the country, I don't feel like he speaks for me..."

The president of the United States does not always speak on behalf of the whole country. Following this trial, I feel that in the following year of 2016 there were a great many Republicans who did not feel nor agree with Donald Trump speaking on behalf of their political party. Yet, Trump won that party's nomination. After capturing the presidency, there was a quite large number of Americans very vocal about the fact that Trump did not speak for them or their country, despite the office he held.

Downey then asked about my personal feelings on the history of race relations in the United States. I answered: "I think racial relations would flourish without U.S. government interference or just about any government interference. For example, I go to church with some black people. I am involved with Saks (my home community) Youth Activities, that is probably close to fifty percent black and get along wonderfully with the black people in that organization and we never needed a government to regulate that or try to force us to get along..."

Different ethnic groups having problems and vying for power with each other is not something that has been confined to the South. That has occurred all over the world from the beginning of mankind. As a student of history, I maintain that government interference (and what is "government" if not a group of fallen mankind, each member with his own prejudices and biases?) has been merely a tool in such conflict and, more often than not, exacerbated all situations.

Downey attempted to paint my viewpoints as controversial, radical, extreme, and therefore "incompatible" with someone who could discharge police duties in the City of Anniston, Alabama. I disagreed that an individual merely having opinions which some would characterize in whatever fashion they may was still someone acting within their constitutional rights and that someone could advocate for something that was legal and still be able to impartially discharge one's duties. I had been doing it for eighteen years. At one point I remarked, "I had political views that I understand are outside the mainstream. I thought in America that was okay... I also believe that I have constitutional and civil rights and have the right to engage in political discourse and political activity..."

Downey mentioned the city's internal investigation of me six years prior and how I had taken steps to attempt to minimize repercussions for city officials having to deal with it. I remarked, "I never anticipated being in this situation. Having to answer for it, sure. Being fired for it? No, sir, never did I anticipate that. I don't understand. I don't know how you sanction something and allow something for nine years and then fire somebody when it was okay for nine years. I cannot get my mind around that."

Downey asked several questions about my speech at the 2013 League national conference and the fact that I identified myself as an Anniston Police officer during it. "I did. I couldn't come up with a way to talk about the interactions of police agencies in my home county without stipulating to the credibility that I knew what I was talking about."

He also asked about me speaking at the 2012 national conference. "In 2012 I spoke about a friend of mine from here that received an award and I talked about how he had come to a conference with me in 2008 as an atheist and through – partly through the League [influence] came to salvation in Christ."

The transcript indicates Phillips called for a ten-minute break about 4:40 p.m. I had been under cross-examination for an hour and a half. We resumed at 4:50.

Downey asked about particulars from the 2013 speech and tried to tie my expression that the police department had been "supportive" of me to implying that the department was supportive of the League of the South. That was certainly not my intention: "When I said the department was supportive of me, I never intended that to mean that the department [was supportive] of the League of the South because, as I pointed out on another page [of the speech transcript] earlier about 'trouncing around in the wilderness among people what don't think like I do' they [my coworkers] were certainly who I had in mind. I never had meant to convey that they were talking about being supportive of the League of the South. They were supportive of me exercising my rights."

Then Downey addressed the issue that gave the city such fits. The fact that, even though I disclosed to the audience that I was an Anniston police officer, I plainly stated that I was speaking only as an individual and not on behalf of that department. The only method the city could contemplate in diminishing this was to assert that I was not serious about it.

BD: "Is it your testimony to this board under oath that you gave that disclaimer in a serious manner?"

JD: "The fact that I even had to give a disclaimer or felt it necessary to did amuse me."

BD: "So you admit it was done in a sarcastic manner?"

JD: "No, sir, not sarcastic. I remember thinking, I can't believe I am even having to say this. But I thought to myself, just in case one of these days down the road someone tries to make the assertion I am speaking on behalf of the police department, I better include this is what I was thinking..."

BD: "So you on the one hand thought there was no connection whatsoever with the Anniston Police Department and you didn't need permission from the police chief to give this speech; but, yet, on the other hand, you felt it necessary to provide a disclaimer which you found amusing?"

JD: "... I would liken it to if a police officer pulls over a car and smells the odor of marijuana, they've got probable cause to search your car. But, to go ahead and get an extra layer of protection, they might ask for consent to search... I thought it would be wise to add an extra layer of protection."

Downey then played a video of my disclaimer and commented, "I will just be honest, it seemed very sarcastic to me, but you represent that you didn't mean to be sarcastic?

JD: "No, sir, not at all. Amusement and sarcasm are two different things."

We reached a point in the transcript I considered to be very important, when I said that the members of my police department were "not on board" with the League. This was important because Downey had struggled so mightily in trying to insinuate that I had said the very opposite. Downey and I both had copies of the 2013 speech transcript in our hands.

BD: "Explain to us what you are saying [at this point in the speech transcript]."

JD: "... I am talking about them being supportive of my ability to be a member of the League of the South and to exercise my constitutional and civil rights. When I say they are just like other Southerners, I'm saying –"

BD: "Before –"

JD: "You asked the question. You asked me to explain the –"

At this point the hearing transcript records that me and Downey are talking at the same time. My attorney, Kenneth Shinbaum, interjected, "Please let the witness finish answering the question."

BD: "Go ahead. We will come back to it."

KS: "Please! You can wait for him to finish. Answer the question. Then ask the next question."

JD: "The next, the *very* next sentence after that is, 'They are not all on board.' In other words, they are not on board with the League of the South now but they have been very supportive, again supportive of me being in there, not agreeing with the League but being very supportive of me being in there. They appear to have taken the next step."

BD: "What step are you referring to?"

JD: "Taking the step of having views that are outside of the mainstream."

Downey asked if I could understand that, following the 17 June 2015 Southern Poverty Law Center hit piece against me "the community" had the perception that APD condoned and supported my membership in the League. I took this opportunity to speak about what occurs when spineless city "leadership" caves to mob justice:

> "People can sometimes draw their own conclusions... when Mr. [Brian] Johnson [the city manager] spoke of the community [being] outraged, I really wonder. Because I'm in the community, too, and I didn't hear any outrage. I wonder who 'the community' is. If it's the same six-to-ten people that about every three months decide to march around here [city hall] and have press conferences and scream... I remember two years ago they got on Allen George. It was [APD] Captain George they got on. They demanded he be fired. I had to do security on him. They were right

out here [pointing to the sidewalk out the window from where I sat inside city hall] and I remember some of the most outrageous things being said that I knew weren't true. And it's the same people. If that's who he's talking about, they are going to be back. You have emboldened them now. Now we see that the mob is ruling the city... Chief Denham sat right here and testified that there were people screaming in this room [demanding that he take action against me after the SPLC article]. And I thought, why weren't they arrested? That's disorderly conduct. And now I am being accused of disorderly conduct in a speech that I gave where I never even raised my voice an octave. The city is accusing me of disorderly conduct and at the same time saying we had to do something here because people were screaming at us. That's where we are at, people scream and that determines the rights and wrongs of an issue... I mean, we have heard that for decades, the same people that go on and on about it and give speeches and have the press conferences and hold signs... this time you have caved into them... this is the first time it's ever worked. We have protests every few months by these same people who are never satisfied and whose very existence is to be agitators and try to get their way by screaming the loudest. Now if *that* was the 'unrest', then the city mishandled the situation."

Downey mentioned that it wasn't just local people who were interested in this situation. "NBC News" and "Anderson Cooper" had taken an interest. I declined to comment about how the national media loves to sensationalize a story about a purported "racist, white Southern cop."

Here is what I did say: "You asked if it would be better for the city had I not given that speech. Yes, I guess it would be better for the city if nobody ever exercised any rights and we just went home and never engaged in any kind of political discourse and never joined a political party, never did anything that might be deemed by Brian Johnson to be distasteful or against what he thinks. I think that would be much better on the city. But thank God we don't live in a country like that."

Or Do We?

We were almost done. "Mr. Doggrell," Downey said, "thank you for your testimony. I don't have any further questions."

The final twelve pages of the 580-page transcript was my attorney's redirect and questions from the two board members who were awake and coherent. Shinbaum first addressed the attention Downey had given to the fact that I refuse to cite the "Pledge of Allegiance."

KS: "Now, earlier you were asked a question from Mr. Downey, do you pledge allegiance to the flag... can you explain why you personally do not pledge allegiance to the flag?"

JD: "Yes, sir. I don't put anything above Christ in my life and I don't pledge (my loyalty) to anything. My allegiance is to Him."

KS: "Do you understand there has been court cases by the United States Supreme Court that says it's unconstitutional to make people say the pledge of allegiance?"

JD: "Yes, sir."

Next, Shinbaum focused on the attention paid by Downey on the fact that I maintained throughout this entire ordeal that I would not "denounce" the League of the South or its members in whole, even if it meant saving my job. I believe we made an excellent point during the testimony of Police Chief Shane Denham. Denham testified that, since my termination, the City had made all employees divulge their memberships in any kind of organizations, and, if any had raised an issue, the employee would be questioned about it and given the opportunity to cease that membership and maintain their employment. When asked by Shinbaum if the City had ever given me such an opportunity, he was forced to admit it had not.

KS: "...[I]s there a difference in the words 'denounce' and 'terminate' your relationship?

JD: "Yes, sir."

KS: "What is the difference?"

JD: "If you just wanted to leave something, you can just leave it, separation without comment in that regard. I guess it would be something like an amicable divorce, some kind of separation. To come out and 'denounce' or trash somebody is a completely different matter."

In the meeting in Chief Denham's office the morning of 19 June 2015, prior to me being fired by press conference later that afternoon, Lt. Nick Bowles asked me why I would not just "flush" the League if it meant saving my job.

KS: "Now, is there a difference between the meaning of... 'flushing' the League as opposed to... to terminate your relationship with the League?"

JD: "Yes, sir. Especially in the context in which it was used. As I said, that was Lt. Bowles's term for it after the use of the word 'denounce' was used by Chief Denham."

KS: "And what did you take the words to 'flush' the League meant... or 'denounce' the League?"

JD: "That I would probably be asked to make some kind of apologetic statement and trash them."

KS: "You have people that you were friends with in the League?"

JD: "Still do."

KS: "Now, you said something about how relationships can improve without court orders... Have you ever heard of a coach named Paul 'Bear' Bryant?"

JD: "I sure have. Done a lot of studying on him."

KS: "Was he ever ordered to give scholarships to African American athletes?"

JD: "Based on my research, that was never something he was ever forced to do, it was something he wanted to do."

KS: "It was your understanding that he did so voluntarily...on his own?"

JD: "Right. Without a government mandate."

KS: "And did that improve the relationships on the University of Alabama football team?"

JD: "I think eventually it did."

KS: "So things can improve in race relationships without governmental intervention?"

JD: "Contrary to what a lot of government employees think, believe it or not, life can actually flourish and things can be a lot better without the government having to hold your hand through it."

KS: "Now...you go to church, am I correct? ... And was that particular church ever ordered by the government to admit both, to have members of both races in the church?"

JD: "No, sir... the church itself changed without any kind of government interference whatsoever."

KS: "No further questions."

Downey: "Nothing further from the City."

16.

GOD RATHER THAN MEN

"Thou shalt have no other gods before me."
— Exodus 20:3

*"Shall the throne of iniquity have fellowship with
thee, which frameth mischief by a law?"*
— Psalm 94:20

17 September 2015

THE PROSECUTION AND THE DEFENSE had rested. It was
the final minutes of the final day of my trial before the Anniston
Civil Service Board appealing my termination as a police officer.
I was on the stand after having undergone about four hours of
testimony. The board attorney asked if any of the board members
had any questions for me.

Two of the three board members had questions. By this time,
the reader should be able to surmise which ones. The two members
who had been present and awake throughout the trial asked.
George Bates remained in his coma-like state seated next to them.

Randy Third asked a question he had already asked one of
the witnesses. "I want to ask Josh one thing. Josh, at any time

did anyone, whether they were your supervisor, or some rank, or just a regular officer or colleague, did any of them ever warn you about your association with this League – [that] it might get you in trouble?"

Seeing that this was the only question Third asked throughout the entirety of the trial, I assume he had it in his mind that surely I had been warned by someone, and that I simply should have known better. If Third used this as his rationale for voting against me, it should be noted that every time it was asked of any witness the answer was always that I had not or the witness was unaware if I had.

I answered it for him again, "Warned me? No, sir...the answer to your question is no."

Then came an interesting discourse with board member Mike Reese.

Reese was an Anniston police officer himself decades ago. He was a subordinate of my father's at the time. He left there to become an agent with the Alabama Beverage Control Board. I remember Chief Denham telling me and a few others during a staff meeting circa 2014 how excited he was that State representative Randy Wood was getting Reese appointed to the vacant spot on the board. Reese was considered to be pro-police. His questions during my trial, his decision, and his private comments relayed to me lead me to determine that he is not necessarily pro-police officer, but pro-government.

I will give Reese credit for one thing. He testified that he actually watched the speech and listened to it. In the 48 hours between the Southern Poverty Law Center's attack piece on me and the city manager firing me, the media's portrayal was that my speech confirmed what a dangerous "racist" I was. The issue of race was never even addressed in the speech. It was primarily about gun rights and the role of government.

Reese alluded to **Dr. Michael Hill** testifying that he did not support the Constitution. (The guilt-by-association and the fact that **Dr.** Hill was apparently the one on trial has been covered in previous chapters. But it carried on even through these final questions.)

"I ask you directly," Reese said, "do you support the Constitution of the United States?"

"I do," I responded. "I took an oath to uphold it and defend it. I do not take that oath lightly."

In what he might have been expecting as a "gotcha" moment, Reese held up the copy of my written oath of office I had just referenced.

"I am holding the oath actually right here... I took it myself, and your dad did. I learned how to police because of your dad. But you say you can't say the pledge. What is the difference because the flag represents a government just like the Constitution represents the government. What is the difference? Tell me that."

The Constitution represents the government? I thought to myself. *I believe it could be more accurately stated that the Constitution represents the protection of the people* from *the government.*

Here was my response: "Pledging allegiance to something is different from upholding some civil document of a civil government. And the pledge is not law. It has its origins from the 19th century. It was written by a socialist named Francis Bellamy, which one objection I have to it is I'm not a socialist. It was written in the aftermath of the war. It has its origins in loyalty oaths that the United States government made our Southern ancestors take to get back in the union. It mentions in there that we are an indivisible union, which I disagree with. If you are not free to leave, you are not free. And we left a government [Great Britain] to form the United States of America. [I have] many objections."

I went on to explain that the Constitution does not declare that a citizen had to hold the government in higher esteem than God, and I believe that is what the Pledge of Allegiance does. I should have also noted what my attorney and I did during my direct testimony, that the Supreme Court has ruled that citizens, including government employees, cannot be compelled to recite the pledge. Reese must have disagreed with that.

Reese moved ahead. "The second thing I ask is, a while ago, I think Mr. Downey asked the question about George Wallace and you immediately without even thinking about it, you brought to mind June 11th, 1963. Why is that date so memorable to you?"

In one of many exchanges where Downey was trying to paint me as a racist, he had condescendingly asked if I knew about Wallace and his "Stand in the Schoolhouse Door." I decided to show him I probably knew more about it than he did by immediately recounting the exact date of it.

I replied, "I study a lot of that and dates I am pretty good with. And he said it, Mr. Downey said it, I interpreted it as very sarcastic, [like] 'Maybe you have heard of this?' and I was thinking, yes, I've heard of that."

Mike asked, "What is your opinion about George Wallace's stand in the door?"

"... I believe that the U.S. government at that time and constitutionally had no kind of authority to do what they did in that situation."

I realized at the time these answers in this forum were not helping me. I also believed that it would not have mattered if I had plainly lied, effusively praised Martin Luther King, picked up a guitar and begun playing "We Shall Overcome" that it would have swayed those board members from their preconceived determination. So, I stuck with the truth.

"And then the last thing," said Reese, referring to the speech I had given two years prior that was the focus of the city's main allegation against me, "I read your speech and I watched your speech word for word, and I have read and watched it again. And one of the things that alarmed me a little bit about the speech, and

I don't think that it was brought out, one of the comments that you were making is if the order came down as far as going door to door and taking up arms...being a police officer we follow orders, that's our duty. And I think your contention might be that if you were given an unlawful order, you wouldn't follow it. Is that correct?"

Reese was referring to the part of my speech where I related a concern among many Southerners:

> If an illegal, unconstitutional order came from Washington, D.C., instructing soldiers and police officers to go door to door and forcefully confiscate firearms from citizens, would the soldiers and officers carry that out? I recounted the determination of county sheriffs across the country who were on record that they would refuse to carry out such orders and considered it a violation of their oath to protect their citizens and uphold the law. I commended them for it.

But by his question here, Reese feels like they *should* do such a thing. He took issue with me saying I would not carry out an illegal order! Apparently, he is okay with police officers going door to door of homes and forcefully confiscating firearms belonging to citizens if someone with the federal government "ordered" them to do so. This even though the federal government has no authority under the United States Constitution to do so. As a matter of fact, they are specifically *forbidden* to do so under the Second Amendment.

"...being a police officer we follow orders, that's what we do." He was "alarmed" that I would advocate that officers should not follow illegal, immoral orders. Self-defense is a Biblical principle, and God Himself has blessed weapon possession and usage for his children to defend themselves. If the federal government acted to confiscate firearms they would be acting in a wicked, unconstitutional manner and officers would be violating their oath if they carried out such an "order."

Here was my answer to Reese's question: "If the order in itself was unlawful, and I took an oath to uphold the law, then I could see where I could make a reasonable argument that you would be breaking the law by upholding an unlawful order."

Reese: "But you also say that you represent — or that you follow the Constitution of the United States and **if an order came down from the president, no matter what it is, whoever the president in office is, if they give an order, as police officers it's up to us to follow orders. Is that right?**"

At this point I was trying to conceal my shock. Here was this former police officer, and one of three men who currently held the fate of my career in his hands, saying that he could not understand how I could not violate my oath and carry out an illegal order. He was saying that, if the president "ordered it," police officers would have no choice but to "follow orders" and turn their guns on their fellow citizens, go door to door, and forcefully confiscate the citizens' firearms. It became obvious to me just how ignorant of the actual content of the Constitution was Mr. Reese. He apparently thinks it allows the federal government to do whatever they want.

Here is how I answered that question: "If they are lawful. And, the context of what I was talking about in that speech and the questions that were asked...the questions that a lot of people have is if this whole gun issue comes down to an unconstitutional order coming from Congress or the president asking or directing the soldiers or peace officers to turn their guns on their fellow people and confiscate them [their firearms], would that be something they would do?"

"Josh," Reese then asked, "do you believe State rights, the sovereignty of the State, over what the federal government mandates you to do?"

"I believe in States rights. To be simplistic about it, I believe that the Constitution should be followed."

Reese: "That's all I have."

He seemed to be unsatisfied with my answer. However, I found his position to be reprehensible.

The federal government does not have unlimited powers. It is restrained by the Constitution. Furthermore, as a Christian, I stand with my heroes of the faith who rejected wickedness and unlawful, corrupt civil authorities who endangered and oppressed the people. I also stand with all my ancestors who took up arms against oppressive government. It is certainly worth noting that there would be no United States of America today were it not for patriots who refused to follow orders from the British crown and parliament. Rather than assist in their own subjugation, they boldly resisted tyranny.

God's intention is that citizens submit to civil government (Romans 13:1-7), but only a *righteous* government. A government would have to be following its own laws (and the Constitution is the "supreme law of the land") and not tyrannizing their people to be acting righteously.

The Hebrew midwives (Exodus 1:15-22) disobeyed and lied to a wicked civil ruler, and in so doing protected innocent lives. They feared God. The priests successfully resisted King Uzziah's efforts to violate the law of God by his attempt to enter the temple (2 Chronicles 26:14-21). Uzziah was stricken with leprosy, and he died. The Apostle Paul wrote four epistles recorded in the Bible while he was incarcerated in prison. They are known as the Prison Epistles. Why was he in prison? For resisting a wicked civil government. Paul feared God.

King Nebuchadnezzar issued an order that all citizens must bow down and worship a pagan image (Daniel 3). Shadrach, Meshach, and Abednego did not "follow orders." They feared God.

Rahab the harlot (Joshua 2) not only lied to her king, but personally harbored the Hebrew spies and assisted in their escape from him, thereby protecting innocent lives. She didn't follow orders. She feared God. And God placed her among the "heroes of faith" in Hebrews 11.

The parents of Moses did not follow orders from the civil authorities. They did not murder their baby son, but concealed him and thus preserved his life. He went on to lead his people out of slavery and write the first five books of the Bible. Should his parents have "followed orders" and killed him?

King Ahaziah sent two different captains, each with fifty men, to arrest Elijah and bring him before the king (2 Kings 1). Elijah was ordered to turn himself in. He refused. Not only did he refuse, but he appealed to God, Who smote the civil authorities in a consuming fire. The death count was 102 before the third captain sent changed his tune. Elijah resisted a wicked government issuing orders meant for his destruction. Elijah understood that he owed no allegiance to an evil ruler violating the law of God. He feared God more than men.

Daniel was a government employee (Daniel 6). A "law" was passed mandating that if someone prayed to anyone except the king he would be thrown into a den of lions. What did Daniel do? Daniel prayed to God. He refused to follow orders pertaining to wicked legislation. He would not dishonor God. He feared God more than men.

I think the point is made. As a Christian, I realize that God's word is preeminent. As Peter and the apostles responded to the civil authorities when brought before them for not following orders, "We ought to obey God rather than men." (Acts 5:29)

We are not required to be accomplices to our own destruction. "Thou shalt not murder," and its positive parallel, thou shalt preserve innocent life, would require an officer to resist an unlawful, unconstitutional "order" from Washington, D.C., to confiscate firearms from citizens. That was the position I put forward in the speech. That is the position I maintain today.

Too many Americans have made a god out of their government, and they worship it like an idol. But God is still God.

17.

DIGGING DITCHES, BUILDING BREASTWORKS, AND FIGHTING CITY HALL

"...the tested genuineness of your faith—more precious than gold that perishes though it is tested by fire—may be found to result in praise and glory and honor at the revelation of Jesus Christ."
—1 Peter 1:7

"...through many tribulations we must enter the kingdom of God."
— Acts 14:22

"And we know that for those who love God all things work together for good for those who are called according to his purpose."
— Romans 8:28

IN THE SUMMER OF 2015, I found myself unemployed for the first time since I had begun my career eighteen years earlier. This left me with plenty of time to prepare my defense for the upcoming trial and to reflect. I remember praying and saying to God, Lord, I know what you have told me, that all things work together for good for those who are called according to Your purpose, but forgive me for admitting I do not see how that can be done with this.

I would like to tell you I was the portrait of unbridled optimism and rock-hard faith throughout the aftermath of that trial. That would be untrue, although my moments of despair were temporary. I did continue to fight, not knowing exactly what was ahead of me.

It took the civil service board less than 24 hours to rubber stamp the city manager's decision. On 18 September, they filed a one-page memorandum. In a short, two-paragraph memorandum with no finding of fact documented, the board summarized their decision by stating, 'It is therefore ordered and adjudged by the Anniston Civil Service Board, that it affirms the decision of the City of Anniston dated June 25, 2015. Done this 18th day of September 2015.'

Thus, the board, less than 24 hours after the closing of the hearing, affirmed the city manager's decision to fire me. The document read that the board had 'fully understood' the evidence presented by both parties, which was patently false in regards to the aloof George Bates, who had been absent for roughly half of the entire trial and mostly asleep for the half he did attend. He could not have possibly read and fully understood the hundreds of pages of testimony he missed, much less have properly conferred and deliberated with the other two members in such a short period of time. Yet, his signature was on top of the list of board members who ended my career. All three board members, including the absent and aloof George Bates, who could not have possibly apprised himself of all the testimony he had missed in such a short time, signed off. I was told by one of my character witnesses that board member Mike Reese had told him during a break in the early part of the trial that "what they are doing to Josh is bullshit, but he'll have to take it to the courts." A mutual friend of mine and Mike's related to me that Mike also predicted I would win "a big paycheck" through a lawsuit. He was wrong about that.

Shinbaum and I began work to appeal the board's decision to Calhoun County Circuit Court and to file a federal lawsuit for violation of constitutional rights. One day, after a long session with him in Montgomery, he phoned me when I arrived at home and said he was including in the filing that the city had violated my rights under the Alabama Religious Freedom Amendment that State citizens had approved at the ballot box in 1998. That amendment reads, in part, "The purpose of the Alabama Religious Freedom Amendment is to guarantee that the freedom of religion is not burdened by state and local law; and to provide a claim or defense to persons whose religious freedom is burdened by government."

Shinbaum explained that throughout our deliberations, and throughout the trial, he determined that all the convictions I had (whether political, cultural, or economic) with which the city took issue were ultimately due to Biblical principles I held concerning my Faith. Therefore, when discussing what rights had been violated, religious rights were at the top of the list. The appeal and lawsuit were filed in October. The "wheels of justice" began their painfully slow turn.

I began trying to find work. I applied for so many jobs I thought carpal tunnel syndrome might be induced. This included police and other jobs. At age 38, I spent a lot of time occupying myself with physical exercise and doing the physical endurance tests required by police agencies upon application for entry-level officers. I passed them, although just prior to Halloween I overdid it and actually acquired a different syndrome, iliotibial band, of which I had been blissfully unaware until then. I received medical treatment and recovered at home. Despite passing the required tests, I never received an interview from any department.

For the first time in my life, I had the humiliation of having to apply for unemployment benefits due to my inability to find a job. I reconciled my feelings on this by acknowledging the fact that I had paid such an enormous amount of taxes to the federal government throughout my life that I was due payback. I began drawing an income that was a fraction of what I was making. As the head of a family of five with a stay-at-home mother, a severe belt-tightening was undertaken.

Once, I was summoned by the unemployment mandates to attend a seminar at a local community college, where I sat with my other unemployed attendees and received a lecture about the process of seeking a livelihood. When the class broke up, we were directed to another room filled with cubicles where each of us sat down for a one-on-one consultation with a representative who would coach us. My rep, who apparently did not watch the news and seemed oblivious to the particulars of my ordeal, looked over my employment history and wisely explained that it would make sense that I seek employment in the criminal justice field, since therein lay the bulk of my experience.

Ah, the irony, I thought. It makes all the sense in the world. I should seek employment in the field that dominated my experience. Alas, with my reputation blackguarded, that avenue was blocked.

Not only was I not accepted by police agencies – I was not welcome anywhere in my home or adjacent counties. I assumed the persona of a leper. Ten years prior, when my first son was born, I had obtained part-time employment at Books-a-Million in Oxford. The store manager, a man named Dave, took an immediate liking to me, brought me in at a slightly higher than usual wage, and informally waived the company prohibition against employees carrying concealed firearms due to my status as a peace officer.

Ten years later and post-trial, Dave would not answer my phone calls. Hoping of a misunderstanding, I decided to personally carry my resume and application to Dave at the store.

I could not say for certain, but I think when Dave saw me, he tried to hide. He made a quick beeline toward the back of the building where his office and the rear entrance were located. Determined, I caught up to him (I had been taking all those physical training tests, you know). He was clearly uncomfortable talking to me, but grudgingly took my paperwork and assured me that he would contact me if any openings materialized. It was just before the Christmas season, and I knew the need in retail for any type of solid, part-time or full-time work for the holiday season.

Dave did not call.

In October I was contacted by a man over the editorial board for *The Anniston Star*. He offered me the opportunity to write an article for publication with my side of the story of my termination from the city. I did so. It appeared in the 3 November 2015 edition of the *Star* under the headline, "Josh Doggrell: How the City of Anniston has Smeared my Reputation." An end-of-the-year summary report published by the *Star* revealed it was one of their most-read online pieces for the year. My family received some supportive calls due to this. In particular, I was contacted by someone from Habitats for Humanity and received a modest check from him.

From June 2015 to January 2016, the Lord provided the financial needs of my family through my lifetime savings account, the meager unemployment benefits, and an organized budget adjustment of considerable proportions. But, since I was determined to fight the city in the courts, that left those expenses.

I had heard the idiom, "You can't fight city hall," all my life. I encountered the cold reality of that. Not wealthy people, we were peasants in the eyes of the coterie of Anniston establishment. When the government takes away your livelihood, that is one thing. When it orchestrates a cover-up of their actions by publicly painting you as a racist and smearing your reputation in the process, it makes it incredibly hard to find employment. Struggling to find money just for provisions and existence, the working man would seem to have no means of mounting the capital for a legal defense. And every time I appeared for a court hearing, deposition, attorney meeting, trial docket, etc., I was the only one in the room not getting paid. My attorney, the judge, the city prosecutor, the police chief, the city manager, human resources, court reporters – all on the clock. The accused and slandered was the only one footing the bill and missing the opportunity for work.

I considered the radical options for obtaining the means for legal defense. Would I sell some of our land? Mortgage our home? Sell vehicles or other possessions? Seek loans from the bank or friends? Fundraisers?

It turns out I had to do none of that. The Lord, indeed, works in mysterious ways.

The League of the South began passing the word, and cards and checks began arriving in my post office box. Unexpectedly, due to my story making national news, I also began receiving gifts from all across the country, and some from outside it, from people whom I did not know. Most of these were accompanied by a few words of encouragement, many with extensive, handwritten letters expressing admiration, spiritual inspiration, and tales of similar trials. Most were one-time gifts, but many were reoccurring. I had a contingent of strangers who sent me various amounts on a regular basis, extolling me to press the fight.

At the beginning of these gifts, I took a notebook and kept a ledger of each person and amount. I resolved to personally respond to each one. Some contributed via a PayPal account set up by a family friend, and I responded electronically to each of them. Most responded through the mail, and I wrote each one, each time, a thank-you note expressing my gratefulness and providing an update on the slow roll of the legal process.

By the time of federal depositions in October 2016, thirteen months following the trial, when asked how much money was raised on behalf of my legal defense, I could testify that the amount roughly met the amount spent, approximately $15,000.

It was during a break in those depositions when I inadvertently found out something about our appeal that enraged me. I heard city prosecutor Bruce Downey speaking to my attorney, Kenneth Shinbaum, about the fact that they had agreed to shelve the appeal we filed in Calhoun County Circuit Court of the civil service board's decision until the outcome of the federal lawsuit.

This was something that I was not consulted about and something with which I would never have agreed. I took my attorney outside for a chat and unloaded on him in the parking lot of city hall. I had spent over a year thinking that, any day, the circuit judge assigned to the case may be reviewing the board's decision, with the hope that he would overturn it and I could go back to work or at least receive earthly vindication. I screamed at Shinbaum, asking him why in the world would he do such a thing. And why would he do it without consulting with his client?

Shinbaum expressed his customary awkward dishevelment when encountered with a situation for which he was not prepared. He attempted to explain to me, without logic, that he thought the move was for the best.

* * *

A good friend of mine had worked for years in a machine strapping and packaging service company in Fort Payne, Alabama. He thought there was a good chance I could find employment there. I interviewed for the job, at which he was present with the boss. The boss decided not to hire me.

I turned to another good friend, who had promised to do whatever he could for me immediately after my firing in June. He was the general manager of Aramark Uniform Services in Birmingham. I went for a tour and interview with his assistants just before Christmas of 2015.

I could tell from my tour of the production plant that I would probably not like this job. (That turned out to be an understatement.) But I was desperate. And I was grateful for what I am sure was a decisive influence from my friend.

On 13 January 2016, I began work at Aramark. Coincidentally, I received a letter from unemployment that, inexplicably, my financial benefits were being discontinued after six months. My hourly rate at Aramark was half of what I had been earning as a police lieutenant in Anniston.

I worked Monday through Friday. The commute was 134 miles each day. I did an orientation in the plant, where I learned the production side of things. Aramark is a company that rents items to businesses such as uniforms, aprons, towels, etc. and the guys who drove the service trucks would deliver cleaned products once a week and collect the dirties to take back to the plant.

The regular drivers who had their own route worked on commission, so most of them worked to grow their route to as many stops and product supplies as they could to increase their paychecks. I was what was called in the business a "jumper," or a support driver. When one of the drivers who ran a regular route had a vacation week scheduled, I would ride with him the week before to see the route and get at least a cursory look at what all was involved.

I was "trained" by a man who was assumed by the bosses to be a good trainer because he made so much money. Turns out the two do not always equate. Because he worked on commission and not by the hour, his daily goal was to get done with the route as quickly as he possibly could so he could get home before his wife got home from work and his kids got home from school and have the house to himself while he consumed gin in his recliner and did the computer work (that he was supposed to be teaching me) for orders and such.

He was not at all concerned that I learned the route or the details of it well. If anything, I believe he figured that when his customers received what they considered poor service from me during his vacation that would justify his job protection, as he would moan to them the problem of finding good help and intimate how fine of a serviceman he was to them.

Service routes like these usually begin early in the morning. In my time at Aramark, I rose in the morning anywhere from 2:00 to 4:00 in order to make it wherever in the State I needed to be. When I rode with someone, I had to meet them somewhere (usually around Birmingham) where I would have to park my personal vehicle in a parking lot where it would set unattended throughout the workday.

The routes and the days were long. I was often paired with a driver who lived in Gadsden, one county to the north of me, because we were two of the only drivers that lived on the east side of Alabama. The problem was the workday always ended at the plant in Birmingham. On Mondays, for instance, I woke at 3:00am, left my house to meet him in Gadsden at 3:45, ran a route that ended in Cherokee County around 2:00pm, drove from there to the plant in Birmingham, arriving about 3:30, unloaded the dirty material from the truck and loaded the clean product for the next day (about one hour), and did the paperwork required (usually about one hour). We would leave Birmingham for Gadsden about 5:30. I would get back in my personal vehicle about 6:30, and arrive back home somewhere around 7:00. Eight hours later, I was up to do it all again.

The hours were long and the labor was hard. Drivers loaded and unloaded their own trucks. All the trucks were equipped with engine governors that restricted the top speed at 65 miles per hour. The whole day was a bustle of frenetic hurriedness. Most drivers did not stop to eat, but brought small items they could consume while driving down the road to the next stop.

I hated it. And I do not mean that such work was beneath me. I have an admiration for the working man who becomes accustomed to such a way of life and finds satisfaction from it. Government workers are often, justifiably, critiqued for the hourly-pay leisureliness and laziness it can breed. But I got to see the other side of the coin. In the private sector, a man can make himself a slave to the dollar, always chasing it and more of it, becoming discontented, resulting in a suffering of spiritual and family life.

My hours at Aramark meant that I was long gone before my family woke. Often, they were involved with extracurricular activities in the evenings when I came home and I would have to go to bed without seeing them. Wednesday night church services were no longer possible for me to attend.

Have you heard of the "Sunday blues" workers often experience at the prospect of returning to work on Monday? I started getting them around midday Saturday. A few times I vomited in the morning just contemplating the day ahead.

Once, at home at rest on a Friday night, I was having what was becoming an all-too-infrequent conversation with my oldest son (eleven years old at the time). I noticed that his facial features had changed from the last time I remembered looking at him. That's when I knew I *had* to find something else.

Off for the Independence Day holiday in July, I wound up getting in touch with our county commissioner, who had recently seen my father in the local grocery store and lamented what I had been through with the city and told him he would assist if I needed a job back home. I called him on it that day. He told me over the phone that if I would begin taking the county civil service tests for jobs, he would help getting me hired if I scored in the selection range.

Another one of those old sayings we hear is, "It helps to have a job is you are looking for a job." Not so with Aramark. I was constantly out of town working when people gave job interviews. With the assurance given me by the commissioner, I took a leap of faith and turned in my notice with Aramark. I worked out a four-week notice with the company at their request, and my last day was 5 August 2016.

I came home and began spending my days studying for the civil service jobs for which I was applying. I took every test I could and scored high on all of them. Each time, I would text message the commissioner when I had an upcoming interview. I began to see the writing on the wall when he sent back short, non-committal messages such as, "Thanks for letting me know."

I interviewed for every job for which I took a test. I was not hired. In October, I was told by a friend familiar with the commissioner something he had related that he cowardly would not reveal to me. Due to the black cloud that surrounded me from my termination from the city, there was not a chance on earth of anyone hiring me in county government. So much for that promise made to my father.

Enter another old friend. His sister was the human resources director at Mohawk Industries in Roanoke, a little over fifty miles from my home. An interview was arranged for 29 September. I was given a tour of their factory, one with an environment that necessitated ear plugs and safety glasses. This did not seem like much of an improvement from Aramark for contented labor, and much more confined.

After the tour, I was interviewed. Refreshingly, the interviewee seemed to not know or care about my reputation as a racist. I think the qualifications for assembly-line worker in his estimation were walking and breathing, and I met those. I remember getting a sick feeling in my gut when I realized that I was getting hired.

After signing up, I stopped at the Roanoke Jack's restaurant to eat before heading home to tell my wife the good news. As I sat looking out the window, I thought to myself, this signifies the end of my hope for the kind of work I enjoyed for so many years. I prayed to God, thanking Him for providing in whatever way He deemed appropriate, and asking Him to help me with the discouragement I was having.

The words to the Bob Wills song "Goin' Away Party" kept coming to me over the smell of French fries as I sat in a corner booth at Jack's:

I'm throwin' a goin' away party

A party for a dream of mine

So put me somewhere off in a corner

With a glass and bottle of your party wine

Don't worry it won't be a loud party

I feel too low to get too high

It's just a sad goin' away party

For a dream I'm telling goodbye

So, in mid-October 2016, I began another unfulfilling yet necessary occupation as an "Assistant Extrusion Operator" with Mohawk. After graduating from the training class just before Christmas, I was put on 12-hour night shifts as a "doffer" on an extrusion line. The work was timed and laborious. I was about to be forty years old and the average age of my coworker was early twenties. They had much less physical difficulty than I did doing the work required, although I believe I was more concerned than most with the quality of the finished product. I often worked without breaks and came in early to get my line ready to compensate for my physical disadvantages.

Even with the accompanying mandatory overtime, I hated this job less than Aramark. No matter how hard the shift was going, I knew when the clock hit 7:00 and the whistle blew, I would finally get to leave. I had a mark to strive for; at Aramark, you were never really sure when you could go home.

In the winter of 2017, I was reading a biography of Nathan Bedford Forrest when a line stuck in my mind. The author was describing the monotonous life of the soldiers between battles, when psychological effects could grip a man's mind. He wrote about how the soldiers would spend their days "digging ditches and building breastworks," which probably seemed at the time to be tedious, unrewarding assignments.

Lord, I thought, that's what I'm doing. I just kept moving. I was doing the labor He had given me to do at this time, hoping for some sort of future deliverance. He had kept me and preserved me through my trials. I was where He wanted me. It was providing for my family. I was not excelling at it, but I was accomplishing it. I was in the midst of a long fight, and I was digging ditches and building breastworks.

On one of my off days in July of 2017, I was sitting in the parking lot of the county administration building back home, waiting to go inside for yet another department interview which, I now knew, was not going to result in a job (*keep moving, digging ditches, building breastworks...*).

I was sitting in that parking lot when I received a social-media message from an old colleague from my days at the sheriff's office. I had not heard from Jeremy Angles in many years. He was now the head of in-house security at a metal plant in Anniston and was looking for good help.

We met and talked. A month later, I turned in my notice at Mohawk. The last time I exited the doors of that prison was Thursday, 10 August 2017. As I was leaving the parking lot, I looked at those massive buildings that comprised Mohawk Industries and prayed. I thanked the Lord for providing it so I could make a living. I knew the job well enough that, if it came to it, I could return and do it again. But I sure hoped it would be the last time I was ever in that parking lot.

A man I had befriended working there told me on our way out to meet him at a nearby gas station. I did, and he bought me a beer. I popped the top just outside the station and it was one of the best I've ever tasted.

I had the weekend off before I started my new job at Huron Valley Steel on Monday. On Saturday, some friends and I headed to Tuscaloosa to see Cody Jinks and Ward Davis in concert.

That same weekend, large crowds gathered in Charlottesville, Virginia, where a "Unite the Right" rally was held. It was occasioned by chaos, disorder, violence, and ineptness from government officials responsible for maintaining order. The League of the South made the fateful decision to participate with the myriad right-wing groups present.

On 16 August 2017, *The Anniston Star* ran a story about the weekend's proceedings. It had contacted me for comment. I thought the decision by the League leadership to participate was a horrible one. And, since my name would now forever be, at least in some way, associated with the League, I had no hesitation in speaking out against it.

> "It saddens me that what was once an intellectual group has aligned themselves with the Klan," said Josh Doggrell, a former Anniston police lieutenant who lost his job in 2015 because of his activities with the League.

> Founded by a former college history teacher, Michael Hill, the League in its early years seemed merely like an edgier version of Confederate "heritage groups" like the Sons of Confederate Veterans. The group's 1994 manifesto praised agrarian ideals and the "chivalric idea of manhood." The group adopted British spellings – "honour" and "colour" – in a rejection of American spellings created by Noah Webster, a northerner.

> News accounts from the 1990s show the League disavowing any support for slavery or segregation, even as watchdog groups warned of racist overtones to the secessionist idea...

> Doggrell, the former Anniston police officer, said he still believes secession would be best for Alabama, though he said he doesn't recognize the League today.

"There are still some good people in the League, as far as I know," he said. The leadership, not rank-and-file members, he said, have driven the shift to white nationalism.

Doggrell said he hasn't been a dues-paying member of the group since 2014. The Anniston Police Department looked into his affiliation with the League in 2009, after he led the formation of a local chapter in Anniston. Doggrell kept his job at the time, but was fired in 2015 after a watchdog group, the Southern Poverty Law Center, posted a video of a 2013 League speech.

It was typical *Star* liberal treatment. Despite the huge variance of degrees of the throngs present, the totality of the participants on the right were characterized as "far-right" protestors, while those on the other side were labeled "anti-racist" protestors. The "expert" cited was someone from the Anti-Defamation League who claimed to study in "extremist" groups and behavior.

But I felt it important that I go on record as opposing the shift the League had taken. I was not the only one. Most of the people I was closest to were also leaving the League. Even the Alabama State chapter, headquartered in Montgomery and host to so many of the League's national conferences over the years (including the one where I gave the speech in 2013), voted to disallow any further such occasions. Following that, they left the League and created the Southern Cultural Center to take its place, founding the new organization on the model of the early League. This organization has my full support.

Returning from Tuscaloosa on 13 August 2017, I shaved my beard and readied my uniform to begin my new job as a security officer at Huron Valley Steel the next day.

* * *

Huron Valley was a godsend. Instead of commuting fifty-to-seventy miles to get to work, I now traveled six. The work was more accustomed to security and criminal justice, to which I was attuned. The pace was slower, more deliberate, and detail oriented. This was more my style. I received affirmation from my superiors. I was comfortable. I was grateful to God.

I was post-police work. I had served my time and paid my dues digging ditches and building breastworks. I was thankful to God that He had delivered me from that. I was doing a job I enjoyed again, for the first time in years. I was working in my hometown again. I was even wearing a badge and a gun again, as incredibly unlikely as that had seemed. I was content. My family life was good. I was forty years old. I figured I could work twenty years for this company and have the possibility of retirement. My career as a lawman was over, and I had come to grips with that. I trusted the Providence of my Lord and found peace that that part of my life was over. I would not pursue it again.

There is an old country song with the line, "If you wanna hear God laugh, tell Him your plans." This is a play on Proverbs 16.

Two years into the job I thought (and hoped) would carry me into old age, I was manning my station when my phone rang. It was the Calhoun County sheriff.

18.

Back In The Saddle

"I will not be bullied by the Anniston City Council and neither will my officers."

"Behold, I am sending you out as sheep in the midst of wolves, so be wise as serpents and innocent as doves. Beware of men, for they will deliver you over to courts and flog you in their synagogues, and you will be dragged before governors and kings for My sake...Brother will deliver brother over to death... and you will be hated by all for My name's sake. But the one who endures to the end will be saved."
— *Matthew 10:16-22*

WHEN HE WAS STILL A CALHOUN County corrections officer, Matthew Wade would occasionally do a ride-along with me during my patrol duties as a deputy sheriff in the late nineties. He soon became a deputy in his own right, and we worked the streets as lawmen together for several years. We became friends.

He left for other jobs, including as a state probation officer, where he was stationed for a brief stint two hundred miles south of me in Dothan, Alabama. He eventually moved back and in 2005 returned to work at the Calhoun County Sheriff's Office as chief deputy. He would hold that position for twelve years, when he was appointed sheriff upon the retirement of the man who held that office.

As has been chronicled here, I left the county sheriff's office to become a police officer for the City of Anniston in 2006. Wade and I largely lost touch over the ensuing years. I worked for Anniston until they fired me in 2015.

In 2017 I saw Wade at a youth recreational baseball game in which my son was playing. My career having been blackballed and my reputation blackguarded as a result of the turmoil with the SPLC and the City of Anniston, I rarely initiated a conversation with anyone I saw that I knew in the "old days." Most of the time, they seemed too disgusted, ashamed, or embarrassed to acknowledge me.

This was fine with me. Under those circumstances, the conversation was bound to be unpleasant, and was therefore unnecessary. I can be civil but refuse to be phony. I would just as soon be left alone.

Wade approached me and spoke, and we had a very good conversation. I was amused and appreciative that the county sheriff did not seem to have the emotional obstacles others did to fellowship with an old friend.

He invited me to visit him at his office and to take me to dinner. I thanked him and we parted ways. To tell the truth, I really thought he was just being overly kind. I could not imagine he would actually want to risk the fallout that might accompany the county sheriff hosting the town leper.

I thought little about it until a little over two years later when my phone rang while I was at work and it was him. He had been contacted by a writer from *The Guardian* magazine, a British rag specializing in neo-Marxist social justice, virtue signaling, and striving to find white supremacists under every bed. They were preparing a story on me for their magazine.

I already knew about it. The writers had contacted me several months prior, asking to interview me. I was hesitant, because I knew how far-left *The Guardian* was, and I predicted (correctly) the angle they were going to take. However, I agreed, because at that point I concluded my reputation could not be damaged further by this issue. One of my regrets of the battle with the City is I took the advice of legal counsel and remained silent in the beginning stages. That was a mistake. I should have come out swinging.

It may perhaps be true that it still plays to the advantage of a defendant in a criminal proceeding to remain silent until trial (and sometimes throughout it, particularly if he is guilty). But in 21st Century America, when a traditional Christian white male Southerner is accused of thought crimes, remaining silent simply allows the leftists to paint the narrative with whatever extremes and inaccuracies they please, selling their pablum to a gullible public who largely believes whatever they are told.

Firm in my belief that my police career was over, I figured, what the heck? I would tell it my way and it may cost the city some additional embarrassment, which they so richly deserved. I also reckoned that, since at the time I was becoming successful at being published as a writer with the few remaining Christian, pro-Western Civilization, pro-South institutions in the world, I could only enhance my conservative credibility if I added *The Guardian* to the Southern Poverty Law Center and the City of Anniston to those who think ill of me.

Unsurprisingly, the city, its position indefensible, refused all requests from *The Guardian* to defend its actions.

The article was finally published on Friday, the 13th of December 2019, under the title, "Extremist Cops: How US Law Enforcement is Failing to Police Itself." To their credit, I was not misquoted. But the article was still full of inaccuracies and the expected far-left slant. For example, they analyzed that I "couched his extremist views in careful terms, often centred on his religious beliefs..."

Several liberal "scholars" were interviewed for the piece, representing various groups self-designated to monitor and oppose boogeymen comprising the purported substantial rise of the "radical right." Along with groups like the Anti-Defamation League and the "Centre for Analysis of the Radical Right," there was Whitney Shepard, "who works at the DC-based organisation Stop Police Terror Project." Here was Whitney's view: "Since the inception of this nation, black people have been under threat from the police... There's not really ever been a time in this country where the police have protected our communities."

Interestingly, the Federal Bureau of Investigation was not so willing to plunge headlong into *The Guradian's* right-wing witch hunt. The authors wrote, "The Bureau may know of some officers who are active members of white supremacist organisations, but it maintains that it's not the FBI's place to remove them from the police force unless they violate federal law. 'We do not and will not police ideology,' an FBI spokesperson wrote in an email, after the Bureau denied repeated requests for an interview."

The Guardian must have been astounded. Like the SPLC and others of the 21st Century, Post-Marxist Left, the cancel culture that they have become believes that even thinking differently from them is something to be silenced by any means necessary. And those thinking and, especially, speaking such nasty thoughts are to be considered criminals.

I was amused that the lefties across the pond were under the impression that our local newspaper was on *my* side. At one point the article stated that when black city councilmen Ben Little and David Reddick "voiced their concerns about local policing two years ago [2017], the local newspaper...responded with the headline: 'NAACP leaders, with little evidence, claim racism by police, courts."

And, later on, "The department's tolerance for Doggrell seemed to be mirrored by some of the local press. When Doggrell held his League chapter's first meeting, in an Anniston diner, he invited a reporter from *The Anniston Star* to cover it. *The Star* published a 380-word account of the meeting that read like the announcement of a new seniors' night at the bingo hall: 'Local Secessionist Hold 1st Meeting.'"

I did agree with *The Guardian* authors on one statement: "Had the video of Doggrell's speech never gone viral, though, it's quite likely he would still be serving on the Anniston police force."

That is exactly correct. As internal affairs Lt. Nick Bowles plainly stated to me in our recorded interview the morning I was fired, "The city is reacting to the public reaction, that's why this is happening."

This was not about right and wrong. No policies or laws were violated. My rights did not matter. This was about base cowering by gutless city officials to the social justice mob.

The Guardian also seemed aghast that they could not find more citizens and city officials to damn me: "A number of residents we spoke to in Anniston remained unsure of why exactly Doggrell had been fired." The magazine quoted "one of the three white [city] council members" as saying, "I heard he was an exemplary police officer...and [exhibited] no sign of racism."

In a probable state of mortification, the authors even included this from the city attorney who led the prosecution of me in the civil service trial: "Unprompted, during our interview, the lawyer Bruce Downey, who defended the city against Doggrell's lawsuit, said he thought Doggrell was a 'very intelligent guy and a deep thinker.'"

During that phone conversation in the late summer of 2019 with Sheriff Wade, he renewed his invitation to visit with him at his office and join him for dinner. Unlike two years prior, this time I accepted.

We were together a couple of hours that day, conversing over a meal, the ride to and from, and afterward in his office. Before leaving home for this meeting, my wife and I joked that he was probably asking to see me so he could offer me a job. We both got a pretty good chuckle from it.

Whether that was his original intention or not, he did just that.

I (half-jokingly) questioned his sanity. I asked if he realized the storm he may be inviting into his life from the professional protestors. He said he did.

For four years, I had been hearing various excuses from people about why the City of Anniston may have had to do what they did to me and why no other police agencies could risk hiring me. It was too risky. Liability was an issue. What if I had to use force against a black man? Would not the "community reaction" Anniston said was why they had to fire me be the same reason any other agency felt they could not hire me?

I was told the black cloud that resulted from my ordeal with Anniston would follow me everywhere I went, and no police agency in the world would hire me. Yet, here I was in an office in Anniston being offered a job as a lawman by the top lawman in the county.

In the ensuing week he and I had a few more conversations. I paid another visit to his office to meet with him and his command staff. I answered some pretty tough questions from them about the possible ramifications to everyone involved with me being a deputy sheriff.

Of course, I prayed about it extensively and consulted my family. It was a pay raise, which we needed. It was my field of experience and expertise. For years I had been praying to God for earthly vindication and it was apparent that we were not going to get that in the courts. But God, in His providence, granted it another way – not through the judiciary, but the executive.

The officials of the City of Anniston washed their hands of me, plainly stating that the merits of the issue did not matter and that they had to "react to the public reaction." Their claim was there was just no way I could ever be a lawman in that town again.

We were about to prove them wrong.

Sheriff Wade swore me in on 12 November 2019. I spent the day with patrol Lt. Falon Hurst, getting issued my equipment. At one point, I brought up the heat that may be headed toward the office. "The sheriff's official policy," said Hurst, "was that you were done wrong and we are moving forward."

I began the departmental training program. In December I attended and graduated from the refresher course (for officers who had already been certified but been out of the profession for over two years) of the State police academy in Tuscaloosa. Graduation was Friday the 13th, incidentally the same day *The Guardian* published their "long read" on me and "extremist" cops.

I went to work as a night-shift patrolman. I had confidence issues early due to being out of it for so long and wondering when the hammer would drop from the media.

Things went well for a while. In the spring of 2020, everyone became completely immersed in Covid hysteria.

Then, in July, they finally figured it out.

The sheriff called me that summer of 2020 and told me Tim Lockette, a reporter for *The Anniston Star,* had contacted him about my employment with the county. Wade told me he informed Lockette that I had already been employed there almost a year and Wade had received no negative feedback on it thus far. Wade, of course, knew this was inevitably coming, and he had already prepared to defend me.

Lockette had also contacted me via text message. I had not responded. Wade told me I could talk to him if I wanted. I did not. I messaged him back informing him I would not be speaking with him about this matter.

The article was published in the *Star* on 7 July 2020, under the headline, "Ex-officer with secessionist ties now working as Calhoun County deputy."

It rehashed my termination with the City of Anniston from four years prior and repeated the characterization of the League of the South as one of the many designated "hate groups" by the self-proclaimed experts at the Southern Poverty Law Center. Quoted was "SPLC senior analyst Howard Graves: 'Our position hasn't changed. Being a deputy or a police officer is a position of public trust.'"

In marked contrast to the police chief of Anniston and other city "leaders," Sheriff Wade possessed the boldness and courage to defend me.

Lockette wrote, "Wade said he's known Doggrell for years, and that the two worked together in the Sheriff's Office before Doggrell moved to the Anniston Police. He described Doggrell as a 'history buff' and said his secessionist views were always known. He said he'd never seen signs of racist leanings from Doggrell."

The sheriff was also quoted as saying, "I gave the man a chance... Show me where the man has done something specific against somebody. You can't..."

In remembrance of and in anticipation of the political storm and howls of protest that did and could possibly envelope the situation once again, Wade declined to lament what this could do to his and his family's own well-being and his professional status. He elected instead to put the focus on me and my family.

"'Know that he is a human being,' Wade said of the deputy. 'Know that his wife and kids have been put through hell after he was called a racist.'"

The sheriff and I had several conversations prior to and following the publication of this article. Both being Christians, we largely spoke about the spiritual effects of it all. I told him about how I was trying to lead my family through this by showing them the perseverance of our Lord despite suffering and tribulation. I remember him specifically telling me he was having conversations with his teenaged son about the value of sticking up for someone.

There was, indeed, another storm. On 14 July, another article appeared in the *Star* under the headline, "Group airs concerns over ex-officer's hiring by sheriff, other matters." The piece detailed the "Anniston Police Citizens Advisory Committee" relating their meeting with the sheriff concerning my employment.

Wade told me that in this time period he also had a meeting with a group of local black pastors, in which he listened to and addressed their concerns.

On 4 August 2020, another *Star* article by Tim Lockette was published with the title, "Confederate monument to be moved to rural park." This detailed a meeting of the Anniston City Council where the members voted 4-1 to move an obelisk honoring Confederate Major John Pelham, a local hero who died defending the South at a battle at Kelley's Ford, Virginia, in 1863. The monument had been erected approximately one hundred years earlier by an Anniston society that still honored the sacrifices of our Confederate ancestors. But it was a convenient target in the aftermath of the death of George Floyd and Social Justice Summer 2020. In addition to whatever it cost the city to move the obelisk to a Confederate park in the northwest portion of the county, the city was also breaking a 2017 State law prohibiting the removal of monuments and renaming of most buildings and streets named for historic figures. The city council willingly put itself at risk of a $25,000 fine for violating that law. But, hey, what's price of social justice?

Even that vote was not unanimous, which was an extreme rarity for that dysfunctional council. However, buried toward the end of the article was this gem: "The council also voted 5-0 to ask Sheriff

Matthew Wade to prohibit Deputy Josh Doggrell from patrolling in Anniston's police jurisdiction, a zone surrounding the city that is patrolled by Anniston police even though it is outside city limits."

The article continued, "[Anniston] Mayor Jack Draper said he was typically reluctant to intervene in a matter involving the sheriff – but not this time. 'While generally speaking a government should not inquire into another government's operations, this is a unique situation."

Responding to this request, Sheriff Wade noted the timing of the decision coming three weeks before city elections "...and that he would decide where to send his deputies. 'I will not be bullied by the Anniston City Council and neither will my officers,' he said."

Perhaps most notable was the reaction from local community activist Glen Ray, Sr. Ray had become president of the Anniston chapter of the NAACP since my separation from the Anniston Police Department. He was vocal to Wade about his displeasure regarding my employment as a deputy. The two of them spoke at length about it.

Soon afterward, Ray filmed a video on one of his social media accounts I viewed. He aired his concerns, but also went on to say he considered other matters as more troubling. He put forward an illustration whereby if he was manning a lifeboat in a sea of water and came upon me and two other particular assistant district attorneys drowning, and he could only save one, it would be me whom he would offer a place on the boat.

Following that, the matter began to dissolve.

At least for now...

There was to be no vindication from the judiciary. It was my hope to get matters out of the local politics of Anniston. However, our federal lawsuit inexplicably landed in the hands of Judge Virginia Hopkins in the Northern District of Alabama. She was a native of Anniston and was still country-clubbing and friends with city leadership at the time. I impressed upon my attorney, Kenneth

Shinbaum, of moving to get the suit out of her hands. For whatever reason, he refused. She sided with the city in the summer of 2017. My attorney informed me via email it would cost me an additional $15,000 to appeal the decision higher. I said no, let's concentrate on the civil service appeal.

That appeal of the civil service board's decision bounced around several judges of the Calhoun County Circuit Court for three years. I pushed for a decision that was never made. When I was hired as a county deputy in November 2019, all judges used my employment as a reason to recuse themselves. The case was then assigned to Etowah County Circuit Judge William Ogletree. Unlike the others, he wasted little time in making a decision, affirming the city's termination of me in a bland opinion in May 2020. Shinbaum again wrote that an appeal of that decision would also cost an additional $15,000, adding the encouraging words that he thought it would be "futile" to do so. I gave him no reply, hoping that my communication with that man would come to a happy conclusion.

Lt. Nick Bowles, my one-time peer colleague at Anniston Police Department who was the lead investigator in the internal affairs investigation that ended my career, was quickly rewarded for his efforts by being promoted to captain at that agency. Then, in July 2020, he was made chief of police upon the retirement of Shane Denham.

The four captains under Chief Bowles are Justin Sanford, Chris Sparks, Matt Caballero, and Clint Parris – all men I worked with and supervised when I was at that agency and mistakenly thought were my friends.

For reasons unknown to me, Bruce Downey, who served as city attorney and the prosecutor against me in my trial, returned to private practice in Anniston some time after federal depositions in 2016.

One year after firing me and testifying against me, Anniston City Manager Brian Johnson left Alabama, taking the same position with Peachtree Corners, Georgia.

On 1 October 2021, I was promoted to sergeant at the sheriff's office. I served as a shift supervisor until June of 2023, when I was moved to the investigative division. I hope to work in this field until I am able to retire.

I have had people tell me I am the only person they have personally known to be "canceled" in such a public way. It is true that I was on the cusp of the latest wave of some type of "cancel culture" when things began to go in motion in the Spring of 2015, although that was just the latest wave in what has been a longstanding practice from the left. Many have paid in ways far more treacherous and costly than my family and I have.

I had a hard time understanding when going through it how this trial would be to my benefit. Difficult as it was to conceive then, I can honestly tell people today that I am glad it happened. It brought a better perspective to my life, it enhanced my spiritual discernment, and it drew me closer to Christ.

I have not had anything to do with the League of the South since 2015. Had my issue with the City of Anniston not come up, the League's own change of direction would have necessitated my withdrawal from it. It is not the same organization with which I was involved for twenty years. Of all the numerous people I met through the League during those years, I know of no one still involved.

I began submitting writings in 2018 and was blessed by God to be published by some of my favorite entities: *Chronicles: A Magazine of American Culture,* the Abbeville Institute, the Fleming Foundation, and American Remnant.

My wife of nineteen years, two sons, daughter and I still live in the same house next door to my parents on family land in the Saks community of Anniston, Alabama. We were never shamed into moving to another part of the country, as was suggested by some. It wouldn't have mattered anyway. There may have been a time in this country when a man could move from his problems and start over elsewhere. The internet has made that an impossibility. (Google my name and see.) I have chosen to embrace it and defend ourselves, rather than leave the enemy to tell the tale.

My wife is still a homemaker and homeschool teacher. We are active in our church. Ours is a simple life with dreams that never stretched beyond the county line.

I still love the South — the Old South, not the wicked and desolate land we now inhabit. I am proud of my ancestors and my roots. I refuse to apologize for being Southern and white.

The only thing that makes me special is being a child of God, a sinner adopted into His family through the blood of Jesus Christ. We are commanded to spread His gospel. My hope is that this book is part of my ministry and my testimony of how He led me out of the darkest period of my life and made me a better disciple and better man in the process. If I can be His instrument in telling others what He has done for me, it is my duty to do so.

> "And the days that I keep my gratitude higher than my expectations, well, I have really good days."

> — Ray Wylie Hubbard

> "Mother Blues"

ABOUT THE AUTHOR

Joshua Doggrell is a blessed Christian Southerner who lives with his wife and three children on family land in Anniston, Alabama. He has been working in the criminal justice field for 25 years. He is a contributing writer for *Chronicles* magazine, The Abbeville Institute, and The Fleming Foundation.

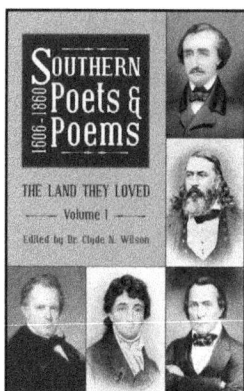

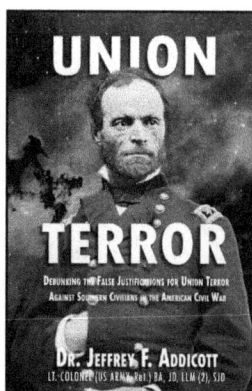

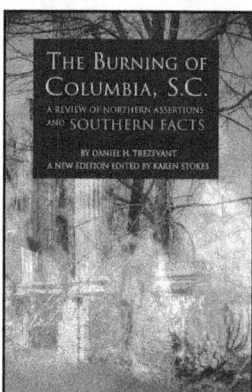

Jeffery Addicott

*Union Terror: Debunking the False
Justifications for Union Terror*

Mark Atkins

Women in Combat: Feminism Goes to War

Joyce Bennett

*Maryland, My Maryland: The Cultural
Cleansing Of A Small Southern State*

Garry Bowers

*Slavery And The Civil War: What Your
History Teacher Didn't Tell You*

*Dixie Days: Reminiscences Of A
Southern Boyhood*

Jerry Brewer

Dismantling the Republic

Andrew P. Calhoun

*My Own Darling Wife: Letters From A
Confederate Volunteer*

John Chodes

Segregation: Federal Policy Or Racism?

*Washington's Kkk: The Union League During
Southern Reconstruction*

Walter Brian Cisco

War Crimes Against Southern Civilians

John Devanny

Continuities: The South in a Time of Revolution

James C. Edwards

*What Really Happened?: Quantrill's Raid On
Lawrence, Kansas*

Ted Ehmann

*Boom & Bust In Bone Valley: Florida's
Phosphate Mining History 1886-2021*

John Avery Emison

*The Deep State Assassination of
Martin Luther King Jr.*

Don Gordon

*Snowball's Chance: My Kidneys Failed,
My Wife Left Me & My Dog Died...*

John R. Graham

Constitutional History of Secession

Paul C. Graham

Confederaphobia

*When The Yankees Come: Former Carolina
Slaves Remember*

*Nonsense on Stilts: The Gettysburg Address
& Lincoln's Imaginary Nation*

Joe D. Haines

*The Diary of Col. John Henry Stover Funk of
the Stonewall Brigade, 1861-1862*

Charles Hayes

The REAL First Thanksgiving

Terry Hulsey

25 Texas Heroes

*The Constitution of Non-State Government:
Field Guide to Texas Secession*

V.P. Hughes

*Col. John Singleton Mosby: In the News
1862-1916*

Joseph Jay

*Sacred Conviction: The South's Stand for
Biblical Authority*

Suzanne Johnson

Maxcy Gregg's Sporting Journals 1842-1858

James R. Kennedy

Dixie Rising: Rules For Rebels

*Nullifying Federal And State Gun Control:
A How-To Guide For Gun Owners*

*When Rebel Was Cool: Growing Up In Dixie,
1950-1965*

Walter D. Kennedy

The South's Struggle:America's Hope

*Lincoln, The Non-Christian President:
Exposing The Myth*

Lincoln, Marx, and the GOP

J.R. & W.D. Kennedy

*Jefferson Davis: High Road to Emancipation
and Constitutional Government*

Yankee Empire: Aggressive Abroad And
   Despotic At Home

Punished With Poverty: The Suffering South

The South Was Right! 3rd Edition

Lewis Liberman

Snowflake Buddies; ABC Leftism For Kids!

Philip Leigh

The Devil's Town: Hot Springs During
   The Gangster Era

U.S. Grant's Failed Presidency

The Causes of the Civil War

The Dreadful Frauds: Critical Race Theory
   And Identity Politics

Jack Marquardt

Around The World In 80 Years: Confessions
   of a Connecticut Confederate

Michael Martin

Southern Grit: Sensing The Siege At Petersburg

Samuel Mitcham

The Greatest Lynching In American History:
   New York, 1863
Confederate Patton: Richard Taylor and
   The Red River Campaign

Charles T. Pace

Lincoln As He Really Was

Southern Independence. Why War? The War
   To Prevent Southern Independence

James R. Roesch

From Founding Fathers To Fire Eaters

Kirkpatrick Sale

Emancipation Hell: The Tragedy Wrought
   By Lincoln's Emancipation Proclamation

Joseph Scotchie

The Asheville Connection: The Making of a
Conservative

Anne W. Smith

Charlottesville Untold: Inside Unite The Right

Robert E. Lee: A History for Kids

Karen Stokes

A Legion Of Devils: Sherman In South Carolina

The Burning of Columbia, S.C.: A Review
   of Northern Assertions and Southern Facts

Fortunes of War: The Adventures of a
   German Confederate

Jack Trotter

Last Train to Dixie

John Theursam

Key West's Civil War

Leslie Tucker

Old Times There Should Not Be Forgotten:
   Cultural Genocide In Dixie

John Vinson

Southerner Take Your Stand!

Howard Ray White

How Southern Families Made America

Understanding Creation And Evolution

Mark R. Winchell

Confessions of a Copperhead: Culture and Politics
   in the Modern South

Clyde N. Wilson

Calhoun: A Statesman for the 21st Century

Lies My Teacher Told Me: The True History
   of the War For Southern Independence

The Yankee Problem: An American Dilemma

Annals Of The Stupid Party: Republicans
   Before Trump

Nullification: Reclaiming The Consent
   of the Governed

The Old South: 50 Essential Books

The War Between The States: 60 Essential Books

Reconstruction and the New South, 1865-1913:
   50 Essential Books

The South 20th Century And Beyond:
   50 Essential Books

Southern Poets and Poems, 1606-1860:
   The Land They Loved, Volume 1

Looking For Mr. Jefferson

Joe Wolverton

What Degree Of Madness?: Madison's Method
To Make American States Again

Walter Kirk Wood

Beyond Slavery: The Northern Romantic
Nationalist Origins Of America's Civil War

Gold-Bug
(Mystery & Suspense Imprint)

Brandi Perry

Splintered: A New Orleans Tale

Martin Wilson

To Jekyll and Hide

Green Altar
(Literary Imprint)

Catharine Brosman

An Aesthetic Education and Other Stories
(2nd Edition)

Chained Tree, Chained Owls: Poems

Aerosols and Other Poems

Randall Ivey

A New England Romance: And Other Southern
Stories

James E. Kibbler, Jr.

Tiller : Clayback County Series, Vol. 4

Thomas Moore

A Fatal Mercy: The Man Who Lost The Civil War

Perrin Lovett

The Substitute, Tom Ironsides 1

Karen Stokes

Belles

Carolina Love Letters

Carolina Twilight

Honor in the Dust

The Immortals

The Soldier's Ghost: A Tale of Charleston

William Thomas

Runaway Haley: An Imagined Family Saga

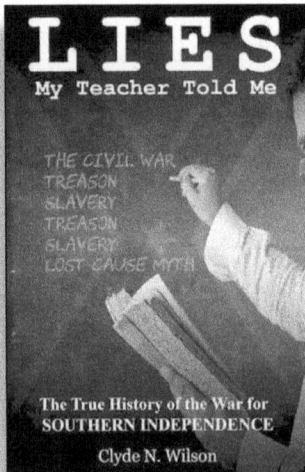

www.ingramcontent.com/pod-product-compliance
Lightning Source LLC
Chambersburg PA
CBHW060042100426
42742CB00014B/2667